The Political Philosophy of Mao Zedong

Manoranjan Mohanty

The Political Philosophy of Mao Zedong
Manoranjan Mohanty

First Published, 1978
Revised Edition, 2012

Published by
AAKAR BOOKS
28 E Pocket IV, Mayur Vihar Phase I, Delhi 110 091
Phone : 011 2279 5505 Telefax : 011 2279 5641
info@aakarbooks.com; www.aakarbooks.com

Printed at
Mudrak, 30 A Patparganj, Delhi 110 091

Contents

Preface to the New Edition 5

Prologue

Mao Zedong Thought: A Twenty-first Century Perspective 7

Introduction 17

1. Theory of New-Democratic Revolution 25
2. Theory of Class Struggle in Socialist Society 75
3. Contradictions in the Modern World 136
4. Four Laws of Materialist Dialectics 165

Appendix 209

Bibliography 219

Index 231

Preface to the New Edition

In this edition I have added a Prologue trying to take a comprehensive view of Mao Zedong Thought, keeping in view some twenty first century concerns and the developments in post-Mao China. This discussion is grounded on the fact that Maoism remains an ideological inspiration for many communist movements in the world, especially in Asia. It also notes that within China, Mao's ideas and perspective continue to be a reference point for assessing the impressive achievements during the reform period.

This book had been out of print for many years. I thank Mr K K Saxena of Aakar Books for undertaking its fresh edition. The only change that has been made in the old version of *The Political Philosophy of Mao Tse-tung* is the replacement of Chinese words in the Wade-Giles system by the Pinyin system.

There has been much debate on each aspect of Mao's life and ideas during the recent decades. But to get an understanding of Mao's Thought and its critique when it was the guiding ideology in China and assess it as a part of world political discourse has its own significance. Status of Maoism and the course of ideological formulations in post-Mao China from Deng Xiaoping's Theory of Building Socialism with Chinese Characteristics and Jiang Zemin's Three Represents to Hu Jintao's notion of Scientific Outlook on Development have been analysed in my book *Maoism and CPC Ideology* as a companion volume to this, also published by Aakar.

July 2012

Manoranjan Mohanty
Institute of Chinese Studies, Delhi

Preface to the First Edition

This study of Mao Tse-tung's thought has been undertaken keeping in view the concrete problems of social transformation that we in the developing countries face today. These are essentially the problems of completing the anti-colonial and anti-feudal revolution. This is an attempt to analyse how the Chinese communist leadership headed by Mao comprehended such problems in China and tried to tackle them.

Mao Tse-tung's thought is the philosophy of the praxis of the Chinese revolution. I have divided this into four major dimensions: (1) the theory of new-democratic revolution which deals with the analysis of the anti-colonial and anti-feudal revolution in China, (2) the theory of class struggle in socialist society or the theory of continuous revolution which underlies the mode of socialist development in China, (3) the Maoist world-view which analyses the nature of the contradictions in the modern world situation and governs China's foreign policy, and (4) the dialectical materialist method as understood by Mao Tse-tung which has been reformulated here in terms of four laws. Together these four dimensions can provide a comprehensive understanding of this important political philosopher of the twentieth century.

Each one of these theories was subjected to diverse interpretations even in Mao's own lifetime, as has been discussed at various places in this book. After the death of Mao some of his ideas have been reinterpreted with the declared objective of correcting certain recent deviations. It has been pointed out that the 'gang of four' had given an idealist interpretation to the theory of continuous revolution by undermining the need for developing the production process. The new programme of all-out modernisation of the economy to turn China into a powerful socialist country by the end of this century has been regarded by some observers as throwing the perspective of the Cultural Revolution overboard. But as our discussion of the theory of continuous revolution shows such a debate had gone on from time to tine in China and each deviation was followed by a corrective since there was no mechanical way of implementing the Basic Line.

Another recent development is the growing international debate on China's Three-Worlds thesis. Ever since the Albanian Party of Labour launched an indirect attack in July 1977 on this, the Chinese have come forward with more and more carefully prepared documents to explain their thesis. Their current international behaviour is essentially determined by their analysis of the present world situation according to the Three-Worlds thesis.

An understanding of China's internal political developments is difficult without a comprehension of the Maoist theory of continuous revolution just as we need to realise the implications of the Maoist world-view for being able to put meaning into China's foreign policy actions. People's China's experiences of the last three decades were greatly influenced by the revolutionary movement which gave birth to it. Hence the necessity of grasping the theory of new-democratic revolution. In this whole process there were the leading actors who consciously tried to analyse the nature of the developing situation by some method in order that they could influence the process. I have attempted to discern and perhaps simplify that method, the method of dialectical materialism.

I have explained the nature of each of these ideas, the context of their evolution and the controversies they have generated. This analysis also identifies the extent of the universal significance of these theories and also their relative particularity in the Chinese situation.

There cannot be any finality of interpretation in political philosophy and in case of Mao Tse-tung there is the additional problem of incomplete information. Yet at this point of history, a theoretical summing-up of the Chinese revolution has its own significance.

Research on this forms part of the project on 'Revolutionary Politics in China' which has been supported by the Indian Council of Social Science Research since 1973. I am grateful to the ICCSR, especially to its ever encouraging leaders J.P. Naik, Ramashray Roy and R. Barman Chandra for their help at various stages of this work. At a critical juncture of the development of Chinese Studies at the University of Delhi, the ICSSR project helped us create a stable nucleus of research activities on the People's Republic of China. I thankfully acknowledge the contribution made by some of our research scholars who at various points of time worked for this project. I especially thank Govindi Joshi, Arttatrana Nayak and Sreemati Chakrvarti. The mass of data collected by this group has not only been used for their individual research projects but has also greatly facilitated my work on China's political experience whose completion awaits gathering of more grassroot level information from China.

This project was almost entirely conducted at the Department of Chinese and Japanese Studies, University of Delhi. The lively intellectual atmosphere which has been built up in this Department is bound to have its imprint on all academic work produced here. We have evolved a tradition of putting each other on dock and also helping each other to get out of it. My deep gratitude to my colleagues especially to Tan Chung and G.D. Deshingkar for their valuable suggestions on several chapters of this book. Tan Chung's calligraphy appears on the cover. Our Department librarians, B.K. Kumar and Attar Chand have never lost patience with my heavy demands on them. B.S. Chitkara's typing assistance has been an asset to me. I record my sincere thanks to all of them.

None of the institutions and persons mentioned above are responsible for any fact or opinion expressed in this book. I fully own all responsibility for them.

Finally, a note on romanisation of Chinese words. The proper names of Chinese leaders appear here in the Wade-Giles system while the place names are according to the international postal code. The other Chinese words, however, have been romanised in accordance with the present-day official Chinese (Pin Yin) system.

Delhi University
May 1978

Manoranjan Mohanty

Prologue

MAO ZEDONG THOUGHT: A TWENTY-FIRST CENTURY PERSPECTIVE

The issues of liberation and social transformation which permeated the philosophy and practice of Mao Zedong in course of the Chinese revolution and socialist construction in the twentieth century continue to engage activists and thinkers in the twenty-first century. In the present day world Mao Zedong's ideas are not only reference point for many contentious discussions on development and revolution there are also many communist parties and organisations in the world who call themselves as Maoists.

Maoism after Mao

When communist parties in different countries split, first over their stand on the ideological debates between the Communist Party of Soviet Union (CPSU) and the CPC during the 1959-1964 the then radical wings had added in parenthesis Marxist. Subsequently, when further splits took place in the wake of the Chinese Cultural Revolution and the issue of armed struggle or parliamentary path to socialism, many parties split further and the radical wings called themselves 'Marxist-Leninist'. When further splits took place among them, the most radical communist formations among them called themselves Maoist. There are two communist parties in South Asia with large scale mass base which carry this name. One is the Communist Party of India (Maoist) formed after the merger of CPI-ML (People's War) and Maoist Communist Centre in 2004 which has an extensive support base in the tribal areas of central India. Another is the Communist Party of Nepal (Maoist) renamed Unified Communist Party of Nepal (Maoist) which was engaged in agrarian armed struggle from 1996 till 2006 when it participated in a popular uprising against the monarchy in Nepal and joined electoral process to win the largest number of seats in the Constituent Assembly and in 2011 led a coalition government in Nepal for the second time. Its political programme presents the Maoist party as an organization committed to a creative Marxist-Leninist-Maoist programme called 'socialism in the 21st century'. Besides these two mass parties there are numerous Maoist parties and groups in different parts of the world.

Yet, the Maoism like Marxism and Leninism was one of the most debated subjects of the twentieth century and is most likely to remain so in the 21st century in the face of the expanding process of capitalist globalization. This is because the formulations advanced by Mao and the later Maoists, challenge some of the dominant assumptions relating to the basic issues of struggle for liberation, equality, justice and self-development in course of social transformation in all societies.

Mao Zedong Thought in China

In China itself assessment of Maoism has varied between official verdict, elite opinions and popular adoration especially in the countryside. In the immediate aftermath of the death of Mao and fall of the Gang of Four in 1976 a powerful current had emerged which was characterised as 'de-Maoization'. But Deng Xiaoping took the lead to reorient that trend and in a CPC Central Committee Plenum in 1981, a Resolution on Certain Questions in Party History for the post-1949 period was passed which set the official framework on treating Mao's role in contemporary China. The Deng leadership followed Mao's own method of discriminating evaluation of Stalin after Khrushchev's de-Stalinization in 1956. According to Mao he was 70 per cent right – for eliminating feudalism, building a strong industrial country and defending the Soviet Union in the face of Nazi and Fascist attacks during the World War II. But he was 30 per cent wrong for abandoning democratic centralism and following absolute centralism and liquidating his opposition. Similarly, without mentioning the proportion, the CPC resolution recorded Mao's contribution in formulating the line and strategy for China's new democratic revolution that created massive popular support for the CPC among the peasantry, defeated the Japanese during the war of 1937-1945 and Guomindang during the civil war of 1946-1949 and founded the People's Republic of China. At the same time, the Resolution squarely criticised the economic ideas and policies of Mao Zedong during the 1958-1976 period starting from the Great Leap Forward till the end of the Cultural Revolution. Repudiation of the Cultural Revolution theory of class struggle paved the way for the reforms and open door line of Deng Xiaoping proclaimed by the Third Plenum of the Eleventh Central Committee in December 1978.

There were signs of greater acknowledgement of Mao's contribution beginning with the celebration in 2009 of the sixtieth anniversary of the founding of the PRC. Many scholars and Party leaders took a holistic view of China's achievements rather than attributing the great economic successes of China only to the thirty years of reforms. As recognised abroad, now it was admitted in Chinese official circles that rural transformation through land reforms, cooperatives and finally collectives during the years of the People's Communes, the effort to universalize literacy and primary health care and bringing women to agricultural work besides building rural infrastructure during the Mao period had created a foundation for the success of the later reforms under Deng and his successors. In his speech on the occasion of the ninetieth anniversary of the founding of the CPC on July 1, 2011 CPC General Secretary acknowledged the 'great theoretical achievement' of Mao Zedong Thought which " resolved in a systematic way the issue of how to accomplish the new democratic revolution and socialist revolution in China, a big semi-colonial and semi-feudal country in the East and made painstaking efforts to explore the issue of what kind of socialism China should build and how to build it, thereby making new and creative contributions to enriching Marxism." (*News from China*,vol XXIII no.7, July 2011, p. 7)

While the CPC discourse on Mao focuses on the theory of new democratic revolution and critique of the Cultural Revolution, the Maoist understanding of the contemporary world has remained an important element of the Maoist discourse the world over. Underlying all three elements are some of the philosophical formulations on dialectics, especially on contradictions and practice which have been the basic premises of forming the Maoist outlook.

Debates on Maoism

The significance of the new democratic revolution was such that despite the criticisms relating to Mao's policies during the Great Leap and the Cultural Revolution, the official evaluation of Mao Zedong in China has remained highly positive. Its theoretical and strategic significance has been vindicated by the fact that many communist movements in former colonies in Asia, Africa and Latin America accepted the new democratic revolution as their political line. The CPC described this perspective as the creative application of Marxism-Leninism to the concrete conditions of the Chinese situation. As such it also opened up possibilities of creative application of revolutionary legacies of the Bolshevik as well as Chinese revolutions to concrete conditions of revolutions in various countries. The two unique aspects of the new democratic revolution were the mobilisation of the peasantry and the broad united front mobilisation on the platform of nationalism which included the national bourgeoisie. Both these dimensions had critical relevance to the populous agrarian societies in the third world which suffered in the hands of colonialism or in the recent decades also neo-colonialism.

Yet, critics of Mao pointed out the fact that Mao undermined working class leadership and promoted 'agrarian socialism' and 'peasant nationalism' deviating from classical Marxist-Leninist premises. Others criticize Mao for aligning with patriotic entrepreneurs temporarily in the early years of 'New Democracy' and attacking them soon after by initiating nationalization policies. The reform and open door policies initiated by Deng, re-emphasized the role of the entrepreneur class as a part of the 'people's democratic dictatorship' and established links between Mao's 'new democratic revolution' and the 'preliminary stage of socialism' in which 'socialist market economy' developed and achieved spectacular economic growth in China.

Mao's ideas on building socialism which led him to launch the Great Leap Forward in 1958 and the Cultural Revolution in 1966 have been subjected to much criticism in China during the reform period and also by development analysts in the liberal and neo-liberal mould all over the world. These mass campaigns caused enormous hardships to millions of people. Yet it is important to understand the Maoist perspective which guided those initiatives. Essentially these campaigns, especially the Cultural Revolution raised qualitative questions about the nature of socialism affirming that socialism was not only about achieving high growth of production as in case of capitalist systems, but it was to be based on the socialist vision of creating an egalitarian society with socialist values and moving towards a classless society.

The Deng leadership had four major criticisms against Mao's theory and the Cultural Revolution. Firstly, socialism was not about poverty, but improving material conditions of people to achieve an egalitarian society. Indeed, the growth rate under the reforms has grown with modern infrastructure and better living conditions for all and substantial reduction in poverty. Second, mass campaigns in the name of fighting class enemies suspended all institutions, led to arbitrary use of power and harassed and killed many innocent people . Indeed, since 1978 the organs of state and the Party have met regularly according to the constitution and even ensured smooth transition of leadership from one generation to another. Third, the theoretical premise that treats culture or ideology as autonomous is , according to the critics, an idealist deviation of Mao which put superstructure independent of the economic base, thus violating the tenets of dialectical and historical materialism. It is this perspective which invoked workers to work not on material incentives but ideological incentives during the Mao era. That perspective put so much emphasis on self-reliance as a principle that during the Great leap Forward there was severe scarcity of food and caused a massive famine in which millions of people perished. The Deng regime stressed the need for 'open door' within the country and worldwide to share the knowledge and resources of others. Fourthly, the egalitarianism promoted during the Cultural Revolution was an attempt to artificially create conditions of equality irrespective of the contribution made by a worker. The many Maoist policies including the People's communes were regarded as 'eating from the iron bowl' or everyone getting the same out of a common fund. The rural communes were dismantled and a Household Contract Responsibility' system was introduced in the early years of the reforms which distributed land equitably in proportion of the number of the members in the family on long term contract for farming by the household.

Yet the debates on the questions raised by Mao on building of socialism are not closed. As the Chinese leadership grapples with the consequences of the reforms and the world debates the social and environmental consequences of neo-liberal globalization the qualitative questions about the nature of socialism in particular and development in general will continue to be raised.

On the nationality question

The ideological focus of the Cultural Revolution on classes and class struggle has clouded a closer discussion on the treatment of ethnicity in the Maoist theoretical framework. But taking Mao's life and works as a whole, it is possible to discern two aspects of his approach to the ethnic question. One being the necessity to protect cultural identity of every group in the process of revolutionary transformation and the other being the need to curb chauvinism either of the small group or the large group. But before that a clarification may be in order. Until the reforms period, this issue was discussed under the category of 'nationality question'. But as China's social science discourse got increasingly reshaped by the Western vocabulary, the same Chinese word 'minzu' was now translated mostly as 'ethnic group'. In the Marxist discourse, a social group with shared cultural identity seeking political safeguards for its identity was always referred to in the writings and policies of Lenin and Stalin and subsequently of Mao as nationality. The preference for the term 'ethnic identity' during the reform period in China during the 1980s coincided with the growing Western emphasis on the significance of non-class social formations as against the primacy of class. In the aftermath of the Cultural Revolution as the attempts were made to de-emphasise class struggle the shift from nationality discourse to ethnic identity was not surprising. But the significance of the cultural identity of a group and evolving a viable policy has remained a challenge throughout the history of the PRC.

The two elements of the Maoist approach to the ethnic question were stated eloquently by Mao in his speech at the enlarged meeting of the CPC Politbureau on 25 April 1956, entitled, On Ten Major Relationships: " We put the emphasis on opposing Han chauvinism. Local nationality chauvinism must be opposed too, but generally that is not where our emphasis lies....The minority nationalities have all contributed to the making of China's history." Discussing the relationship between the Hans and the minority nationalities he mentioned how "all through the ages, the reactionary rulers, chiefly from Han nationality, sowed feelings of estrangement among our various nationalities and bullied the minority peoples". In this speech as far back as in 1956 Mao had described the treatment of the minority nationalities in the Soviet Union as ''abnormal" and called upon the CPC to learn lessons from it. Indeed, this was one of the contradictions which got accentuated in the succeeding years leading to the collapse of the USSR in 1991.

How was the nationality question or the "human factor" handled by the Chinese regime under Mao and by his successors? The record is not very encouraging. Even though the Maoist approach of the 1956-57 broadly continues to remain the official perspective of the CPC its performance on the ground has failed to eliminate discontent in the minority areas. Even before coming to power, the CPC under Mao's leadership had pursued the policy of forging solidarity between the Hans and the minority nationalities. The Jiangxi Soviet Constitution of 1931had a provision for right to self-determination of nationalities including the right to secession. In course of the Long March the Red Army travelled through the minority nationality areas and secured much support among them in the north-western region. The PRC Constitution of 1954 affirmed by its later versions regards the PRC as a multi-national state. Article 4 of the PRC Constitution declares all nationalities of China as equal, protects the rights of minority nationalities and prohibits discrimination against and oppression of them. The six big minority areas (inner Mongolia, Heilongjiang, Guangxi, Tibet, Ningxia and Xinjiang) were constituted as Autonomous Regions with their own constitutions and autonomous organs of power. There are 55 minority nationalities whose language and culture are recognized and protected by law.

Yet the CPC policy has failed to respond to the democratic aspirations of minority groups of Xinjiang and Tibet. Two strands of thought which evolved as major currents in the modern history of China also have origins in Maoist practice, have contributed to this situation. Firstly, the stress on nationalism and building a united China was a great commitment of the CPC during the anti-Japanese War, further reinforced during the cold war which kept Taiwan as a separate entity. Therefore the Chinese regimes treated territorial sovereignty as a firm value ruthlessly suppressing any challenge posed by minority groups. Secondly, during the Cultural Revolution when Mao was at the helm of affairs, the CPC faction in power promoted the idea that socialism would create conditions of equality irrespective of race, gender and ethnic identity. Religion was considered as an obstacle to that process. Religious practices were suppressed and religious places including mosques in Xinjiang and Buddhist monasteries in Tibet, in addition to Confucian temples in many parts of China were vandalised. Even though Mao Zedong was referred to as the "great leader of all the nationalities of China" the Cultural Revolution greatly alienated China's minority nationalities from the CPC.

During the reforms period Deng Xiaoping and his successors took a number of major steps to recover ground and win over minorities. However, even the numerous economic and cultural initiatives did not adequately respond to the political urges of the minority nationalities. Political leadership, especially Party leadership in the regions still remained in the hands of the Hans. Rebellious campaigns and self-determination movements persist in Tibet and Xinjiang which are regarded as "separatist" and subjected to severe repression in contemporary China. Paradoxically, Maoism which took culture and superstructure seriously in its treatment of dialectical and historical materialism did not ensure correct handling of this contradiction among people in China.

Mao in the history of political thought

Maoism does not figure prominently either in the Western discourses on Marxism or the discourses on development and transformation in the West. Paradoxically, communist movements and discourses on social transformation in the Asian, African and Latin American countries derive a lot of insights and inspiration from the Maoist tradition. That is because they find the ideological creativity in Mao Zedong's theory and political practice as attractive. In the two philosophical essays of Mao, On Practice and On Contradiction, both written in 1937, the essential point made by Mao is that theory has to be derived from practice. Hence the innovative idea of new democratic revolution and many new formulations on socialism, howsoever controversial they may be. While the new democratic revolution focussed on unity of people for national liberation, the theory of socialism stressed equality. In both cases, social differentiation was made essentially on class lines. The concept of 'people' (*renmin*) in People's Liberation Army, people's democracy and People's Republic of China clearly meant, as Mao put it, ninety five per cent of the population against the enemies. This concept of people, representing the broadest possible spectrum of a united front was the central theme for revolution as well as social transformation according to the Maoist framework. But in practice, it often pursued class politics in such a way that it did not adequately respect the relative autonomy of ethnic identity.

On the gender issue the famous statement 'Women hold up half the sky', is attributed to Mao. During the Yanan period many women were placed in high positions and a large number of women had joined the PLA. The PLA soldiers were scrupulous in maintaining dignity and rights of women in the war zones. The reform of the family under the Marriage Law in 1950 was a radical measure giving choice and equal rights in many spheres to women and men. The people's communes released women from household work and gave them opportunities to do agricultural work in the fields earning work points along with men. However, they got less work points than men. Mao is credited for taking many steps towards liberation of women. But the structural inequalities accruing from property rights, job opportunities and above all feudal cultural beliefs still remain. Women are yet to obtain high leadership positions to any significant measure in the Chinese state or Party. The reforms may have accentuated gender inequities as men move to specialized technical jobs in a situation of high growth. Thus the trend of gender equity visible during the Maoist era may not have been sustained in the reform era as the dialectical relationship between class and gender with autonomous importance given to gender remained unresolved in China.

Mao Zedong Thought initiated several innovative formulations on revolution and social transformation which continue to reverberate leading to intense political debates on the nature of democracy, socialism and human future in the twenty-first century throughout the world.

FURTHER READINGS

Dirlik, Arif, Paul Healy and Nick Knight, *Critical Perspectives on Mao Zedong's Thought* (Amherst, N.Y.: Humanity Books, second edition, 1997).

Fitzgerald, C.P., *Mao Tse-tung and China* (London: Hodder and Stoughton, 1976).

Meisner, Maurice, *Mao Zedong: A Political and Intellectual Potrait* (Cambridge: Polity, 2007).

Pence, Jonathan, *Mao Zedong: A Life* (London: Penguin, 2006).

Resolution on CPC History (1949-81) (Beijing: Foreign Languages Press, 1981).

Introduction

PHILOSOPHY OF THE CHINESE REVOLUTION

In recent years the study of political philosophy has become more lively. Instead of textual analysis of the classics of Western political thinkers, scholars have made determined bid to study the ideas as a part of their historical processes. Besides, categories of thought, concepts of analysis and theoretical frameworks are no longer limited to the 'masters of Western political thought'. Political philosophies of non-Western traditions have begun to attract almost similar attention. Moreover, the assumption that all political philosophy was exhausted in the ancient times has been proved facile because it went counter to the basic law of knowledge that with more practice the body of knowledge gathered possibilities of further growth. In fact, the human experiences of the twentieth century have posed more philosophical questions than was the case ever before in the history of mankind.

But it is not easy to study the political philosophy of a recent revolutionary era. Events and personalities may be too recent to offer themselves for considered assessment. Yet their importance is sometimes too great to indefinitely postpone philosophical comprehension of the momentous processes. Moreover, isolated judgement on specific events may be both superficial and misleading. Therefore, a deeper historical and philosophical understanding of a movement is necessary. This becomes even more difficult because there are obviously strong and passionate feelings about recent historical developments. Interests and attitudes may be so sensitive as to render an objective understanding of recent revolutions difficult. But these risks do not appear insurmountable when one remembers how important it is to comprehend the philosophy of modern revolutions. It is with this realisation that this study of the philosophy of the Chinese revolution has been undertaken.

The philosophy of the Chinese revolution is the product of the revolutionary movement in China during the last hundred years or so. Out of these, the last fifty years of Chinese history have seen the rise of certain political philosophical dimensions of the revolutionary movement with far-reaching implications. These dimensions were not the product of the personal imagination of Mao Zedong. They evolved gradually through a variety of successful and unsuccessful experiments by the Communist Party of China (CPC) headed by Chairman Mao since 1935. Mao's creative contribution lay in periodic 'summing up' or theorisation of the practical as well as philosophical lessons of the movement from time to time. So what we call 'political philosophy of Mao Zedong' or 'Mao Zedong Thought' is indeed the political philosophy of the Chinese revolutionary movement during the past half a century. Only a study of the historical process can explain the meaning of Mao Zedong's political ideas.

The Chinese revolutionary movement did not end in 1949, it developed into a new stage of social reconstruction after the establishment of the People's Republic. In case of China the continuity has been too pronounced to allow a separation of the two periods at 1949. Therefore, the theory of new-democratic revolution, which guided the movement till Liberation, is closely linked with the theory of class struggle in socialist construction in China.

The theory of new-democratic revolution sought to grapple with problems of anti-colonial and anti-feudal struggle. How does a peasant society fight against the formidable power of imperialism and feudalism was the problem taken up by the CPC in the 1920s. After a series of setbacks the CPC formulated the line of united front and people's war which finally brought the Chinese to victory. After completing the tasks of the new-democratic revolution, the CPC embarked on the building of socialism in China. The resources in the Chinese society, the CPC's revolutionary legacy, and the developments in the international communist movement created conditions warranting a new orientation to China's development process. Then Mao Zedong formulated the line of continuing revolutionary class struggle throughout the period of socialism—a line which stressed mass mobilisation and mass enthusiasm as the main basis of socialist construction. It also envisaged dialectical resolving of several development contradictions like the ones between industry and agriculture, city and countryside, workers and peasants, mental and manual labour. This theory conceived of the two-line struggle as a permanent safeguard against political degeneration. Thus these two theories, new-democratic revolution and continuous revolution, provide keys to the understanding of the revolutionary development in China during this century.

In this study the evolution of these two theories has been discussed in detail to show how the political context at different periods of time gave rise to the various dimensions of these theories. Some literature on Maoist 'guerilla warfare', 'military principles', and 'strategic doctrine' is available. But, in my view, these military dimensions can be comprehended only if we take a full view of the political framework of new-democratic revolution as a whole. As I argue in Chapter 1 unless the relationship between strategy and ideology is correctly understood we cannot separate the general from the particular in the context of the strategic experiences of the CPC. Many revolutionaries outside China have failed to grasp this difference. In Chapter 1, I have also tried to show how hard it is to practise new democracy after the seizure of political power.

My study of 'the theory of continuing the revolution under the dictatorship of the proletariat' mainly asks the theoretical question how to ensure a desirable quality of socialist development. As the evolution of this theory in course of intense inner-party struggles in China shows the story of this perspective is neither a story of success nor that of failure for the Maoist section of the CPC leadership. But clearly it is the chronicle of a series of attempts to steer the course of development in a large peasant society. The perspective of class struggle points at a certain path of development. But as we will see in Chapter 2 the difficulties, both theoretical and practical, in implementing this line are no less than its promise.

China provides a case of intimate link between internal politics and international politics. The CPC's practice of new-democratic revolution is very much reflected in the People's Republic of China's (PRC's) world-view and international behaviour since 1949. This is why the CPC's world-view is a legitimate part of its philosophy. The world-view as formulated by the CPC sees the world situation in terms of increasing struggle against imperialism conducted through an international united front with reliance on armed struggle as the main form of struggle. I have tried to show in Chapter 3 that this world-view represents an essential continuity since the CPC's Seventh Congress in 1945. I have compared the CPC's theoretical formulations on the modern world situation with its formulation during the period of the Sino-Soviet polemics in the 1960s and also with its three-worlds thesis of the 1970s, and argued that except for the redefinition of the Soviet Union as 'social-imperialist' the CPC has maintained its earlier approach. However, in spite of this approach, the Chinese foreign policy behaviour has raised serious questions in recent years. These are related to the handling of the contradiction between the superpowers and the issue of peaceful coexistence.

Finally, the basic methodology of the philosophy of the Chinese revolution has to be understood in some depth. Mao Zedong's materialist dialectics are perhaps one of the least studied aspects of his political thought even though they provide the maximum clues to the understanding of the theory and practice of the Chinese revolution. In Chapter 4, I have made an attempt to reconstruct the ideas of materialist dialectics putting the Maoist writings and the Chinese revolutionary experiences together with the earlier Marxist ideas. I have formulated four laws, the Law of Unity of Knowing and Doing, the Law of Analysis, the Law of Synthesis, and the Law of Particularity which have been put forth as essential tools for comprehending reality and changing it or for understanding a problem and solving it. But as we will see later these laws themselves are subject to the process of dialectical development. But an understanding of these laws is helpful in understanding all the other aspects of the philosophy of the Chinese revolution.

A comprehensive study of Mao Zedong's political philosophy or the philosophy of the Chinese revolution may not be adequately done without bringing the Chinese revolution into the historical perspective of China's long tradition. As the Chinese communists themselves have frequently admitted, old social values like Confucianism die hard. Therefore, an inquiry into how the new political theories overcame the force of the old society would be interesting. But unfortunately the whole debate on this question has come to hover within a circle of oft-repeated arguments. The efforts to draw isolated parallels between Mao's ideas with those of the classical Chinese thinkers are as unexciting as to seek their sources among Western liberal thinkers or for that matter among Marxist theorists.[1] These studies tend to lose the overall character of Maoist theories and above all ignore their close links with the actual social environment as it developed in China in recent times. Our study takes a total look at the theories and the basis of their development in course of the revolutionary movement.

How Marxist are these theories? First of all, official Soviet denunciations of 'Maoism' as a 'petty bourgeois chauvinistic ideology' clearly seems to generate from the present level of Sino-Soviet confrontation. This has to be viewed against the background of the fact that the Soviet assessment of Mao from 1930 till 1957 was absolutely different from the present one.[2] Some Western authors have regarded Mao as a Marxist but not a Leninist since Mao steered the course of the Chinese revolution on an agrarian revolutionary path.[3] Our study of the new-democratic revolution suggests that even though the Bolshevik revolution had a different character, it was Lenin who authored the lines of united front and agrarian revolution at least in their elementary form. As we will see in this study, Mao's ideas on dialectical materialism heavily rely on Engels and Lenin. Perhaps in order to underline the dependence of Mao's ideas on Marxism-Leninism the CPC writings carefully use the term 'Mao Zedong Thought' (*Mao Zedong Si-xiang*).[4] Besides, during the last decade the number of Mao Zedong's non-Marxist admirers has multiplied in the West. These 'radicals' do not see much of Marxism-Leninism in Mao's thought and rather see in him a body of humanist, egalitarian ideas for building a community devoid of all the ills of the Western industrial society.[5] As we will see in this study, none of these Maoist theories can stand independent of the basic postulates of Marxism like dialectical materialism, class struggle, dictatorship of the proletariat, and the communist party. Therefore, appreciating Mao aside of Marxism is like learning yoga without knowing of Hinduism.

NOTES

1. Putting Maoist ideas in the Chinese traditional context Richard Solomon has tried to point out a basic continuity of thought and behaviour in China (see Richard Solomon, *Mao's Revolution and the Chinese Political Culture,* Berkeley: University of California Press, 1971). However, Solomon fails to explain to what extent the modern socio-economic forces have generated a revolutionary situation causing discontinuities in some realms. Solomon's effort to apply the functionalist notion of political culture to explain the Chinese developments is painstaking but arbitrary. This is where Frederic Wakeman's attempt to identify the sources of Mao's ideas is less constrained by the usual functionalist prejudices. He traces Mao's ideas into Chinese and western traditions of idealism and human will on the one hand and materialism and utilitarianism on the other. However, Wakeman seems to exaggerate the role of the subjective force in this synthesis. It is very tempting and extremely easy to visualise an idealist Mao in whom human will ventures to change the course of history. But the meaning and force of Mao's ideas arise only from their roots in the reality of the revolutionary movement (see Frederic Wakeman, *History and Will: Philosophical Perspectives of Mao Tse-tung's Thought,* Berkeley: University of California Press, 1973).
2. V. Feoktistov, 'Phases of Maoism's Ideological Evolution', *Far Eastern Affairs,* No. 2 (1975) sees it as a 'system' of chauvinistic, militarist, petty bourgeois ideas. Lev Delyusin, on the other hand, thinks that it is not a system of coherent ideas, but a 'system of slogans' (see Lev Delyusin, *The Socio-Political Essence of Maoism,* New Delhi: Sterling Publishers, n.d., p. 10).
3. The ideology and strategy of China's new-democratic revolution made Benjamin Schwartz to show the glaring differences between Mao and Lenin, (see Benjamin Schwartz, *Chinese Communism and the Rise of Mao,* Cambridge, Mass: Harvard University Press, 1951, Ch. XIII; see also Arthur Cohen, *Communism of Mao Tse-tung,* Chicago: The University of Chicago Press, 1964). The theory and policies behind the Cultural Revolution moved Stuart Schram to see Mao's further departures from Leninism (see H.C. d'Encausse and Stuart, Schram, *Marxism and Asia,* London: Allen Lane; The Penguin Press, 1969, pp.

101-2). Franz Schurmann also thought that the Cultural Revolution was an attack on the Leninist organisational system which Mao and his colleagues had so imaginatively built up (see his postscript in *Ideology and Organisation in Communist China,* 2nd ed., Berkeley: University of California Press, 1968).

4. During the Cultural Revolution the term Marxism-Leninism-Mao Tsetung Thought (without the hyphen in Mao Tse-tung's name and Thought with capital T) was first used. The couple of instances of the use of Maoism (*Mao zhu-yi*) were never favoured officially. However, if we keep the nature of Mao's various ideas and theories in mind they can easily justify the use of the term 'Maoism'. Originally in 1945 Mao's ideas were described as 'thoughts' because his theory of new democratic revolution was an *application* of the Marxist theory to the Chinese conditions.
5. See for example, Committee of Concerned Asian Scholars, *Inside the People's Republic*, New York: Bantam, 1972.

1

Theory of New-Democratic Revolution

I. THE ISSUES

Achievement of national independence and liberation from colonial and feudal oppression have been the most significant processes in Asia, Africa, and Latin America since the Second World War. In these processes, the revolutionary movements and freedom struggles in China, India, Algeria, Indo-China, and Angola spanning through the last three decades have posed several crucial questions of revolutionary strategy as well as national reconstruction. Each experience has had its uniqueness and has contributed to the total body of ideas influencing the process of social transformation in the third world today. The Chinese experience in waging a liberation struggle and consolidating its achievements after seizing political power has raised several fundamental issues of revolutionary strategy as well as social reconstruction. The Chinese experience acquired significance because a peasant society with a large population and an ancient tradition underwent a convulsion under the leadership of a communist party which did not emulate the strategy of the Bolshevik revolution even though it was born out of the latter and had accepted the latter as the most important inspiration.

Isolated items of China's revolutionary experience have attracted so much attention that the basic character of the whole experience is rarely understood. This is why a comprehensive understanding of the theory of new-democratic revolution becomes important; especially because some of the critical issues of social transformation in the third world can be grappled with better from the positive as well as the negative aspects of the Chinese experiences before and after 1949.

In the following words Premier Hua Guofeng summed up Mao Zedong's theory of people's democratic revolution, in his speech at the mass memorial meeting in Peking on 18 September 1976:

> During the period of the new-democratic revolution, Chairman Mao analysed Chinese history and existing conditions and the principal contradiction in Chinese society, correctly answered the questions of the targets, tasks, motive, forces, character, perspectives and transformation of the new-democratic revolution in China, and laid down the general line and general policy of our Party for that historical period, that is, the new-democratic revolution against imperialism, feudalism and bureaucrat-capitalism waged by the broad masses of the people under the leadership of the proletariat. Chairman Mao pointed out that the seizure of political power by armed force in China could be achieved only by following the road of building rural base are encircling the cities from the countryside and finally seizing the cities, and not by any other road. Summing up the historical experience of our Party Chairman Mao pointed out that the three principal magic weapons for the Chinese Communist Party to defeat the enemy in the Chinese revolution were a Communist Party built on the Marxist-Leninist revolutionary theory and in the Marxist-Leninist revolutionary style, an army under the leadership of such a party and a united front of all revolutionary classes and all revolutionary groups under the leadership of such a party.

Indeed for many years Mao Zedong was known all over the world mainly for his strategic principles which led the Chinese revolution to victory in 1949. This was specially to because numerous communist revolutionary groups in the third world countries had formulated their revolutionary strategies under the inspiration of the Chinese new-democratic revolution. In a peasant society subjected to colonial exploitation and imperialist aggression the growth of a small communist force into a massive revolutionary tide that swept into victory was undoubtedly a rare historical experience. The strategic and organisational principles which brought this about were bound to generate interest all over the world. But an under standing of the underlying theory of new-democratic revolution has continued to be confounded by many controversies. Was the theory a Maoist innovation or was it the logical outcome of the policies of the Communist International (Comintern)? Was it an opportunist rationalisation of an arrangement forced upon CPC in the face of the Japanese aggression or was it a theoretical formulation with universal relevance in colonial situations? Was there some consistency between the new-democratic revolution and the people's democratic state which was set up in China in 1949 in terms of political and economic practice? And above all, does this theory represent the core postulates of Marxism or is it Mao's first major deviation from Marxist-Leninist path? At the same time, one may ask, what was passed for Maoist strategy, a body of universally applicable principles or was there a Maoist revolutionary outlook under which various strategies could be formulated in accordance with the demands of a prevailing environment?

It will be argued in this essay that Mao's theory of new democracy was the culmination of a series of conceptual as well as practical developments starting with the May Fourth Movement of 1919 and the 1920 Congress of the Comintern. Nevertheless as a comprehensive formulation it could be regarded as Mao's contribution to revolutionary theory. Every theory evolves in course of practice. Therefore, to some extent this theory was a strategic necessity in the situation of the late 1930s in China. But its continued practice even after the Sino-Japanese war suggested that it was more than an opportunistic rationalisation to get the support of the Guomindang (Kuomintang popularty know as KMT). The international influence of the so-called 'China path' in the year following the Second World War also supports this view. We also find some measure of consistency between the strategy of the revolution and the policies during the early years of the People's Republic of China (PRC). The policies during the 1949-56 period were basically of people's democratic nature rather than of socialistic nature. Our analysis suggests that the theory of new-democratic revolution applied Marxist-Leninist theory of revolution to the conditions of the colonial East without sacrificing any of its core postulates. Finally this analysis suggests that the core elements of the theory of new-democratic revolution constitute the Maoist revolutionary outlook on the basis of which appropriate strategies can be formulated to suit the demands of the various stages of a revolutionary movement. Under Mao Zedong's leadership the CPC changed its strategy from stage to stage. The CPC experience demonstrates that the character of revolutionary strategy is such that it is a dialectical synthesis of the ideological considerations and environmental demands. However, there are conceptual as well as practical problems in Mao's formulations which have surfaced in practice both in China and elsewhere.

II. DEVELOPMENT OF THE PERSPECTIVE

Mao Zedong published 'On New Democracy' in January 1940 in the midst of the Sino-Japanese war.[1] In this essay he defined the nature of the current stage of the Chinese revolution most explicitly and discussed the crucial questions arising out of it. It is this essay and the writings on strategy and philosophy by Mao during the three preceding years which acquired a distinct character for the CPC's revolutionary outlook. In 1945 the CPC Constitution acknowledged Marxism-Leninism and 'the combined principles derived from the practical experience of the Chinese revolution—the ideas of Mao Zedong—as the guiding principles of all its work'. This revolutionary outlook assumed further legitimation in the international communist movement.[2] But 1940 was only a culmination of a least a twenty-year long process of an evolving perspective.

The formulation of appropriate political lines for the Chinese revolution had bothered the Chinese revolutionaries for long and the Comintern since 1920. The revolutionaries in China had carried out various experiments from time to time since the May Fourth Movement of 1919. Till 1927 the CPC was a willing partner of the international communist movement following the decisions of the Comintern. Thereafter, the clash of political lines among the Comintern and the various factions within the CPC brought to the fore the whole range of strategic policies, many of which were simultaneously practised in China. Most of these policies, were costly adventures. But the cumulative experience derived from them nurtured the CPC in the right direction and as a result gradually a perspective of anti-feudal an anti-imperialist revolution developed. Thus, all the ideological and strategic elements of the new-democratic revolution could be traced back to the developments of the preceding twenty years. The concept of a broad united front, the agrarian character of the revolution in the colonies, the principles of a people's war, and all the corollaries of these elements gradually got linked with each other.

Under the impact of the Bolshevik revolution and in the wake of the turmoil of the First World War developments in China took a new turn. The May Fourth Movement stirred students, intellectuals, and workers in the cities of eastern China into an unprecedented demonstration of mass nationalism. The new nationalism clearly acquired an anti-imperialist character and at the same time it was firmly tied with programmes of social transformation and political integration of China. In these circumstances various revolutionary groups, communist and non-communist, tried to plan united action. This movement released forces which eventually became the basic elements of the new-democratic revolution.

The united front question was first discussed in depth in the Second Congress of the Third International in July 1920. The famous controversy between Lenin and M.N. Roy in this Congress took up the issue to decide whether the communists in colonial societies should join the nationalist struggles led by the bourgeoisie or should the communists organise the masses independently. M.N. Roy argued at this time in favour of the second line. He thought that if the communists joined the nationalist movements under the leadership of the bourgeoisie then the movements would not grow in the direction of first democratic and then socialist revolution. Lenin, on the other hand, noted that the proletarian movements in the colonies were still weak and anti-colonial tasks were the primary tasks of the revolution. So he favoured the formation of broad united front even under the leadership of the national bourgeoisie. In his opinion the proletariat should participate in the freedom struggles to further advance the movement against colonialism. He clearly had the Indian and the Chinese situations in mind where the major movements were led by the Congress and the Kuomintang respectively. A compromise was arrived at by the Congress which allowed flexible strategy to be pursued according to the needs of the situations but accepting suitable united front arrangements as the main principle.[3] The concept of united front even at this stage meant not only collaboration between the national bourgeoisie and the proletariat, but also alliance between the workers and the peasants. The peasant question was the main agenda in the Petrograd Congress of the Toilers of Far East in January-February 1922, which was attended by representatives from both the KMT and the CPC. There the 1920 thesis was reiterated and along with it, the Congress stressed the need for mobilisation of the peasants in the colonies and united fronts to carry out the national democratic movements.[4]

It was in this context that the CPC was founded in July 1921 on the initiative of the Comintern. Since the two urgent tasks facing all the revolutionaries in China were unification of the disintegrated nation and achieving freedom from the colonial powers the very first manifesto of the CPC talked about united efforts on the part of all progressive forces in China to achieve these pressing goals.[5] The contacts between Sun Yat-sen and Lenin bore fruit and in 1924 a united front government was set up in China bringing the CPC and the KMT together. This united front was the result of both an internal demand from the Chinese revolutionary groups as well as the Comintern advice in accordance with its 1920 line.

During this period the Comintern as well as the CPC defined the character of the Chinese revolution as bourgeois-democratic revolution in which the major goal of unification of the country was to be achieved by joint efforts of all revolutionary forces.[6] But the practice of the united front developed enormous strains after the death of Sun Yat-sen in 1925. On the one hand, the trade union movement in the cities of eastern China made fast progress as was evident from the many strikes of the workers, since 1922. On the other, the new KMT leader, Chiang Kai-shek started getting weary of the rise of communist influence in the cities. By 1926 the united front had shown enough cracks. That was also the year of the Northern Expedition to defeat the warlords. At this time Chiang started purging communists from the administrative councils. By the end of 1926 the viability of the united front was being questioned within the CPC leadership. The Controversy as to whether CPC Secretary-General Chen Duxiu advocated an early dissolution of the united front or did he 'capitulate' at the KMT offensive would never be resolved. But Stalin persisting to vindicate his policy of united front in China in the face of Trotsky's virulent criticisms against it, advised the CPC to unite with the left faction of the KMT and try for a military seizure of power by defeating the rightist faction of KMT led by Chiang Kai-shek. Even though the Comintern had two prominent representatives in China in M.N. Roy and Borodin, this line ended in a miserable failure. Chiang Kai-shek dealt a heavy blow on the communist cadres in April 1927 and only a small section of the CPC escaped to the countryside of Kiangsi.

Thus the first united front was a failure. But in retrospect we may say that the CPC learnt many lessons about the utility as well as the limitations of the united front. It never gave up the approach itself. Several lessons were to be learned from this 'Great Revolution which was betrayed by the KMT reactionaries'. The CPC did not have an army of its own so it could not meet the rightist armed onslaught. Their movement was concentrated in the cities where they fell easy prey to the Kuomintang forces. Finally, they were perhaps excessively dependent on the Comintern advice.

In July, 1928 the Sixth Congress of the CPC was held in Moscow and a new line was formulated for the Chinese revolution. This followed the decisions of the Ninth Enlarged Plenum of the Executive Committee of the Comintern in February 1928. These resolutions have been subjected to very different interpretations. However, undoubtedly the Comintern now stressed the need for militant labour organisation in order to establish the proletarian leadership of the Chinese revolution. It asked for propagating the idea of Soviets, developing the agrarian movement and arming the workers and peasants. It also recognised the unevenness of the Chinese revolution in different spheres and in different regions. These decisions were so general that within their purview Li Li-san advocated the line of sudden nation-wide proletarian armed insurrection in the cities. On the other hand, in the Soviet areas of Kiangsi, Mao pursued the line of setting up revolutionary bases and carrying on agrarian armed struggle while also claiming to pursue the Comintern line.

The debates on political and strategic lines first between Mao and Li Lisan, and then between Mao and Wang Ming became very bitter. But the CPC faction led by Mao gradually asserted one basic thing about the nature of the Chinese revolution, namely its agrarian character. Earlier in 1926 Mao had carried out an investigation on the peasant movement in Human and published his famous report the following year in which he had glorified the revolutionary potential of the peasant masses. After 1927 the organisation of the 'Workers and Peasants Red Army' and its work in defending the base areas in the face of the KMT attacks and carrying out agrarian reforms in the Soviet areas had shown promising results. In carrying out agrarian reforms the Government of the Soviet areas first pursued a radical policy of confiscating the land of landlords and rich peasants. But later it decided to win over the rich peasants and concentrate its attack on the landlords.[7] Thus the CPC became deeply involved in the concrete problems of agrarian armed struggle. By the early 1930s the CPC leaders in the Soviet areas were convinced that the main character of the Chinese revolution was to be agrarian armed struggle with peasants playing a leading revolutionary role.

In the meantime the intensification of the Japanese aggression in Manchuria had produced a qualitatively new situation in China. The government of the Chinese Soviet Republic reacted sharply to this and declared war against Japan in April 1932. In September 1933, that is, after four KMT campaigns of encirclement and annihilation against the Soviet forces had already taken place, the Chinese Soviet government made an appeal for united efforts to resist Japan. In January 1934 in his report to the Second Congress of the Soviets Mao Zedong discussed the seriousness of the national peril and announced the Chinese Soviet government's 'readiness for joint anti-Japanese military movement' on three conditions. First, the KMT should stop its anti-communist offensive; second, it should guarantee civil rights; and third, masses should be armed and anti-Japanese armed volunteers should be trained.[8] But Chiang Kai-shek's strategy was first to 'suppress the communist bandits' and then face the Japanese. Thus by the time the Red Army was forced to abandon Juichin and start on the Long March their slogan of the anti-Japanese united front had begun to acquire wide support.

But as yet new-democratic united front had not been developed into a full-scale revolutionary theory. In the 1934 report Mao still spoke of the continuing bourgeois-democratic revolution in China. But a rudimentary form of people's democracy can be seen in his exposition of 'Soviet democracy' which he described as 'worker peasant democratic dictatorship', a 'dictatorship against landlords and bourgeoisie'.[9] But the differentiation of the bourgeoisie which later became an important aspect of the new-democratic united front was still not visible in the CPC strategy. However, Mao stressed the agrarian character of their revolution which would have to be both anti-imperialist and anti-feudal. Thus, by 1934 some important dimensions of new democracy had become clear even though the concept of the united front of classes, the strategic principles of the war, and the overall political orientation were still not developed.

The Long March of 1934-35 was among other things a massive propaganda campaign for forging an anti-Japanese united front and stopping the civil war. Already this slogan had persuaded some KMT forces to come to terms with the Red Army. On 1 August 1935 the CPC—now with Mao as its Chairman—issued an 'Appeal to the whole of China to Resist Japan and Save the Country' (*Kang-ri jiu-guo*). The CPC carried out its propaganda campaign also through the mass organisations and demonstrations in cities. They established secret contacts with various KMT armies. All this seemed to pay off well when the public opinion in China gathered momentum in favour of organising united resistance against Japan. In 1936 the CPC made several formal proposals to the KMT in this connection. In Shensi the Red Army moderated their land policies and offered to carry out only democratic measures. On 26 August 1936 the CPC wrote to the KMT: 'We are prepared to form a strong revolutionary front with you as was the case during... the Great Chinese Revolution of 1925-27...(that) is the only proper way to save our country today.'[10] But Chiang Kai-shek persistently rejected the idea and started preparations for another bandit-suppression campaign in Shaanxi. The Xi'an incident, during which the forces of the Dong Bei Army led by Chang Hsueh-liang and the Shaanxi troops led by Yang Hu-cheng, took Chiang as prisoner and asked him to form an anti-Japanese united front with the CPC in December 1936, finally forced him to change his line.

We have recalled these developments to show that clearly the CPC had taken the initiative to form an anti-Japanese united front. Its united front line later coincided with the comintern's call for world-wide united front against fascism. But it was not on the basis of the

Comintern directive that the CPC formulated its line. Actually in the Seventh World Congress in August 1935 Georgi Dimitrov congratulated the CPC for its united front efforts and said:

> We therefore approve the initiative taken by our courageous brother Party of China in the creation of a most extensive anti-imperialist united front against Japanese imperialism and its Chinese agents, jointly with all those organised forces which are ready to wage a real struggle for the salvation of their country and their people.

The Chinese delegates including Wang Ming also reported to the Congress on the advance made by the CPC's united front campaign.[11]

A comparison of the Comintern Seventh Congress line and the CPC's united front line would show a number of differences in their orientations and emphases. Dimitrov's speech was primarily addressed to the Social Democrats in Europe with whom the Communists should forge a 'proletarian united front' and 'unity of action' at all levels. Then the spoke of 'anti-fascist people's front' which he described as 'fighting alliance between the proletariat, on the one hand, and the toiling peasantry and the basic masses of the urban petty bourgeoisie constituting the majority in the population of even the industrially developed countries on the other.' Only a small section of Dimitrov's speech was devoted to 'anti-imperialist united front' in the colonies in case of which the Comintern also suggested broad-based united fronts. The CPC formulation cannot be regarded as inconsistent with the Comintern's for actually Comintern did not spell out the line for the colonies. For China it has merely approved what the CPC was already doing. Moreover, the CPC went a step further with its decision to include the national bourgeoisie within the united front. This was perhaps necessary to justify association with the KMT at that stage.[12]

The CPC had adopted a dual approach towards the KMT since 1932. On the one hand, it continued the campaign against the KMT as the 'government of national betrayal' and on the other it called for united front with the KMT against the Japanese. Even in 1935 the CPC spoke of 'broad anti-fascist and anti-KMT united front.' But in 1936 they sent formal proposals to the KMT government. Perhaps it was an objective necessity to get the support of the KMT in order to meet the Japanese challenge. The KMT was still the dominant political authority in China; it had a large army, and the international community regarded the KMT and its leader Chiang Kai-shek as the leader of the Chinese people. Therefore, the CPC was genuinely interested in a united front with them, to save the nation from imperialist aggression.

The need for united effort was so great that the CPC reformulated its revolutionary programme of social transformation by moving a step backward. Instead of advocating a socialist programme of confiscation and redistribution, the CPC authorities in the Shaanxi region decided on taking only democratic anti-feudal measures of land reforms, rent reduction, and elementary cooperativisation. After the formation of the Border Region under the united front arrangement in 1937 the CPC conducted elections in the Shaanxi-Gansu-Ningxia Border Region and a united front government was formed. There were many non-communist activists in the new administrative set up at all levels. In May 1937 Mao referred to 'new-democratic republic' (*xin de min-hu gong-zhe-guo*) as a suitable system for China.[13] Shortly afterwards, the Finance Commissioner of the Border Region government Lin Bochu spelled out the framework of 'a new-democratic system' for the Border Region. The overall orientation of all policies in the Border Region was national mobilisation for war. Thus by the time Mao wrote his 'On New Democracy' in January 1940 the CPC was already practising it in the areas under its control.[14]

In 1937 both Mao and Lin Bochu had described Sun Yat-sen's 'Three people's Principles' as the basis of the united front policies. Sun's principles of nationalism, Democracy and People's Livelihood, and the policies of united front between the CPC and the KMT, alliance between China and the Soviet Union and the worker peasant alliance as formulated in 1924 still carried enormous weight in the minds of the Chinese people. As the CPC put it, the KMT's betrayal of all these principles had brought unprecedented miseries to the Chinese people. Therefore, a united front of the entire Chinese nation could be built on the basis of the programme charted out by the father of modern China, Sun Yat-sen. As Mao later explained in his essay of 1940, the programme of the new-democratic revolution was an extension of the Three People's Principles.[15] Such a link with the legacy of Sun Yat-sen proved very effective in achieving wider popular appeal for the new policies.

Thus the actual situation as it developed in China in the face of Japanese aggression influenced the CPC's policies and led it towards a political line of united front. This was further complicated by the operative military situation on the war front. The superior military strength of the Japanese armed forces had succeeded in their occupation of the whole of eastern China within a few months in 1937. This situation was to be tackled by a decimated Red Army now renamed as the Eighth Route Army and the New Fourth Army which had to fight mainly on its own because of tenuous united front arrangements with the KMT forces. In these circumstances Mao Zedong summed up the Red Army's military experiences during the Jiangxi Soviet period and drew important lessons for the new situation. The idea of 'revolutionary base area' had vindicated itself during the previous years. But exclusive reliance on professional and positional warfare did not always pay off especially when the army was poorly armed. Therefore, the revolutionaries would have to resort to guerilla warfare and launch attacks on the cities from the countryside. Thus on the basis of experiences in a developing military situation Mao Zedong formulated a series of strategic and tactical principles of a 'people's war' as a part of the programme of united front resistance to Japanese imperialism.

From the foregoing it is obvious that the second united front was very different from the first. Now the CPC had its own armed forces and its own areas which it did not surrender. It maintained 'independence and the initiative' in the united front while at the same time forging joint programmes against Japan. While the KMT had a purely military view of the united front, the CPC regarded it as a revolutionary programme with political, economic, cultural, and, of course, military dimensions. The CPC carried out patriotic political mobilisations, land reforms and production movements, set up the Anti-Japanese University in Yenan, and initiated a host of cultural and literary programmes. Above all, the CPC linked the policies of the united front with its programme of revolution in China and formulated a theory of new democratic revolution.

The evolution of the CPC's new democratic perspective thus, was a gradual process. It was a brick-by-brick construction by the CPC in course of many trial-and-error encounters. Enough evidence is available now to disprove the once popular view that the second united front in China was a product of the Comintern directive. Nor is it appropriate to attribute the CPC's new-democratic theory to any one or two factors like patriotic mobilisation against Japan or this combined with an appealing programme of social transformation.[16] Perhaps, instead of looking for single causes of victory of revolutions, the question should be recast in terms of explaining the nature and outcome of historical processes. The process of the Chinese revolution had a zigzag course and there were periodic theorisations of its experiences. The 1940 theorisation by Mao was an articulation of an already developing process. The negative lessons of the first united front and the Jiangxi Soviet period gave rise to positive alternatives in the wake of the imperialist aggression and finally a political perspective of anti-imperialist and anti-feudal united front emerged.

III. IDEOLOGY AND STRATEGY OF THE NEW-DEMOCRATIC REVOLUTION

The theory of new-democratic revolution is an application of the Marxist theory of bourgeois-democratic revolution to the colonial situations. According to Marx, in the process of development of societies feudalism is overthrown by a bourgeois-democratic revolution as a consequence of which capitalist system is established. When capitalism reaches its point of saturation it starts decaying and it is replaced by a socialist system through a proletarian revolution. This formulation was obviously based on the experiences of the industrial societies of Europe. In colonial situations where liberation from colonialism is as important as fighting against feudalism, some modification of the original formulation of Marx was needed. This modification was first undertaken by the Comintern under Lenin's leadership in 1920 when the tasks of anti-colonial struggle were sought to be combined with anti-feudal revolution.

Based on the experiences of the Chinese revolutionary movement Mao Zedong suggested that in semi-colonial and semi-feudal conditions like those which obtained in China, the bourgeois-democratic revolution had to take the form of a new or people's democratic revolution which was to be both anti-colonial and anti-feudal. It was a more advanced form than the bourgeois-democratic revolution because it was led by worker in alliance with the peasants. This would create conditions for a smooth transition to socialism.

Even though Mao frequently said that China's new-democratic revolution was a part of the proletarian-socialist world revolution it was 'not yet itself a proletarian-socialist revolution in its social character,'[17] because at this stage a section of the bourgeoisie was not only allowed to carry on its economic activity but also was a partner in the united front. Thus, the new-democratic revolution was conceived as an intermediate stage of revolution between bourgeois-democratic and socialist revolutions and it was to take place in semi-colonial and semi-feudal situations.

Even though this overall perspective can be traced back to the Comintern, the articulation of certain elements of this theory can be attributed to the CPC leadership headed by Mao. Even though the idea of the four-class united front consisting of the workers, peasants, petty bourgeoisie, and the national bourgeoisie was a Comintern formulation, the particular policy regarding the united front that regulated the class relations within and without and the role of the communist party in it was a CPC innovation. Equally significant was the set of policies regarding the agrarian revolutionary war which guided the mobilisation of the peasants, building of a people's army, setting up of revolutionary bases, and attacking the cities from the countryside.

Chart 1
A Comparative Chart of Revolutions

Stage of revolution	*Enemy class*	*Leading class*	*Its allies*	*Form of the emergent state*
Bourgeois-democratic revolution	Feudal class	Bourgeoisie	Petty bourgeoisie peasantry, workers	Bourgeois democracy
New-democratic revolution	Imperialists, landlords comprador bourgeoisie	Proletariat in alliance with peasants	Petty bourgeoisie, national bourgeoisie	People's democracy or people' democtatic dictatorship (United front of workers, peasants, petty bourgeoisie and national bourgeoisie in power)
Socialist revolution	Bourgeoisie	Proletariat	Peasantry	Socialist democracy or dictatorship of the proletariat

Contradictions in the Chinese Revolutionary Environment

The characterisation of modern Chinese society has raised many controversial issues regarding the applicability of Marxist categories to China. Even among the Marxist, opinions have differed as to whether the traditional Chinese society down to the twentieth century demonstrated Marx's 'Asiatic mode of production.' In the 1920s and 1930s Marxist scholars in China debated the extent of the development of capitalism in China. While some argued that the Chinese society was still essentially feudal, others pointed at the increasing trends of commodity production and money economy in China since the middle of the nineteenth century and characterised it as a capitalist society.[18] These characterisations were important because they would decide the nature of the revolution, its motive forces, and targets.

For the CPC Mao presented a definitive class analysis in December 1939 and said that the last hundred years' experiences had changed China's feudal society into a colonial, semi-colonial, and semi-feudal country. He pointed out that 'in their aggression against China the imperialist powers have on the one hand hastened the disintegration of feudal society and the growth of elements of capitalism, thereby transforming a feudal into a semi-feudal society, and on the other imposed their ruthless rule on China, reducing an independent country to a semi-colonial and colonial country.[19] In this characterisation particular emphasis was laid on the fact that to some extent national capitalism had developed in China alongside the operation of colonial economic control, but it had not become a dominant force. Thus after the 1911 revolution there was first the warlord-bureaucrat rule of the landlord class and then the joint dictatorship of the landlords and the big bourgeoisie. They were subservient to, if not agents of, imperialists.

The situation in China represented a convergence of some elements of the feudal epoch with some elements of the capitalist epoch. So the contradictions between imperialism and the Chinese nation, and between feudalism and the great masses of the people were described by Mao as the 'basic contradictions in modern Chinese society' (*Jian-dai zhong-guo she-hui de zhu-yoo mao-dun*).[20] Mao referred to the existence of the contradiction between the bourgeoise and the proletariat but did not describe it as a basic contradiction though theoretically it ought to be one. This was perhaps because even though a section of the bourgeoisie sided with colonialism, another section could be regarded as belonging to the united front of the Chinese masses. In 'On New Democracy' Mao clarified this further and described the contradiction between the comprador-bourgeoisie and the proletariat as a basic contradiction. Thus the contradictions between imperialism, feudalism and comprador-bourgeoisie on the one hand, and the workers, peasants, petty bourgeoisie and national bourgeoisie on the other were regarded as the basic contradictions in the societies which were colonial, semi-colonial, and semi-feudal.

According to the laws of materialist dialectics each contradiction had its particularity at a definite stage of the historical process. During the Sino-Japanese war the contradiction between imperialism and the Chinese nation was the principal contradiction which determined the state of all other contradictions.[21]

However, the contradictions keep on developing with the changing position of their aspects. As the situation changed after the defeat of Japan in 1945, the principal contradiction was no longer the same. In 1946 it became clear to the CPC that the KMT represented the three enemy classes, so the contradiction between the KMT and the revolutionary classes became the principal contradiction during the third civil war.[22]

United Front

The dialectical law of synthesis demanded the resolution of the principal contradiction to help the development of the Chinese social process. Therefore, once the principal enemy was identified all other forces were to be united to struggle against the enemy. This is why the Comintern had suggested the notion of an anti-imperialist united front. The CPC developed it further in three ways: (1) by maintaining independence and initiative, (2) by including national bourgeoisie in the united front, and (3) by integrating the united front with an overall programme of people's democratic revolution.

As discussed earlier, the CPC was reluctant to hand over either its army or the areas under its control to the KMT government in 1937. Even after the suffering and losses during the Long March the CPC still commanded a sizeable Red Army. Moreover in the

Shaanxi-Gansu-Ningxia region it controlled vast territories. So the CPC leadership did not want to repeat the arrangement of the first united front. Their insistence on retaining independence was so strong that the arrangements were never fully formalised even though political and military coordination started to take effect in 1937. This policy was also reflected in the united front bodies which were set up in the border regions on the basis of the 'three-thirds-system'. Mao asked the communists to play the leading role in all these bodies.[23]

The national bourgeoisie was regarded as a constituent of the united front. The contradiction between the national bouregoisie and the proletariat was non-antagonistic because both classes had a common interest in fighting against imperialism and feudalism. Yet since the new-democratic revolution was always described as a transition to socialism the national bourgeoisie was bound to be sceptical about cooperating with the proletariat. So it had a dual character. This was recognised by Lenin in 1920 and the Comintern's political lines reflected this. On this question both Trotsky and M.N. Roy held the view that basically the national bourgeoisie was interested in suppressing proletarian movements. In 1926 Mao had pointed out the 'inconsistent attitude' of the 'middle bourgeoisie' towards the Chinese revolution.[24] In his major essays during the Sino-Japanese war, he maintained the same view when he differentiated the national bourgeoisie from the big comprador bourgeoisie, spoke of its dual character, and stressed the need for its inclusion in the united front. In 1935 he assured the national bourgeoisie that 'the people's republic will not expropriate private property other than imperialist and feudal property and so, far from confiscating the national bourgeoisie's industrial and commercial enterprises, it will encourage their development.'[25] In 1939 Mao described this class as a 'good ally of ours' though he cautioned the CPC to follow a 'prudent policy.'[26]

The significance of this formulation is in its actual practice. This formulation attracted a large number of 'middle elements' in Chinese society to work with the communists. This also challenged the claim of the KMT to national leadership. The non-communist intellectuals in the cities started accepting the credentials of the CPC as the main anti-imperialist force. This was in return for CPC's seriousness about the united front. In 1949 on the eve of Liberation, Mao Zedong explained in his essay 'On The People's Democratic Dictatorship' how greatly China needed to continue industrial production with the help of the national bourgeoisie. He said:

> To counter imperialist oppression and to raise her backward economy to a higher level, China must utilize all the factors of urban and rural capitalism that are beneficial and not harmful to the national economy and the people's livelihood; and we must unite with the national bourgeoisie in common struggle. Our present policy is to regulate capitalism, not to destroy it.[27]

On the basis of this perspective China was proclaimed a People's Republic with 'People's democratic front' in power. In 1949 Mao defined *people*: 'At the present stage in China, they are the working class, the peasantry, the urban petty bourgeoisie and the national bourgeoisie.'[28] The contradictions among them were non-antagonistic. After the seizure of political power these four classes established a 'joint dictatorship' which was called 'People's Democratic Dictatorship.' This system ensured democracy for the four classes which constituted over ninety per cent of the population. Since every state according to Marx was a class dictatorship the people's democratic state was also a dictatorship insofar as it denied freedom to the enemy classes. Explaining the united front political system Mao said: 'the state system of a joint dictatorship of all the revolutionary classes and the system of government, democratic centralism—these constitute the politics of New Democracy.'[29]

The other innovative element in the CPC's practice of the united front was its revolutionary character. First of all, this time the united front was not only 'from above' as a political arrangement between party leaders. It was also 'from below', *i.e.*, a class alliance at the grass-root level.[30] These alliances would be sham unless measures were taken to further the common interests of these classes. Therefore, anti-imperialist mobilisation was combined with democratic reforms. As we saw earlier, the CPC gage up its programme of socialist transformation and adopted only democratic measures on the lines suggested by Sun Yat-sen's Three People's principles. This allowed many rich peasants and even landlords to join the united front. But the overall programme of democratic transformation was maintained.

The political, organisational, ideological, and military principles of the united front made it a comprehensive revolutionary programme. Politically the CPC invited non-communists and national bourgeoisie to share power with it. Organisationally, the communist party built itself on the principle of mass line with close reliance on the masses. Militarily, the communists gave shape to a politicised army capable of waging guerilla war and operating from revolutionary bases. Ideologically, the communists propagated new-democratic idea among the Chinese people and Marxism-Leninism among the members of the CPC. The new-democratic culture was described as popular, national and scientific; and this did have wide-spread appeal. It is this attempt to raise what is generally regarded a 'tactic' of united front to a higher level that made it coterminous with the 'theory of new-democratic revolution' which made 'united front' one of the 'magic weapons' of the Chinese revolution.

Organisation and Leadership

Another 'magic weapon' of the Chinese revolution according to Mao was the communist party. It is interesting to see how Mao reconciled the notion of communist leadership with the idea of united front, and both these with a strategy of agrarian revolution.

Among the four classes which constituted the united front, the majority class was the peasantry. The poor peasantry and the landless were the most exploited classes in modern China and they constituted nearly 70 per cent of the rural population. In the Hunan Report of 1927 Mao noted the growing political consciousness among the peasantry and said: 'The only group in the country-side that has always put up the bitterest fight is the poor peasants. Throughout the period of underground organisation and that of open organisation, it was they who fought, who organised, and who did the revolutionary work.'[31] The experiences of 1924-27 had taught the lesson that exclusive attention to city workers would not advance the process of revolution in the existing Chinese conditions. So in the early days of the Jiangxi Soviet, Mao concluded that the Chinese revolution was going to be essentially an agrarian revolution. In 'Why Is It That Red Political Power Can Exist in China?' Mao said: '...the content of China's democratic revolution consists in overthrowing the rule of imperialism and its warlord tools in China so as to complete the national revolution, and in carrying out the agrarian revolution so as to eliminate the feudal exploitation of the peasants by the landlord class.'[32] The formation of the Workers and Peasants Red Army and its growing peasant composition had materially demonstrated the revolutionary role of the Chinese peasantry. As Lin Biao pointed out in 1965, 'the peasants were the most reliable and the most numerous ally of the proletariat and constituted the main force in the War of Resistance.'[33]

While the agrarian character of the Chinese revolution unfolded gradually, concrete theoretical problems also arose out of this. In China a proletarian class had emerged as a result of the growth of industrialisation after the First World War. In 1939 Mao put the number of industrial workers at 2.5 to 3 million and workers in small-scale industries and handicrafts at 12 million, excluding the rural labourers.[34] The total number of workers was still a small percentage of the Chinese population. However, the CPC's early strength was confined to the workers' unions in the cities. Moreover, the communist party by definition is the 'vanguard of the proletariat'. Because of this, in 1928 the Comintern had stressed that the workers must exercise leadership in the revolution. Both Li Lisan and Wang Ming had formulated strategies on that basis. Mao, on the other hand, pleaded for a line of agrarian revolution under proletarian leadership.

Mao's formulation sounded contradictory to his critics. But by 1939-40 he clarified this question by suggesting that in the new-democratic revolution the proletariat exercised the leadership in alliance with the peasants and the peasants were the 'biggest motive force' or the 'main force' of the Chinese revolution.[35] This formulation justified the leading role of the CPC as the 'vanguard of the proletariat' and at the same time it explained the strategy of setting up rural base areas and mobilising the peasants and finally encircling the cities. The partial convergence of the feudal and capitalist epochs in the Chinese situation implied the revolutionary role of both the peasants and the workers. Moreover, history did not provide any instance of the bourgeoisie completing the democratic revolution. So workers' leadership in this revolution was meant to ensure not only completion of the democratic tasks but also transition to the socialist stage.

The formulation that peasants were the 'main force' of the revolution has been subjected to diverse interpretations. With regard to a comparable period of the Russian revolution From 1905 to February 1917 Stalin had described the 'proletariat' as the 'main force' and the peasantry as the 'reserve'.[36] During the proletarian revolution the peasantry became an *ally* of the proletariat. Mao's excessive reliance on the peasantry had invited the accusation of 'peasant mentality' and 'petty-bourgeois romanticism' from his Marxist critics. Original Marxist scepticism about the peasants' revolutionary ability continued to linger in the minds of European Marxists.[37]

Actually, developments since the beginning of the twentieth century have led to a modification of the orthodox Marxist view on the peasantry. Lenin's study of Russian agriculture showed that with the development of capitalism in agriculture 'the former isolation of the uncouth farmer from the rest of the world was broken down.[38] In the colonial societies where colonial and feudal oppression jointly impoverished the masses, new political organisations grew up and political consciousness spread among the peasants.[39] As Mao's Hunan Report showed and as subsequent political movements in China and other colonial situations demonstrated, the development of modern communications, and organisational facilities have changed the environment of the peasants. They no longer remained isolated, individualist, inert, and irrational. The Chinese revolutionary experience proved that they can acquire proletarian virtues of solidarity, rationality, and forward-looking ability.

Besides, the Chinese communists were compelled by their environment to heavily rely on the peasantry. During the Sino-Japanese war the Japanese troops were concentrated in the cities and they also controlled the main lines of communication. As Lin Biao explained in 1965: 'Owing to the shortage of troops they were unable to occupy the vast countryside which remained the vulnerable sector of the enemy's rule.'[40] Hence the communist forces operated in the countryside. Their army was almost wholly composed of peasant recruits. Funds and supplies needed for a protracted war also came chiefly from the peasants. This is why the Chinese revolutionary movement has been sometimes officially described as 'peasant revolutionary war' which Lin Piao summed up thus: 'To rely on the peasants, build rural base areas and use the countryside to encircle and finally capture the cities—such was the way to victory in the Chinese revolution.'[41]

Mass Line

There was little doubt about the fact that the communist party must lead the agrarian revolution. Within the framework of the new-democratic revolution the CPC gradually evolved two important organisational characteristics. Firstly, it should practise mass line (*Qun-zhong lu-xian*) so that it can sustain its mass support. Secondly, it should constantly engage in ideological work so that its grasp over revolutionary theory would be continuously strengthened.

The objective reality confronting the CPC during the Sino-Japanese war made it imperative for it to derive its primary resources from the organised strength of the people. To ensure close links between the party and the people Mao coined the term 'mass line' by which he meant 'from the masses, to the masses.' This orientation of work was explained thus by Mao in June 1943:

> Take the ideas of the masses (scattered and unsystematic ideas) and concentrate them (through study turn them into concentrated and systematic ideas), then go to the masses and propagate and explain these ideas until the masses embrace them as their own, hold fast to them and translate them into action, and test the correctness of these ideas in such action ...And so on, over and over again in an endless spiral, with the ideas becoming more correct...each time.[42]

According to this orientation all policies should involve the masses at the stages of formulation, implementation as well as reformulation. This is how the Leninist organisational principle of democratic centralism was translated into a practical mode of functioning by the CPC. The CPC's experience suggested that without commitment to and strategic dependence on the masses, centralism was likely to prevail over democracy.[43]

While practising mass line the party was expected both to reflect the desires of the masses and at the same time lead them by raising their political consciousness. On this point Mao has said: 'If we tried to go on the offensive when the masses are not yet awakened, that would be adventurism.'[44] And commandism is wrong in any type of work, because in overstepping the level of political consciousness of the masses and violating the principle of voluntary mass action it reflects the disease of impetuosity.[45] Mao also condemned tailism: 'In falling below the level of political consciousness of the masses and violating the principle of leading the masses forward, it reflects the disease of dilatoriness.'[46] According to Mao an organisation must dialectically synthesise the existing consciousness of the people with the possible development of the revolution.

These orientations of the revolutionary organisation were gradually articulated and absorbed into the overall ideology of the CPC in the middle of the 1940s. During the Zheng Feng campaign of 1942-44 the Maoist leadership undertook to sum up its theoretical principles and launched a movement of ideological education among the party members. At that time the objectives of the campaign seemed to be to check bureaucratism within the party and tighten the party organisation under Mao's leadership.[47] But the campaign also reflected an unusual stress on ideological education and political campaign. Since then the CPC has continued to uphold the importance of ideology in all spheres of its activity.

The Maoist notion of ideology is not merely functional, it is the theoretical basis for strategic action. However, mechanical understanding of Marxist ideology was always deplored by Mao.[48] At the time of the Zheng Feng campaign the Maoist leadership emphasised the need for 'creatively applying the truth of Marxism-Leninism to the concrete conditions of China.' This attempt at 'sinicisation of Marxism' on the one hand provided a flexible character to ideology and on the other hand maintained the universal Marxist character of the Chinese revolutionary movement. By putting enormous stress on ideological education Mao, in effect, made this dialectical inculcation of ideology pervasive among his party-men. They were to be Marxists, but not dogmatists. They were to grasp both the universality of the contradictions which Marx and Lenin had demonstrated, at the same time they were to comprehend the particularity of the contradictions in their own situation and find out ways of resolving them.

Mao wrote in 1945 that 'Ideological education is the key link to be grasped in uniting the whole party for great political struggles.'[49]

The pervasive role of ideology in Chinese communist practice was later demonstrated during the Cultural Revolution in the late 1960s. Between the Zheng Feng campaign and the Cultural Revolution the CPC showed a basic commitment to ideological education as a catalytic force. The high premium on ideological education in the People's Liberation Army (PLA), resorting to numerous ideological campaigns against decadent institutions and ideas, and above all undertaking political compaigns in inner-party struggles have become conspicuous features of the Chinese political process. The emphasis on thought transformation in the PRC in fact carried over the ideological orientation of the Yenan years.

This is how 'a communist party built on the Marxist-Leninist revolutionary theory and in the Marxist-Leninist revolutionary style' became an important element of the theory of new-democratic revolution. But even in the Chinese experience implementing the mass line has not been easy. Very often it has meant popular legitimation of a central directive. Especially in situations of leadership conflicts the ruling group invariably used all the resources at its disposal to rally popular opinion in favour of its policy. It is not at all clear to what extent the norms of mass line have been internalised at various levels of the Chinese polity.

The Maoist emphasis on ideological education has no doubt reaped many dividends. It is responsible for a high degree of work-motivation, service mentality, solidarity, and unity in China. But since every campaign reflects the ideological orientation of the ruling group and every ruling group gives its own interpretation of Marxism, this system gives ample opportunities for wrong policies to rally popular support. In other words revisionists can also make good use of this mass line and ideological campaign and can even succeed at least temporarily.

Besides identifying the contradictions and building up a revolutionary party, a revolutionary movement requires a revolutionary army trained in the principles of revolutionary war. In fact, Mao once said that 'without a people's army the people have nothing'. According to the theory of new-democratic revolution there must be an army under the leadership of the party which must master the principles of people's war.

Principles of People's War

Mao Zedong regarded people's war as the main component of new-democratic revolution, but he frequently pointed out that only as a part of a comprehensive political programme of revolution the military principles were significant. Moreover, the principles of people's war as practised during the 1930s and 1940s in China were heavily dependent upon the political and ideological dimensions of the people's democratic revolution. This is why the following statement from Lin Piao's 1965 essay may lead to confusion unless it is put in proper perspective. Lin wrote:

> The special feature of the Chinese revolution was armed revolution against armed counter-revolution. The main form of struggle was war and the main form of organisation was the army which was under the absolute leadership of the Communist Party, while all the other forms of organisation and struggle led by our Party were coordinated, directly or indirectly, with the war.[50]

Taken literally this passage can be construed as taking revolution as a purely military affair. But actually in the same essay Lin Piao elaborated the comprehensive theory of new-democratic revolution and discussed the principles of people's war within that framework.

Many commentators have equated the theory of new-democratic revolution with 'Maoist revolutionary strategy'. This leads to conceptual confusion and may even mislead revolutionaries following the theory. In the Marxist framework strategy as a plan of action is a dialectical synthesis of environmental needs and ideological goals. Every plan of action must fulfil the demands of a particular situation. But at the same time it must lead towards the realisation of the long-term goals of a movement. A correct strategy must not be opportunist, succumbing completely to the immediate environment forgetting the ideological objectives. Nor should it be dogmatic by mechanically deducing programmes from ideological statements without taking into account the resource position and the other factors existing at a particular stage. Therefore, the concept of strategy is below the level of theory and ideology. Consequently, even when an organisation follows an ideology or a theory it has to pursue different strategies of action at different stages of the revolutionary movement.

Mao Zedong's notion of practice suggests the contingent character of strategy. He said in 1937: '... ideas, theories, plans or programmes are usually altered partially or sometimes even wholly, because of the discovery of unforeseen circumstances in the course of practice.'[51] He was even more explicit when he said: 'In a revolutionary period the situation changes very rapidly, if the knowledge of revolutionaries does not change rapidly, if the knowledge of revolutionaries does not change rapidly in accordance with the changed situation, they will be unable to lead the revolution to victory.'[52]

The reference to the 'stages' in China's revolutionary war frequently appears in Mao's writings. Writing in December 1936 he discussed the two previous stages—1924-27 and 1927-36—and the corresponding strategic implications. The new stage of 'national revolutionary war' against Japan inaugurated a new strategy.[53] In an important article in October 1939 Mao referred to the period 1936-1939 as the third stage and said that there were three distinct stages of development in each of the three questions, United Front, Armed Struggle, and Party-Building.[54]

Mao identified the three stages of the protracted war in the following manner and suggested appropriate strategy for each stage: The first stage covers the period of the enemy's strategic offensive and our strategic defensive. The second stage will be the period of the enemy's strategic consolidation and our preparation for the counter-offensive. The second stage will be the period of the enemy's strategic consolidation and our preparation for the counter-offensive. The third stage will be the period of our strategic counter-offensive and the enemy's strategic retreat.'[55] Mao's discussion of 'strategic problems' and 'strategic principles' also conformed to this view of strategy. At one place he mentioned thirty-six strategic problems which ranged from the very general to the very particular. Among the general problems he spoke of 'giving proper consideration to the relation between the enemy and ourselves, between various campaigns or between various operational stages, giving proper consideration to the *special features contained in the general situation.*'[56] In another important essay Mao devoted a full section to the 'changes in the Party's Military Strategy in the Civil War and the National War.'[57] In this he discussed the strategies in the two 'strategic periods' of the civil war between the KMT and the CPC, and the two 'strategic periods' of the war of resistance against Japan.

All this implies that while certain broad principles of waging a people's war governed the CPC's strategic experiences, the actual components of strategy varied from stage to stage. Therefore, it is important to distinguish between the elements of CPC's revolutionary strategy at specific stages of the movement from the principles of people's war which were part of the theory of new-democratic revolution. As any theory and ideology, the new-democratic revolution also needed to be concretised in specific situations in an appropriate form of strategy. This distinction between ideology and strategy has often been absent in interpretations of Mao Zedong's revolutionary strategy.[58]

Among the essential principles of people's war the most important is the organisation of a people's army. Right from the initial days of the Red Army Mao Zedong regarded it as a political arm of the revolution whose activities were not limited to fighting. Mao said in 1929:

> The Chinese Red Army is an armed body for carrying out the political tasks of revolution. Especially at present, the Red Army should certainly not confine itself to fighting; besides fighting... it should shoulder such important tasks as doing propaganda among the masses, organising the masses, arming them, helping them to establish revolutionary political power and setting up party organisation.[59]

During the Sino-Japanese war, out of necessity the Eighth Route Army and the New Fourth Army also tried to adopt mass line mode of functioning. Many steps were taken by the CPC to create harmonious relationship between army and the people, and between the officers and soldiers within the army. The so-called Three-Eight Combination popularised the norms of army behaviour towards people and created enormous amount of popular sympathy and support for the red forces.[60] The democratic measures within the army which reduced the gulf of status and privilege between soliders and the officers also succeeded in creating an egalitarian tradition in a hierarchy-prone organisation.[61] Above all, Mao repeatedly challenged any tendency of military operating independently of party leadership. His famous statement when quoted in full suggests this clearly: 'Every Communist must grasp the truth, "political power grows out of the barrel of a gun". Our principle is that the Party commands the gun and the gun must never be allowed to command the Party.'[62]

Thus a people's army must be a politically-motivated organisation practising democracy within itself and working under the leadership of the party and deriving its fighting strength from the people. This is an important principle of the people's war. Besides this, the three essential principles of people's war guiding formulation of strategy are: (1) protracted war using guerilla, mobile and positional warfare; (2) establishment of revolutionary base areas; and (3) policy of self-reliance.

Inspired by Sun Tzu's *Art of War* (fourth century B.C.) Mao thought that by resorting to guerilla warfare a militarily weak organisation can face the challenge of a strong enemy and can slowly increase its own strength. According to Mao guerilla warfare was a weapon that a nation inferior in arms and military equipment may employ against a more powerful aggressor nation.'[63] However, people's war did not make use of guerilla warfare in exclusion to other forms of warfare. During the first two stages of the protracted war, guerilla warfare was the primary form of warfare while in the third stage the regular form of positional warfare was the primary form.[64] The extent to which guerilla warfare, mobile warfare, and positional warfare should be used would depend on the nature of the particular stage of development of the war. The important implication of this is that the particular sequence of stages which occurred during the Sino-Japanese war need not be replicated in the same order in every war situation. Accordingly the appropriate combinations of these forms of warfare would depend on the needs of a specific situation.[65] All that the principles of people's war suggest is that if a weak army faced a strong enemy, then it must rely on the masses and engage in guerilla warfare in appropriate measure.

The famous tactical and operational principles of the Chinese revolutionary war were only applicable to specific military situations. Therefore, in spite of their success in China they could not be regarded as universal principles of people's war. However, these tactics reinforce our understanding of the nature of strategy. The 'Ten Principles of Operation' lay enormous stress on initiative, flexibility, and planning.[66]

In all these the basic motive is to make the maximum use of the number of the revolutionary forces to gradually reduce the size of the enemy forces. In order to guard the size of the revolutionary army one principle says, 'Fight no battle unprepared'. Many of the principles put emphasis on human capabilities like determination, will, courage, and sacrifice.

Li Zepeng, in an important commentary on the Ten Principles of Operation, has discussed the principle of 'strategically pitting one against ten, tactically pitting ten against one' and has said: 'the method of fighting by "concentrating a superior force to destroy the enemy forces one by one" is a concentrated expression in military struggle of the concept of tactically taking the enemy seriously.'[67] 'Strategically pitting one against ten' means 'despising the enemy strategically' or facing the enemy boldly and confidently. At the same time, in actual operations enemy's strength must be fully noted and met with superior strength. In this approach Mao takes into account the dual nature of the enemy which is weak in ultimate analysis, but strong and powerful in the immediate context. This broad approach therefore, justifies the use of guerilla warfare to start with. But the actual operational deployment of forces has no rigid rules according to the principles of people's war.[68]

Another important principle of people's war is the establishment of base areas in the countryside from where cities could be attacked. In an agrarian revolution using the countryside for strategic purposes has its own justification. But the actual nature of the base area, the extent of political consolidation, social transformation, and military activity in those places varied from case to case.'

According to Mao base areas were 'strategic bases on which the guerilla forces rely in performing their strategic task and achieving the object of preserving and expanding themselves and destroying and driving out the enemy.'[69] Base areas must be distinguished from 'guerilla zones' where guerilla operations are carried on. There may not be any base in these zones. A further distinction should be made between 'base areas' and 'liberated areas'. The former are meant primarily to support guerilla war operations whereas the latter are taken to have been permanently liberated from enemy control. The base areas may be given up for strategic whereas political power is established in liberated areas soon after liberation. It is true that in the base areas political and economic transformation is generally carried out in order to popularise the ideological programme of the party.

During the Jiangxi Soviet period Mao explained as to 'Why is it that Red Political Power Can Exist in China?' 'Red Political Power' is not entirely identical with 'revolutionary base area.' It is more like a 'liberated area.' There were six major Soviet areas in China during the period 1927-34 which were frequently attacked by the KMT forces. These areas were put under a central Chinese Soviet government which carried out various socio-economic reforms. In these areas the Red Army practised rudimentary forms of guerilla warfare. Mao gave several reasons for the emergence and survival of red political power. One reason was 'the incessant splits and wars within China's comprador and landlord classes and between the warlords supported by imperialism.'[70] The splits within the enemy caused by their internal contradictions seem to be a crucial factor making it possible for revolutionaries to try to set up political power in some areas.

According to Mao the revolutionaries on their part must fulfil the following conditions to be able to establish red political power: (1) a sound mass base, (2) a sound party organisation, (3) a fairly strong Red Army, (4) terrain favourable to military operations, and (5) economic resources sufficient for sustenance.[71] It is thus clear that Mao puts severe conditions to ensure that only at an advanced stage of organisation and strategic experience goals like establishment of base areas and political power should be entertained.

Revolutionary base areas are central to guerilla war operations. These are chosen areas not easily vulnerable to attacks by the enemy army. With the support of the people of that area the revolutionary army maintains its supplies, recruits, and trains soldiers; and uses the areas for retreats. They become centres of coordination and planning. Speaking of their importance Lin Biao wrote: 'In the anti- Japanese base areas, we carried out democratic reforms, improved the livelihood of the people and mobilised and organised the peasant masses. They later became the spring-boards for the People's War of Liberation.'[72]

It may be interesting to note here that the idea of revolutionary base has not been accepted by the guerilla forces everywhere in the world. Che Guevara regarded this as unsuitable for the Latin American situation. Che and his onetime defender Regis Debray thought that the idea of base area was practicable only if a certain combination of favourable circumstances existed, namely (1) an extensive territory, (2) a high density rural population, (3) the existence of common borders with a friendly country, and (4) the absence of airborne enemy troops.[73] All four conditions existed in China. The third condition though a rare condition normally, also existed for Vietnam having borders with China. But the fourth condition is hardly met in any recent case of national liberation movement. Airborne troops are always deployed in case the army fails to suppress the guerillas. Thus the idea of a base area must not be mechanically accepted. For the initial phase of guerilla warfare Che thought of 'a moving base' or mobile guerilla bands for carrying out political activities and for building an army.[74]

Yet another principle of people's war is the policy of self-reliance. A prolonged war by a weak army surrounded by powerful enemies can be sustained only if the soldiers and their organisation do not depend excessively on outside supplies. Thus from the days of the Jiangsi Soviet the notion of self-reliance was a military and economic necessity for the CPC. During the Sino-Japanese war it became more so when the CPC forces found themselves blockaded both by the Japanese forces and the KMT forces. To begin with the Red Army was armed mostly with native weapons and later they started manufacturing rifles. The economic drive for self-sufficiency in food and other essential goods was regarded as a part of the military programme. The Great Production Movement of 1940 was a demonstration of this. Measures for agrarian reforms, regulation of the system of distribution, and ensuring financial stability in the base areas and liberated areas signified the policy of self-reliance.

The principle of self-reliance has become such an important element of the CPC's ideology that it has guided China's post-Liberation policies as well. Talking about this in the context of liberation struggles Mao once said '...oppressed people rely first of all on their own struggle and then, only then, on international assistance...'[75] Lin Biao voiced the same view in 1965 when he said: 'Revolution or People's War in any country is the business of the masses in that country and should be carried out by their own efforts; there is no other way.'[76] at the same time Mao did regard new-democratic revolution as a part of the world proletarian revolution and appealed to the socialist and democratic forces to assist each other. But international assistance could not be the primary source of strength of a movement.

The ideology and strategy of the new-democratic revolution thus, constitute a comprehensive and interrelated set of ideas. In a semi-colonial and semi-feudal situation, first, the basic contradictions have to be identified. In every stage of the revolutionary process the principal contradiction has to be determined and consequently, a united front must be formed against the principal enemy. This united front which included the national bourgeoisie should be led by the working class. The overall character of the revolution has to be that of an agrarian revolution, so the peasants play the role of the 'main force'. The communist party has to play a leading role in this by functioning as a mass line organisation. But without an army loved by the people the movement cannot make any headway. Hence, the necessity of a people's army which has to heavily rely on guerilla warfare against the enemy forces. It sets up revolutionary base areas where it practises self-reliance in military as well as economic resources to the maximum possible extent. It is from the countryside that the people's army encircles the cities. This is the package of the new-democratic revolution.

IV. AN ASSESSMENT

People's Democratic Dictatorship

With the establishment of the People's Republic of China on 1 October 1949 the CPC claimed that the character of the new State was the people's democratic dictatorship and its political, economic and cultural policies were in the nature of new-democratic policies. In formal respects this was undoubtedly so. But in practice the distinction between people's democracy and socialism or between people's democratic dictatorship and proletarian dictatorship blurred very fast.

The Common Programme which was like a united front manifesto adopted by the First Plenary Session of the Chinese People's Political Consultative Conference on 29 September 1949 declared: 'The Chinese People's Democratic Dictatorship is the state power of the people's democratic united front, composed of the Chinese working class, peasantry, petty bourgeoisie, national bourgeoisie and other patriotic democratic elements, based on the alliance of workers and peasants, and led by the working class.'[77] The same thing was reiterated in Article 1 of China's provisional constitution called 'The organic Law'. Article 3 of the Common Programme announced that the State would 'protect the economic interests and private property of workers, peasants, the petty bourgeoisie and the national bourgeoisie.' At the same time, programmes of agrarian reform and industrial development with a leading State sector were also announced.

The Chinese People's Political Consultative Conference (CPPCC) was described as the organisational form of the People's democratic united front. Article 13 of the Common Programme provided for all the four classes to be represented in the CPPCC through their political parties. In fact, among the 661 delegates to the CPPCC in September 1949 there were 13 political parties besides the CPC, among these parties the breakaway KMT Revolutionary Committee, the Democratic League, and the Democratic Party of Workers and Peasants were prominent. In addition there were delegates from sixteen mass organisations, the PLA and overseas Chinese being among these organisations.

After two initial years of rehabilitation the new regime undertook a series of economic measures for social transformation. As far as the agricultural sector was concerned the programmes of land reforms as well as cooperativisation were clearly within the framework of 'People's economy of New Democracy'. Sun Yat-sen had given the slogan of 'Land to the tiller' and the Common Programme had announced the development of cooperative economy. (Art, 29). The establishment of Agricultural Producers' Cooperatives (APCs) all over the country in 1955-56 and raising them to an advanced level in 1956 maintained the democratic character of agrarian development because private ownership of land was still retained.[78]

In the industrial sector, however, the picture was different. The strategy of the First Five Year Plan was patterned after the Soviet model and had put its main emphasis on heavy industry. The whole programme involved a strong role for the state sector. Moreover, since the major industrial enterprises were owned by the imperialists and comprador bourgeoisie before Liberation the government acquired a dominant economic role by overthrowing them. After the CPC decided to 'utilise, restrict and transform capitalist industry and commerce' in 1953, many of those capitalist enterprises were turned into jointly managed undertakings. However, some degree of private ownership in industry continued to exist till 1958.[79]

In the political sphere non-communist political parties continued to exist in China. The prominent among them were the China Democratic League, the Kuomintang Revolutionary Committee, the China Association for Promoting Democracy, and the China Peasants' and Workers' Democratic Party. But very soon it became clear that they had ceased to be competitors of power. However, both in the National People's Congress as well as in the State Council there were many non-communist members and the CPC Central Committee continued to have a United Front Department at least till the Cultural Revolution.[80] The Hundred Flowers Campaign of 1956 was another instance of the new-democratic character of politics at that time. But by then a group in the CPC leadership had decided in favour of a swift transition to the period of proletarian dictatorship, so this campaign was promptly followed by an Anti-Rightist Campaign.

The transition from new democracy to socialism was not delayed. The First Five Year Plan inaugurated in 1953 made it quite clear. It became clearer in 1954 when the Constitution of the PRC came explicitly as an instrument of transition. The Preamble of the 1954 Constitution said: 'The period from the founding of the People's Republic of China to the attainment of a socialist society is one of transition... This Constitution... reflects the basic needs of the State in the period of transition, as well as the general desire of the people to build a socialist society.' At the same time some provisions of the Constitution indicated that the period of new democracy was not over. For example, capitalist ownership was recognised as a form of ownership (Articles 5, 10). But it also said that there would be gradual transformation into socialist ownership. On the whole, the Constitution of 1954 was a qualitatively advanced step over the Common Programme because it left no doubt that China was moving towards a socialist form of state.

In practice, the Chinese State was a dictatorship because in every post-revolutionary situation power needs to be consolidated. There were added reasons of economic development which called for a powerful State sector, thus curbing the rights of the capitalists right from the start. There were also two practical advantages of the new-democratic form of State. Firstly, the Chinese communists avoided the intense antagonism that is usually created between the workers and the national bourgeoisie and made possible a peaceful and gradual transformation of the capitalist industry without causing disruption of the production process. Secondly, under the new-democratic scheme the Chinese government could go slow in both agricultural reforms as well as industrial construction, and actually in agriculture they carried out only democratic measures. The sphere where it was somewhat unreal was the sphere of political freedoms where at best it provided some psychological security to some non-communists. A certain degree of conformity between the assurances of the new-democratic revolution and the performance of the people's democratic dictatorship is to be seem only in the economic sphere.[81]

It cannot be said with finality as to when the new democratic phase came to an end in China. Some people think that the establishment of the PRC itself was the end of the new-democratic phase.[82] Seizure of political power is only one stage of revolution. Only when the major programmes of socio-economic change are fulfilled a revolution can be said to have been completed. From this perspective, the year 1956 could be described as the end of the new-democratic phase, for by then new democratic economic measures were fully implemented. Agriculture was cooperativised and socialist transformation had started. With a sense of fulfilment of tasks of a phase of revolution, the CPC Eighth Congress met in 1956 and designed a 'General Line for Socialist Construction.'

Now we know that the CPC leadership was divided by 1956 over the pace and nature of socialist transformation. According to the Maoists, the Liu Shaoqi group and their philosopher-spokesman Yang Xianzhen advocated the continuing of the new-democratic economy so that the joint sector, including the capitalists could continue to function efficiently. Yang is said to have advocated a theory of 'synthesised economic base' which called for full use of both the public and the private sectors. He said: 'In the period of transition the economic base of the State power of the socialist type' was of a 'synthesised nature', 'embracing both the socialist sector and the capitalist sector and the sector of individual peasant economy as well'; they can develop in a balanced and coordinated way; the socialist super-structure should 'serve the entire economic base including the capitalist economy, and 'also the bourgeoisie'.[83] Their argument was the since China's production level was still low the newly established economic system should be continued for some time. As against this Mao argued for a speedy changeover to socialist form of ownership both in agriculture and in industry. He wrote 'On the Question of Agricultural Cooperation' in 1955 and advised the Party to take note of people's enthusiasm and move in the direction of collectivisation of agriculture. Yang Xianzhen had argued that when the productive forces were highly developed condition would be favourable to the creation of socialist form of organisation. This was taken by the Maoists as negating the conscious role of human forces in accelerating socialist development.[84]

The Great Leap Forward and the establishment of the People's Communes in 1958 definitely heralded the period of socialism in China. Ever since that time the Chinese State has become the 'dictatorship of the proletariat' where the CPC as the 'vanguard of the proletariat' controlled State power. Even though China continues the name of the 'People's Republic of China' and some institutions of the new-democratic period like the CPPCC continue to exist nominally in China, it has become a socialist State since 1958. In 1966 the Cultural Revolution was described as a movement to consolidate the socialist State and further socialist construction. Moreover, it was no longer confined to new-democratic culture which was broadly anti-feudal and anti-colonial, but it was a 'proletarian' cultural revolution appropriate for the socialist stage. By implication, the 1954 Constitution was outdated by 1958 and its long overdue revision took place only in 1975 when the new Constitution adopted by the Fourth National People's Congress declared China a socialist State, gave the CPC its vanguard role in exercising state power, generally legitimated only socialist forms of ownership, and made the communes permanent organisation.

Comparison with East European People's Democracies

After the establishment of new regimes in eastern Europe in the aftermath of the Second World War Marxist writers used the concept 'people's democracy' to characterise the new forms of State. In theoretical commentaries on the new States, people's democracy was described as 'a form of the dictatorship of the proletariat' and 'a preliminary stage' of it.[85] According to Dimitrov people's democracy brought about the transition from capitalism to socialism without the establishment of the Soviet order and it must perform the functions of proletarian dictatorship by organising socialist economy.[86] Soviet writers explained the character of the anti-fascist movements in eastern Europe which were also fighting against 'landlords and big bourgeoisie' and said that these movements acquired momentum under the leadership of the working class and the communist parties, and with the help of the Soviet Army these movements succeeded in establishing the new regimes.

The new systems in eastern Europe allowed non-communist political parties to function and provided for three forms of ownership—socialist, cooperative and private (including capitalist). It was explained by the theoreticians that these countries still needed to prepare conditions for making a transition to the stage of the dictatorship of the proletariat. This called for full mobilisation of the economic forces, public as well as private. In agrarian societies like Albania and Rumania more steps were needed to complete the tasks of the democratic revolution before socialist transformation could be attempted.[87]

The East European concept of people's democracy was similar to the Maoist notion of new-democracy in some respects. Both possessed the anti-imperialist and anti-feudal content. Each concept meant a stage prior to the establishment of the Soviet type of dictatorship of the proletariat. Both in China and in eastern Europe the working class assumed the leading role during this period giving a dominant role to the communist party which was to facilitate a smooth transition to socialism. Finally, in practice bourgeoisie was partially tolerated in both situations after the victory of the revolutionaries.

But the comparison cannot be stretched too far. The overall character of the revolutionary processes in China and eastern Europe had some basic differences. China experienced a long-drawn agrarian revolutionary war and in course of that war a four-class united front was forged. Mao Zedong formulated the theory of new-democracy in

1939-1940 as a transitional stage prior to socialism. On the other hand, only after the revolutionaries has seized political power in eastern Europe with the help of the Soviet Army, the Soviet theoreticians conceptualised this situation in term of 'people's democracy' as a form of the dictatorship of proletariat. Moreover, as a Marxist writer put it in 1950: 'In contradistinction from the Soviet Union where the socialist proletarian revolution was carried out without any external aid and exclusively with internal forces, the socialist revolution in the People's Democracies was based in its sources on the aid and power of the Soviet Union and its Army.'[88] The East European movement did not have the same character as the Chinese new-democratic revolution leading to the establishment of new democracy or people's democracy. The triple objectives of ensuring a leading role for the communist party in them, taking them as less advanced forms of State power than the USSR's, and describing them in terms acceptable to the West seem to have guided this conceptualisation. These objectives were not altogether absent in the Chinese case. But the continuity between the revolutionary movement and the new form of State was more pronounced in China. In the East European cases the people's democracy was described as the embryo of the dictatorship of the proletariat and by 1951-1952 many countries had announced the beginning of the transition to socialism. In China the distinction between new- democracy and the dictatorship of the proletariat, even though short-lived in practice was more sharply demonstrated.

In the Soviet writings some difference was clearly noticeable in the treatment of Chinese revolution and the East European revolutions. An authoritative article said in 1951 that 'The Chinese Revolution is the example of the carrying out in practice of the Leninist-Stalinist theses on the policy, strategy and tactics of Communist Parties in the agrarian, anti-feudal, anti-imperialist countries.'[89] This confined the comparability of the Chinese revolution to the colonial situations. The article also said that 'The revolutionary power established in China...represents in its content something in the nature of the democratic dictatorship of the working class and peasantry.' Describing the Chinese State as the first stage of the people's democracy facing numerous tasks (the second stage being dictatorship of the proletariat) the author said: 'The successful solution of these tasks, which are of a general democratic character, will occupy a more or less considerable historical period of time and create all the necessary conditions for the transition in the future to the new State to socialist construction.' Hence in the eyes of Soviet writers China was in a historically backward stage of development than East Europe which was ready to enter into the stage of socialism. During 1950-51 efforts were made to formulate new constitutions in these countries since 'the people's democracies passed the period of reconstruction to socialism'.[90] This was in fact proved in the subsequent years when rapid industrialisation took place in the East European countries. But ironically, in spite of China's slower economic growth the transition to socialism and consolidation of the dictatorship of the proletariat in China was faster and more rigorous than in many countries of eastern Europe where some capitalist forms of ownership and management continued to exist.

International Significance

No revolution in history has been duplicated ever and China's new-democratic revolution was not. The nature of revolutionary strategy is such that the actual revolutionary programmes have been different from situation to situation. But we can still assess the international significance of the Chinese revolution in two ways, first by asking to what extent the theory of new-democratic revolution has become part of the body of universal ideas on revolution and secondly by seeing the changed balance of forces in Asia and the world by the birth of the PRC. On both these points the Chinese revolution scores highly.

The China path or the ideology and strategy of the new-democratic revolution was more or less endorsed by the Communist Party of the Soviet Union as the appropriate road to revolution in the colonial societies during the period 1949-50.[91] Even before that the Telengana people's armed struggle in India (1945-48) and the armed struggle in Malaya and Indo-China soon after the Second World War demonstrated parallel theoretical orientation. The history of the Indian communist movement since 1948 can be easily described as the history of the debates on the theory of new-democratic revolution by the different shades of the communist movement. The first split in the Communist Party of India (CPI) took place in 1964 when a section of the communists denounced the path of peaceful transition to socialism and upheld the path of 'people's democracy' and formed the Communist Party of India (Marxist) (CPI-M). In 1967 the CPI (M) was further split when a section in it declared the immediate necessity of revolutionary armed struggle claiming itself to be the true adherent of the path of people's democratic revolution.[92] In other parts of the world, especially in liberation movements in South-East Asia and Africa, new-democratic principles of united front and people's war were also practised.

Two levels of confusion exist in the theoretical and practical understanding of the new-democratic revolution. At one level many military writers and some social scientists have provided a reductionist view of this by first equating new-democratic revolution with people's war and then by equating people's war with guerilla war. This is why some authors have created a 'paradigm of people's war' based on their understanding of the Chinese revolutionary war and have been puzzled over the variety and even contradictory characteristics of the revolutionary struggles in the recent decades.[93] The puzzles would be minimised if it is realised that the theory of new-democratic revolution constitutes only a broad perspective within which different strategies could be pursued depending on the situation in various countries in different times. The second confusion has arisen in cases of several revolutionary groups in the third world who have tried to mechanically apply the Maoist class analysis of pre-Liberation China to their own countries at present times. This has resulted in superficial understanding of social contradictions causing faulty revolutionary strategies.[94]

As to the impact of the emergence of the PRC there is little controversy on its enormity. Hua Guofeng said in his memorial speech on 18 September 1976: 'The victory of the Chinese people's revolution led by Chairman Mao changed the situation in the East and in the world, blazing a new trail for the cause of liberation of the oppressed nations and oppressed people.[95] The impact was felt immediately when North Korea survived the American invasion. The momentum generated by the victory of the Chinese revolution does not seem to end yet as was indicated by the victory of liberation forces of Indo-China in 1975.

Yet the totality of the experiences of the Chinese people's

democratic revolution before and after 1949 leaves many questions unanswered. The four-class united front which won Liberation in China did not last very long. On the other hand, in the freedom struggles in other parts of Asia and Africa either the illusion of united front was not created before independence or a programme of united national action was put into practice for a longer period, However, in these latter cases the price was paid for following either course. Either these countries suffered because of hasty nationalisations with a low base of production or they allowed the growth of powerful social forces controlling the economics process. This meant delay in taking measures for social justice. In this process the question of political form became more and more clouded. The colonial powers had handed down their own political structures to their colonies. In some countries they were tried and consolidated until socio-economic crisis put them on further trial. In other countries old institutions were thrown overboard and new centralised regimes carried out the process of change, promising appropriate political forms in future. They also seem to have been stuck up in political status quo. In this respect too the Chinese experience had a certain uniqueness. The dominance of a popular communist party which was armed and well-organised was the fact of Chinese political life since 1949 and that could bring about the transition first to people's democracy and then to socialism in China.

NOTES

1. 'On New Democracy' was first published in the first issue of *Chinese Culture* in January 1940. It is included in the *Selected Works of Mao Tse-tung* (hereafter referred to as *SW*), Peking: Foreign Language Press, 1965, Vol. II, pp. 339-84.
2. Conrad Brandt *et al.* (eds.), *A Documentary History of Chinese Communism,* London: George Allen & Unwin, 1952, p. 422.
3. 'Theses on the National and Colonial Question' in Jane Degras (ed.) *The Communist International 1919–1943 Documents,* London: Oxford University Press, 1956, Vol. I, p. 143.
4. Ibid., p. 143.
5. 'Until such time as the Chinese proletariat is able to seize power in its own hands, considering the present political and economic conditions of China's development and all the historical processes now going on

in China, the proletariat's urgent task is to act jointly with the democratic party to establish a united front of democratic revolution to struggle for the overthrow of the military and for the organisation of a real democratic government.' The Manifesto was released on 10 June 1922. See Conrad Brandt *et al.*, op. cit., p. 62.

6. While the Manifesto of the Second National Congress (July 1922) spoke of the 'democratic revolution' that of the Third National Congress described the current movement as the 'national revolution' (ibid., pp. 64, 71). The Comintern documents used the term 'national democratic revolution.' Stalin's characterisation of the Chinese revolution underwent some changes between 1925 and 1928. In 1925 he had said: 'Communists in these countries must pass from a united national front policy to the policy of a revolutionary bloc of the workers and the petty bourgeoisie.' [See Helen Carrere d'Encausse and Stuart R. Schram (eds.), *Marxism and Asia*, London: Allen Lane, The Penguin Press, 1969, p. 226] In 1926 he likened it with the Russian revolution of 1905 (ibid., p.227). In a speech on 1 August 1927 he said that the first stage was 'an all-national united front' mainly against imperialism; the second stage would be a bourgeois-democratic revolution which was principally against feudalism, and the third stage would be a Soviet, *i.e.*, socialist revolution (ibid., pp. 229-30). Later Mao combined the first two stages into one by the concept of new-democratic revolution.
7. For this Mao was accused by Wang Ming of showing 'rich peasant mentality'. The Executive Committee of the Comintern had said in its Resolution on the Chinese Question (23 July 1930): 'In the Soviet Areas the centre of the party's attention should be one of solving the land question. The land revolution should not be for the rich peasantry but for the poor and middle peasants and the strength of spurring the revolution should be the hired hands and poor peasants' (see Hyobam Pak (ed.). *Documents of the Chinese Communist Party 1927–1930*, Hond Kong: Union Research Institute, 1971, p. 570). This was perhaps an indirect criticism of the land policy in the Chinese Soviet areas.
8. Victor Yakhontoff, *The Chinese Soviets*, New York: Coward-McCann, 1934. Mao's Report appears here as an appendix.
9. See also the Constitution of the Soviet Republic of China which was adopted on 7 November 1931.Conrad Brandt *et al.*, (eds.), op. cit., p. 220.
10. Quoted in *The Chinese Communist Movement: A Report of the United States War Department, July 1945*, Stanford: University Press, 1968, p. 39.

11. Special Number of *International Press Correspondence*, Vol. 15, No. 37, 20 August 1935, pp. 971-2.
12. Ibid., p. 965. A recent study of the Chinese Revolution by the Communist Party of India, however, holds that, 'it was only after the seventh congress of the Communist International in 1935 that the CCP was able to evolve a correct united-front line against Japanese Imperialism.' Mohit Sen, *The Chinese Revolution and Maoism*, New Delhi: Communist Party of India, 1975, p. 10.
13. Mao said on 3 May 1937: 'What will be the composition of the new democratic republic? It will consist of the proletariat, the peasantry, the urban petty bourgeoisie, and all those in the country who agree with the national and democratic revolution...' Thus the essence of the new-democratic united front was set out in his report entitled 'The Tasks of the Chinese Communist Party in the period of Resistance to Japan'. *SW* I, p. 271.
14. For the practice of the new-democratic policies in the Shen-Kan-Ning Border Region see Mark Selden, *The Yenan Way in Revolutionary China*, Cambridge, Mass.: Harvard University Press, 1971, Ch.4.
15. 'On New Democracy', *SW* II, pp. 362-3.
16. Chalmers Johnson has argued that the Chinese communists' nationalist performance and their ability to mobilise the patriotism of the Chinese peasants against Japanese aggression, rather than their programme of social revolution led the CPC to victory. See *Peasant Nationalism and Communist Power*, Stanford: Stanford University Press, 1962. Shanti Swarup takes a different position by saying that the CPC's ability to combine the national revolution with a social revolution in the face of warlord challenges made their strategy effective, See Swarup's A *Study of the Chinese Communist Movement 1927-1934*, Oxford: Clarendon Press, 1966. Mark Selden (op. cit.) emphassies the fact that the CPC's programme of transforming the countryside provided substance to the wartime united front and rallied extensive mass support for them.
17. 'On New Democracy', *SW* II, p. 347.
18. A good summary of these debates is provided by Benjamin Schwartz, 'A Marxist Controversy on China'. *The Far Eastern Quarterly*, Vol. XIII, No. 2, February 1954. Schwartz merely states the problems without evaluating the various interpretations. He says: 'It is thus no wonder that China's economic structure which Marx himself never studied closely seems to fit all of Marx's categories of modes of production and none at all.'
19. 'Chinese Revolution and Chinese Communist Party', *SW* II, p. 312.
20. *SW* II, p. 313. *Mao Ze-dong Xuan-ji*, Peking, 1968, p. 594.

21. *SW* II, p. 313.
22. Mao, 'Smas Chiang Kai-shek's Offensive by a War of Self-defence'–*SW* IV.
23. *SW* II, p. 418.
24. Describing them as 'national bourgeoisie' Mao said that 'they feel the need for revolution and favour the revolutionary movement against imperialism and the warlords...but they become suspicious of the revolution when they sense that... the revolution is threatening the hope of their class to attain the status of a big bourgeoisie'. ('Analysis of the Classes in Chinese Society', *SW* I, p. 14). This portion was not changed from its original version published in *Zhong-guo Nong-min.* See in Stuart Schram, *The Political Thought of Mao Zedong,* New York: Praeger, 1963, p. 145.
25. 'On Tactic against Japanese Imperialism' (27 December 1935), *SW* I, p. 169.
26. 'Chinese Revolution and Chinese Communist Party', *SW* II, p. 321.
27. *SW* IV, p. 421.
28. *SW* IV, p. 417.
29. 'On New Democracy', *SW* II, p. 352.
30. Lyman P. Van Slyke, *Enemies and Friends: United Front in Chinese Communist History,* Stanford: Stanford University Press, 1967.
31. Stuart Schram, op. cit., p. 183. In the *Selected Works* this statement was revised to read: 'The poor peasants have always been the main force in the bitter fight in the countryside.... They are the most responsive to Communist Party leadership'. *SW* I, p. 32.
32. *SW* I, p. 64.
33. Lin Piao, 'Long Live the Victory of People's War' in Martin Ebon, *Lin Piao: Life and Writings of China's New Ruler*, New York: Stein and Day 1970, p. 211.
34. 'Chinese Revolution and Chinese Communist Party', *SW* II, p. 324.
35. *SW* II, p. 324.
36. J. Stalin, *The Foundations of Leninism,* Moscow: Foreign Languages Publishing House, 1954, pp. 78-9.
37. Marx's classic description of the French peasantry is often recalled: '...the great mass of the French nation is formed by simple addition of homologous magnitudes, much as potatoes in a sack form a sack of potatoes...they cannot represent themselves, they must be represented'. 'Eighteenth Brumaire of Louis Bonaparte' in Lewis S. Feuer (ed.), *Basic Writings on Politics and Philosophy, Karl Marx and Frederick Engels*, New York: Anchor Books, 1959, p. 338.
38. V. I. Lenin, *Collected Works,* Moscow: Foreign Language Publishing House, 1960, Vol. 3, p. 313.

39. David Mitrany makes an interesting point about Marx: 'What distinguished Marx from his Utopian predecessors was that he, like the economists, regarded the agrarian problem from the angle of production rather than from that of social organisation' see *Marx Against the Pesant*, New York: Collier Books, 1951, p. 36.
40. Lin Piao, op. cit., p. 212.
41. Ibid., p. 211.
42. 'Some Questions Concerning Methods of Leadership', *SW* III, p. 119.
43. In the post-Liberation period mass line continues to be an important political principle of the CPC. Some authors have regarded it only as a 'leadership principle', for example, John, W. Lewis, *Leadership in communist China*, Ithaca: Cornell University Press, 1964. James Townsend takes it as a mode of political participation but says that it only works as an effective way to implement centrally formulated policies, see *Political Participation in Communist China*, Berkeley: University of California Press, 1967. Actually, there seems to be a shift in the practice of mass line in post-Liberation China. Even though the Great Leap Forward strategy demonstrated strategic dependence on the masses there has been an overall trend of centralisation in the recent decades.
44. *SW* IV, p. 243.
45. 'On Coalition Government', *SW* VIII, p. 316.
46. Ibid.
47. Mark Selden, op. cit., p. 210.
48. 'We should regard it not as a dogma, but as a guide to action.' 'The Role of the Chinese Communist Party in the National War', *SW* II, p. 208.
49. 'On Coalition Government', *SW* III, p. 315.
50. Lin Piao, op. cit., p. 214. If this article is ever taken up for attack by Lin Piao's critics in China this passage would be one of the first targets.
51. 'On Practice', *SW* I, p. 306.
52. Ibid.
53. 'Problems of Strategy in China's Revolutionary War', *SW* I, p. 191.
54. 'Introducing the Communist', *SW* II.
55. 'On Protracted War', *SW* II, pp. 136-7.
56. 'Strategy in China's Revolutionary War', *SW* I, pp. 185-6.
57. 'Problems of War and Strategy', *SW* II, p. 227.
58. Benjamin Schwartz describes five features of Maoist strategy in *Chinese Communism and the Rise of Mao*, New York: Harper, Second edition, 1958, pp. 189-90. But he does not take into account the overall character of new-democratic revolution. Ralph L. Powell takes a more comprehensive view. According to him, 'the total doctrine consists of

closely coordinated political, economic, and psychological policies as well as military strategy, tactics and techniques', see 'Maoist Military Doctrines', *Asian Survey*, Vol. VIII, No. 4, April 1968, p. 239. However, Powell does not explain on what theoretical basis the various elements fit together.

59. 'On Correcting Mistaken Ideas in the Party', *SW* I, p. 106.
60. Since October 1947 a standardised description of this is: *Three main rules of discipline:* (1) Obey orders in all your actions, (2) Do not take a single needle or piece of thread from the masses and (3) Turn in everything captured. *The Eight points of attention:* (1) speak politely, (2) pay fairly for what you buy, (3) return everything you borrow, (4) pay for anything you damage, (5) do not hit or swear at people, (6) do not damage crops, (7) do not take liberties with women, and (8) do not ill-treat captives. See note 7 in Lin Piao, op. cit.
61. Ho Lung discusses political, economic and military democracy in the army in 'Democratic Tradition of the Chinese People's Liberation Army', *Peking Review,* Vol. VIII. No. 32, 6 August 1965.
62. 'Problems of War and Strategy', *SW* II, p. 224.
63. Samuel Griffith, *Mao Tse-tung on Guerrilla Warfare*, New York: Praeger 1961, p. 42. For comparison between Mao's principles with Sun Tzu's see Griffith (ed.) *Sun Tzu, The Art of War,* London: Oxford University Press 1963.
64. 'Problems of War and Strategy', *SW* II, p. 227.
65. This is why guerilla wars in post-Second World War years have not been identical with the Chinese revolutionary war. This is interpreted by Chalmers Johnson as disintegration and abandonment of the Chinese people's war strategy by rebels outside China. See his *Autopsy of People's War,* Berkeley: University of California Press, 1974.
66. 'The Present Situation and Our Tasks', *SW* IV, p. 161-2.
67. Li Tso-peng, 'Strategically Pitting One Against Ten, Tactically Pitting Ten Against One–An Exposition of Comrade Mao Tse-tung's Thinking On The Strategy of the People's War.' *Peking Review*, Vol. VIII. No. 15, 9 April 1965, p. 13.
68. 'If we ignore the difference between strategy and tactics and stress the need to "pit one against ten"in specific battles, we will surely commit the mistake of underestimating the enemy and making reckless moves.' Ibid.
69. 'Problems of Strategy in Guerilla War,' *SW* II, p. 93.
70. *SW* I, p. 65.
71. 'The Struggle in the Chingkang Mountains', *SW* I, p. 73.
72. Lin Piao, op. cit., p. 213.

73. Regis Debray, *Revolution in the Revolution?*, New York: Grove Press, 1967.
74. Che Guevara put heavy reliance on the 'mobile guerilla band'. See Chapter II in his *Guerilla Warfare,* New York: Vintage, 1961. In the Vietnamese people's war the concept of revolutionary base took a differenı form altogether because of the existence of the liberated North Vietnam. See Vo Ngyuen Giap, *People's War People's Army,* New York: Bantam, 1962. However, without making references to China Giap mentions so many similar principles of people's war which the Vietnamese practised. Later years of the Vietnam war demonstrated these further.
75. 'Talk with African Friends' (8 August 1963), quoted in *Questions from Chairman Mao Tse-tung,* Peking, 1967, p. 177.
76. Lin Piao, op. cit., p. 222. He further said: 'If one does not operate by one's own efforts, does not independently ponder and solve the problems of the revolution in one's own country and does not rely on the strength of the masses, but leans wholly on foreign aid even though this be aid from Socialist countries which persist in revolution—no victory can be won, or be consolidated even if it is won'(p. 225).
77. Document 2 in Theodor H. E. Chen (ed.), *The Chinese Communist Regime: Documents and Commentary,* New York: Praeger, 1967, p. 35.
78. Even in 1955 nearly 50 per cent of the peasant households were still involved in Mutual Aid Teams and only 14 per cent had come under the APC's. In 1956 this reached the height of 96 per cent, all of which were made into Advanced APCs in 1957. See Helen and Yi-cheng Yin, *Economic Statistics of Mainland China* (1949-1957), Cambridge, Mass: Harvard University Press, 1960, p. 38.
79. Socialist Transformation of Private Industry (Percentage Distribution of Gross Output Value, Handicrafts Excluded.

Year	*Socialist industry (State enterprises*	*Advanced State capitalism (Joint State-private enterprises*	*Elementary State capitalism (Private enterprises executing orders and processing goods for the state)*	*Private industry (i.e., produced and marketed by private industry on its own)*
1953	57.5	5.7	22.8	14.0
1954	62.8	12.3	19.6	5.3
1955	67.7	16.1	13.2	3.0
1956	67.5	32.5		

Source: *Ten Great Years* (Peking: 1960) p. 38.

This reflected a quick process of transformation.
At the Sixth Plenum of the Seventh Central Committee in September 1955 Mao criticised those who advocated the policy of going slow. He said: 'The Four Great Freedom' and 'consolidation of the new-democratic order' are the programmes of the bourgeoisie and run counter to the resolutions of the 2nd Plenary session. *Miscellany of Mao Tse-tung Thought, JPRS*, No. 61269-1, p. 22.

80. Li Wei-han was the director of the United Front Work Department of the CPC from 1949 till 1960. In 1965 Hsu Ping was mentioned in that capacity. Since the Cultural Revolution no reference to the United Front Department has been noticed in the Chinese press. In the early years of the PRC two of the four Vice-Premiers and nine of the sixteen members of the Government Administrative Council were non-communists. In 1954 forty out of seventy-nine members of the Standing Committee of the NPC were non-communists. In the Second NPC in 1959 this was reduced to about a dozen out of the sixty-two members. The non-communist political parties like China Democratic League continued to function at least till 1958 when the League elected its Third Central Committee. As late as November 1965 there was mention of its Chairman Yang Ming-hsuan in the press. But the CPPCC which had elected its Fourth National Committee in 1964 continues to be mentioned even now.
81. Robert North like many other Western Commentators regards new-democracy as a communist tactic or 'actually a weapon for neutralising or destroying opposition and seizing control of or squeezing out all non-communist elements within the country.' *Moscow and Chinese Communists*, Stanford: Stanford University Press, 1963, p. 30.
82. But that does not appear to be Mao's view. Mao said in December 1956: 'The bourgeois democratic revolution is over and presents no more problem. Now the socialist revolution has been essentially accomplished, but not yet fully accomplished...' *Miscellany of Mao Tse-tung Thought*, op. cit., p. 37.
83. *Three Major Struggles on China's Philosophical Front,* Peking: Foreign Language Press, 1973, p. 16.
84. In 1964 when Yang's views were taken up for widespread criticism his 1941-42 articles 'On New Democracy' were made the targets. In two major articles ('More on the Question of Nature of Society in the Resist-Japan Base Areas behind the Enemy Line' of August 1941 and 'Some Incorrect Views on New Democracy' of February 1942), Yang had suggested that after overthrowing imperialism and monopoly capitalism the new democratic regime was going to encourage 'non-monopolistic private capitalism' whose growth was stifled before and also 'state-

monopoly capitalism' which had to play a leading role in building a new-democratic economy. Yang also emphasised the fact that the new-democratic regime had a bourgeois character. In these views the Maoists saw a scheme of capitalist development in China. They pointed out that even though the national-bourgeiosie was a partner in the new-democratic front it was not the leader. The working class played the leading role. This fact was missed by Yang's analysis. This is how the Maoists justified swift transition to socialism. See Lu Wen, 'A Refutation of Comrade Yang Hsien-chen's absurd Views which Distort New Democracy to Mean Capitalism', *Jing-ji yan-jiu* (Economic Research), No. 2, 20 February 1965, *SCMM*, No. 464, (12 April 1965).

85. A. Sobolov, 'People's Democracy as a form of Political Organisation of Society', Bolshevik, No. 19, October 1951, translated version in *Communist Review*, January 1952, p. 321. The author starts by quoting Stalin who said that the Soviet were not the only type of revolutionary organisation: 'Comrade Stalin teaches that the regime of the countries of people's democracy in Central and South-East Europe fulfils the functions of the dictatorship of the proletariat and that the States of people's democracy are one of the forms of the dictatorship of the proletariat.'
86. Georgi Dimitrov, 'Bulgaria on the Road to Socialism', *World News and Views,* Vol. 29, No. 2, 8 January 1948.
87. See 'From the People's Democracies', *World News and Views,* Vol. 32. No. 32., 16 August 1952. The socio-economic developments in Yugoslavia which were hardly different from the other East European States were given a different treatment by the pro-Soviet Press. See Miron Constantinesev, 'Legalising Capitalism in Yugoslavia', *World News and Views,* Vol. 31, No. 45, 10 November 1951. The material similarity between the Yugoslav and other systems showed that in spite of their polemics all the East European States had politically adopted 'dictatorship of proletariat' while economically still remaining far from it. Whether that lag has been bridged as yet is open to debate'.
88. Hilary Mine, 'People's Democracy and the Dictatorship of the Proletariat', *World News and Views,* Vol. 30, No. 17, 29 April 1950. This author clearly states that dictatorship of the proletariat has two manifestations, the Soviet form and the people's democratic form.
89. A. Sobolov, op. cit.
90. Neil Stewart, 'Local Government in People Democracy', *World News and Views,* Vol. 31. No. 5, 3 February 1951. See also David Turner, 'The New Polish Constitution', in *World News and Views,* Vol. 32, No. 19, 17 May 1952.

91. See A. Sobolov, op. cit. However, the *Pravda* editorial of 5 October 1949 entitled 'Historic Victory of the Chinese People' did not comment on the strategic principles of the Chinese revolution though it mentioned how the CPC and 'the glorious son of the Chinese people, steeled leader of the CPC, Mao Tse-tung' had applied Leninist and Stalinist principles (*World News and Views,* Vol. 29, No. 42, 15 October 1949). In fact, the Soviet leaders cautioned that 'it would be dangerous to consider the Chinese revolution as a sort of "stereo-type" for popular-democratic revolutions in other Asian countries' (E.M. Zhukov's speech in Moscow in November 1951. Cited in note 3 to the Preface, *Marxism and Asia,* op. cit., p. 274).
92. My study of the revolutionary strategy of the Indian Maoists shows the contradictions between the theory of new-democracy and the strategy of the CPI (Marxist-Leninist). *Revolutionary Strategy, Maoist Outlook and India's Naxalites*, Ph. D. Dissertation, 1971, University of California, Berkeley. See also my *Revolutionary Violence: A Study of the Maoist Movement in India*, New Delhi: Sterling, 1977.
93. See Chalmers Johnson op. cit. Johnson shows how the people's war as practised by the CPC during the Sino-Japanese war, which had succeeded because of patriotic mobilisation of the peasants, was abortively experimented in various countries in the 1960s and had failed because the same situation did not exist in the other cases.
94. The CPI (Marxist-Leninist) ignored the differences between the pre-Liberation Chinese situation and the contemporary Indian situation in formulating their programme. When the organisation was split in 1971 this was admitted by most of the revolutionaries.
95. This echoed the sentiments of the Chinese leaders ever since 1949. Addressing the World Federation of Trade Unions in Peking in November 1949 Liu Shao-ch'i had said: 'The way taken by the Chinese people in defeating imperialism and its lackeys... is the way that should be taken by the peoples of many colonial and semi-colonial countries in their fight for national independence and people's democracy' (*Marxism and Asia*, op. cit., p. 271). In 1965 Lin Piao said: 'The victory of the Chinese people's revolutionary war breached the imperialist front in the East, wrought a great change in the world balance of forces and accelerated the revolutionary movement among the people of all countries. From then on the national liberation movement in Asia, Africa, and Latin America entered a new historical period' (Lin Piao, op. cit., p. 199).

2

Theory of Class Struggle in Socialist Society

THE CPC'S BASIC LINE

When the Chinese memorial tributes to Chairman Mao described him as the greatest Marxist of our times, they prominently mentioned his 'theory of continuing the revolution under the dictatorship of the proletariat' and his 'discovery' that classes and class struggle still continued in socialist society even after the abolition of the bourgeois ownership of the means of production. Even though this may appear to be the most controversial of the theoretical issues debated between the Chinese and the Soviet communists, and understanding of this theory is the key to the grasping of policy debates and political developments in PRC which opened up vast number of intellectual and practical issues of social transformation that have evoked keen interest among Marxists as well as liberals.

'The correctness of the ideological and political line decides everything'. This has been a widely quoted instruction from Mao Zedong since August-September 1970 when the Second Plenum of the Ninth Central Committee of the CPC was held. Ever since that session several campaigns were launched in China to educate the masses on the questions concerning the line (*lu-xian*). Liu Shaoqi and Lin Biao were accused of paying lip service to the party line while actually pursuing an ant-party line. The campaigns against them were described as the major struggles within the party between two lines, the revolutionary line and the counter revolutionary line. The presently upheld policies in China are described as being in conformity with 'Chairman Mao's proletarian revolutionary line.'

'Chairman Mao's proletarian revolutionary line' has very broad, as well as very specific meanings depending on the context. But the overall orientation to socialist construction in China that Mao sought to give to the CPC is described as the Basic Line. The development of this Basic Line is a revealing story of inner-party struggles, policy debates, and ideological controversies.

I. WHAT IS THE LINE

In Chinese Communist writings terms like theory (*li-lun*), line (*lu-xian*), programme (*gang-ling*), strategy (*zhan-lüe*), policy (*zheng-ce*), and tactics (*ce-lüe*) are used frequently. Of these terms, by and large, theory, strategy, and policy belong to a descending order of generality and abstraction. In terms of time-space relevance, theory remains higher than strategy and strategy higher than policy. Line and programme by themselves cannot be easily categorised in the same way. Certain lines and programmes can be as specific as to belong to the policy level. Certain other lines can be as general as to belong to the theory level. Therefore, the context and the exact description of a line or a programme should be seriously studied in order that its contents and character are determined.

Over the years, the Chinese communists have used a term, 'basic line' (*ji-ben lu-xian*) which Mao 'developed fully' at the Tenth Plenum of The Eighth Central Committee in September 1962. This was described as 'the theory of contradictions, classes and class struggle in a socialist society and of making revolution under the dictatorship of the proletariat' until 7 November 1967 when the term 'Theory of continuing the revolution under the dictatorship of the proletariat' was first used.[1] Both the basic Line and the Theory have been developing over the years. The Constitution of the CPC passed by the Ninth Congress and also the revised Constitution of the Tenth and Eleventh Congresses stated the Basic Line as well as the Theory in identical words in the first chapter of the document entitled 'General Programme' (*zong gang*). Idea of 'Basic', in this case and, perhaps, generally within the Chinese communist framework, belongs to the realm of theory and ideology having high time-space relevance.[2]

The notion of General Line (*zong lu-xian*) is slightly below the Basic Line in its scope. Two examples of the statement of General Line can help us in understanding this distinction. One is the General Line of Socialist Construction (GLSC) which Mao suggested in early 1958 and which Liu Shaoqi put forward before the Second Session of the Eighth Congress of the CPC in May that year. This statement of strategic principles for economic, social, political, and cultural development is associated with the Great Leap Forward. This refers to 'going all out, aiming high and achieving greater, faster, better and more economical results.' This has also acquire new dimensions over the years and has been restated in the Party's General Programmes of 1969, 1973 and 1977. Another example is the CPC's proposal concerning the General Line of the International Communist Movement (GLICM) Published on 14 June 1963. This spelled out the CPC's interpretation of Marxism-Leninism in the light of the prevailing international environment. Both these General Lines made contributions to Marxist theory in a general way. But they were tied to the conditions prevailing at the time of their formulation. Both were more directly action-oriented than theory or ideology.

However, a General Line is wider in its time-space relevance than a policy or a specific line. The CPC's line on agricultural development like other similar lines is derived from the GLSC. The policy towards the third world is a specific line based on the GLICM. At the same time a General Line is not a strategy, which is a plan formulation. Various strategies based on their objectives and resources can emerge out of a General Line. Thus General Line belongs to the realm of 'outlook' which is less universal than ideology and more than strategy.[3]

It may be said that because Mao has been credited with formulating the 'Basic Line' and the 'Theory of Continuing the Revolution', so it is justified to use the term 'Maoism'. This argument may be strengthened by the fact that Mao also developed the Theory of New Democracy. However, this description, *Mao zhu-yi,* was avoided even at the height of the talk about Mao's genius during the Cultural Revolution. Since the middle of 1970 Mao had himself initiated the process of de-emphasising the genius notion. Therefore, the CPC has continued to make a distinction between *zhu-yi* (ism) and *si-xiang* (thought). It uses the term 'Mao Zedong Thought' probably because the main character of the totality of Mao's ideas is less fundamentally universal than Marx's or Lenin's.[4]

Use of the term Mao Zedong Thought or Maoist outlook does not imply that the Basic Line should be brought below the theoretical level. Similarly, use of the term 'Maoist' should not necessarily raise the General Line to the theoretical or ideological level. At the points of the formulation of the Basic Line and the General Line and at the major points of restatement, their differences in time-space relevance have been clarified.

The understanding of the difference between Basic Line and General Line is as important as the understanding of the meaning and functions of the term 'line' itself. Being the concentrated expression of the interests, demands, and world outlook of a definite class and the guide to all action, the line has a fundamental bearing on the entire situation. This concept of *lu-xian* implies roughly what we understand by 'perspective'. This is meant to place an idea or term within a framework so that a relatively sounder meaning of the idea or the term is obtained. Many people only take the meaning of a term without realising that if the perspective changed, the meaning might be different. Like theory, ideology and outlook, the term 'line' is an integrative concept integrating a more general term with less general.

As said earlier, it is the context and the description of the line that determines its scope and nature. Just as Basic and General refer to two levels of generality of the line, other qualifiers determine the scope of the line. An oft-used concept is Mass Line (*qun-zhong lu-xian*) which refers to a perspective of thought and action that relies on the masses. Similarly, Party Line refers to the totality of party's perspective. In all such cases the concept of line implies that a general principle is linked with a particular idea or act.

In Marxist outlook special emphasis is laid on the general dimensions so that a Marxist is not lost in a welter of particulars. At the same time the dialectical materialist theory of knowledge says that the general theory arises out of the particulars. As Mao has explained this in his essays 'On Contradiction' and 'On Practice', general theories are proved or disproved and are constantly enriched in the course of practical experiences.[5] That is why all general concepts, like theory, ideology, outlook, and line are dynamic concepts acquiring new dimensions gradually. But their basic function remains as providing meaning to less general concepts.

This is why Marxists believe that inadequate theoretical knowledge leads to serious mistakes. Mistakes at the level of policy, tactics, and operations are less serious than mistakes at the level of strategy. Mistakes arising out of the deviations from the General Line would be even more serious. Deviation from the Basic Line would certainly be regarded non-proletarian and revisionist. Opposition to General Line is also regarded as revisionism in China. But, violation of the theory of the continuing revolution is even more serious. The important assumption here is that mistakes at one level mostly take place because of incorrect or inadequate grasp over the line at the next higher level.[6]

Ever since the Second Plenum of the Ninth Central Committee (23 August-6 September 1970) when Mao initiated a campaign of 'Education in Ideology and Political Line' the importance of 'line' has been stressed in China in an unprecedented manner. As we shall see later, the perspective of 'the struggle between the two lines' was at the stage firmly added to the theory of continuous revolution, Mao's instruction that 'the correctness or the incorrectness of the ideological and political line decides everything' has become popular since the Second Plenum. He attributed the mistakes committed during the Cultural Revolution to the incorrectness of the ideological and political line which Lin Biao and Chen Boda were upholding. This means that Lin and Chen, just as Peng Dehuai and Liu Shaoqi did before, committed mistakes at the ideological level and political level. Therefore, they were responsible for the many deviations at various levels of policy and practice.[7] This is why Mao launched a campaign to 'study seriously' so that one did not remain a sham Marxist. Thus, the emphasis on line emerges from the Marxist belief that correct theory applied dialectically leads to correct practice.

This preoccupation with perspective does not put ideas above matter nor does it make theory independent of practice. We shall return to this question later. Here it should be stated that this notion of line is both dynamic and developmental with line continuously interacting with practice. In fact, the actual experiences in the implementation of policies during 1955-57 led to the formulation of the General Line of Socialist Construction in 1958. More domestic and international experiences led to the formulation of the Basic Line in 1962, which was a more general concept. Further experiences during the Socialist Education Movement, developments in the international communist movement, and other factors led to a further advance in this direction and the theory of continuing the revolution was put forward in 1967. Experiences during the past few years have added new dimensions to this theory. Thus, there has been a gradual development from less to more general conceptualisation for solving the problems of socialist revolution and construction in China.

Each step in this process has been motivated by important considerations. A Study of these considerations is interesting both for seeing the nature of progress in the socialist construction in China and also for understanding the magnitude of theoretical and ideological problems that the CPC has confronted from time to time.

II. LINE DURING SOCIALIST TRANSFORMATION

In 1952 the Central Committee of the CPC had formulated its general line for the period of transition from people's democracy to socialism. That was the year when rehabilitation of national economy had been completed. So the CPC decided to begin socialist transformation or movement towards collective and State ownership in the various fields by eliminating bourgeois ownership of the means of production. For this transitional period the party's general line was 'to bring about, step by step, socialist transformation of agriculture, handicrafts and capitalist industry and commerce over a fairly long period.' This was written into the Constitution of the People's Republic of China in 1954.[8] The first Five Year Plan, which was launched in 1953, embodied policies of agrarian and industrial development in that direction.

In his Political Report to the Eighth Party Congress in September 1956, Liu Shaoqi announced that 'In the second half of last year and the first half of this, our Party led that people on to win a total and decisive victory in the socialist transformation of agriculture, handicrafts and capitalist industry and commerce.... (resulting in) a series of fundamental changes in our country's internal and external relations.'[9] A major implication of this statement was that by the middle of 1956 not only that the tasks of the people's democratic revolution, i.e., eliminating imperialist vestiges and feudal relations, had been completed but also that the tasks of the first phase of socialist revolution, i.e., agriculture had been fulfilled. Therefore, the next phase of socialist revolution, namely, socialist construction began in the middle of 1956.

As we saw in Chapter 1, the State power in the phase of the people's democratic revolution was vested in the united front of four classes—the proletariat, the peasantry, the petty bourgeoisie, and the national bourgeoisie under the leadership of the proletariat. The organisational form then was the people's democratic dictatorship. According to the Chinese communist theoreticians because the proletariat had assumed the leadership in the people's democratic revolution, it could peacefully lead the revolution to the next stage, i.e., socialist revolution. Therefore, the people's democratic state gradually evolved to become the dictatorship of the proletariat which is the organisational form of the new stage of socialist revolution. The deliberations of the Eighth Party Congress in 1956 suggest that China entered the stage of the dictatorship of the proletariat that year.

Several instances which do not conform to the foregoing classification are often mentioned to suggest that terms like people's democratic dictatorship are purely 'utilitarian formulations' by the communists. One is the fact that even after 1956 the Chinese State has been sometimes referred to as people's democratic dictatorship. Besides, the communist writings sometimes use the expression 'People's Democratic Dictatorship, that is, the Dictatorship of the Proletariat'. Another instance is the continuance of bourgeois ownership in some sectors even after 1956.

About the first point the documents of the Eighth Party Congress provide ample clarification. Urging the partymen to continue to consolidate the 'people's democratic dictatorship', Liu's Political Report said that, 'After the founding of the PRC, the people's democratic dictatorship began to shoulder the task of bringing about the transition from capitalism to socialism... such State power, in its essence, can only be the dictatorship of the proletatriat'.[10] In the same Report Liu goes on to say that even during the new phase other democratic forces, classes, and parties participate in exercising State power because the 'proletariat can establish the dictatorship of the great majority over the reactionary classes, and achieve socialism only by entering into an alliance with the broad masses of people who are capable of embracing socialism.'[11] This is why institutions like the CPPCC and the Ministry of United Front Work continued to exist in China even after 1956.

On the other hand, the role of the national bourgeoisie in the period after 1956 does create some confusion about the characterisation of State power. The line adopted at the 1956 Congress approved the then prevailing policy of 'utilisation, restriction and transformation' by the State of the capitalist industry and commerce. Thus for some more years the national bourgeoisie continued as the owner of some enterprises under a system of State capitalism according to which the State procured raw materials for the private industry and acted as the sole purchaser from it. However, by the time the Cultural Revolution began in 1966 the ownership rights of the remaining bourgeois elements had been completely abolished.[12] Therefore, the continuing of bourgeois elements after 1956 was more of a spill-over and should not affect the characterisation of the period since 1956 as the dictatorship of the proletariat.

This experience in the early fifties is described by the Maoists in China as an instance of continuing the revolution under the leadership of the proletariat from the democratic stage to the socialist stage. This is further developed to propound the 'theory of continuing the revolution under the dictatorship of the proletariat' in the long transitional period from socialism to communism.

The Eighth Congress of the CPC undertook as its main task the formulation of a General Line for the stage of socialist construction. The First Five Year Plan was to be completed in 1957 and the Second Five Year Plan to be launched in 1958. Liu Shaoqi identified the main objectives underlying the new line to be the fulfilment of the tasks of socialist industrialisation and the strengthening of the international cooperation between the countries of the socialist camp. He defined the task of the Second Five Year Plan as follows:

1. To continue industrial construction centered on heavy industry, promote technical reconstruction of our national economy and lay a firm foundation for the socialist industrialisation of our country;

2. To continue our efforts in socialist transformation and to consolidate and extend the system of collective ownership and ownership by the whole people;
3. To develop the production of our industry, agriculture and handicrafts, and correspondingly develop our transport and commerce, on the basis of developing capital construction and completing socialist transformation:
4. To make energetic efforts to train personnel for construction and strengthen scientific research so as to meet the needs of socialist economic and cultural development; and
5. To strengthen the national defence and raise the level of material and cultural well-being of the people on the basis of the growth of industrial and agricultural production.[13]

This was the basis of the concrete outline of the Second Five Year Plan which Chou En-lai presented to the same session of the Eighth Congress.[14]

The General Line which Liu put forward in the name of the Central Committee represented little of the Maoist outlook. It was the continuation of the Soviet model of development which had guided the First Five Year Plan. Perhaps, that is why, the Soviet commentators have regarded the Eighth Congress of 1956 as the greatest event in the history of the PRC because, according to them a genuine programme for socialist construction had been drawn up only in that Congress.[15] There is enough evidence to show that the resolution of this Congress were not to Mao's liking. Liu's Report makes no mention of Mao in the proposals and the Resolution of the Congress mentions him only once towards the end. There is a criticism of 'leftist' mistakes by 'some comrades' which presumably is a reference to Mao's proposals to accelerate socialist transformation of agriculture. The Constitution of the CPC passed by this Congress eliminated the mention of the 'ideas of Mao Zedong' which had been incorporated since the Seventh Congress in 1945.

The General Line of 1956 was clearly more production-oriented than anything else. There was no accent on advancing socialist organisation. In fact, only a peripheral treatment was given to culture in the list of tasks, and even there it was dependent on the growth of production. This point has been substantiated by Zhou Enlai in his Report to the Tenth Congress. Chou says that Chen Boda and Liu Shaoqi 'had smuggled into the Resolution of the Eighth Congress' that the 'major contradiction in our country was not the contradiction between the proletariat and the bourgeoisie', but that 'between the advance socialist system and the backward productive forces of society'. We shall discuss the question of this major contradiction later. Here we should note that the General Line of 1956 represented a certain pattern of socialist construction which was different from that of Mao's. It may not be wrong to say that the line that was adopted for new-democratic construction and socialist transformation was, in a way, extended for the period of socialist construction. Later commenting on the 1956 Congress Mao said:

> ... resolution of the 8th Party Congress...said that the contradiction between the bourgeoisie and the proletariat had been fundamentally resolved. This statement was not incorrect, but fundamental resolution is not equivalent to complete resolution. Once the problem of political authority was resolved, the problem of ownership was fundamentally resolved, but in the economic and political spheres there was not a complete resolution.[16]

It is this viewpoint of unresolved class contradictions which became the governing consideration for Mao in the subsequent years.

III. GENERAL LINE FOR SOCIALIST CONSTRUCTION

The Second Session of the Eighth Party Congress which took place in May 1958 is a major landmark from the viewpoint of the Maoists. It formulated a new General Line for socialist construction which replaced the 1956 Line and which initiated the ideological and organisational development in China along Maoist lines. The process that reached the high point in 1958 had, indeed, started earlier and in the course of zigzag struggle it acquired the status of a theory in 1962 and took the form of the Great Proletarian Cultural Revolution in 1966.

The germ of the Maoist line can be seen in Mao's speech. 'On the Question of Agricultural Cooperation' of 31 July 1955. In this he analyses the successful expansion of the agricultural cooperatives and says that the process of cooperativisation must be accelerated. He points out that in several areas elements of capitalist agriculture were appearing, therefore, there should be a rapid movement in the direction of the socialist ownership of agriculture. Mao's stress on rapid establishment of semi-socialist cooperatives or higher agricultural producers' cooperatives was reiterated in his Preface to the book *Socialist Upsurge in China's Countryside* written in December 1955. In this Mao criticises the rightists in the CPC who wanted to slow down the process of socialist transformation in agriculture. He not only argues in favour of consolidating the semi-socialist mode of farming, but suggests the same rapid pace of transformation of the entire economy. He says: '...If the needs of this expanding agriculture are to be met, the socialist transformation of China's handicrafts and capitalist industry and commerce should also be speeded up.'[17]

Mao advanced the same line in January 1956 when under his initiative the Politbureau prepared the Draft Programme for Agricultural Development in the People's Republic of China for 1956-67. Mao's pleas for accelerated development of socialist ownership in agriculture as well as industry were regarded as 'leftist' by Liu Shaoqi. Therefore, the General Line of 1956 did not reflect his thinking. In fact, the Soviet writers take Mao's December 1955 Preface as the beginning of Mao's attempts to disrupt the normal development of socialist production in China, because in that Preface Mao called for the 'breaking of the old framework.'[18]

There were developments in 1956 which tremendously affected the ideological controversies inside China. The Twentieth Congress of the CPSU which was held in February denounced Stalin and advanced new formulations regarding the nature of the Soviet State, the peaceful transition to socialism, etc. The CPSU Congress preceded the CPC Congress held in September. The other significant development took place shortly after the CPC Congress was over. That was the counter-revolutionary upheaval in Hungary in October 1956. Both the developments embodied serious ideological questions which Mao and the other leaders tried to ponder over.'

The *People's Daily* editorial of 5 April 1956 entitled, 'On the Historical Experience of the Dictatorship of the Proletariat' dealt with the Stalin question. Emphasising the point that the dictatorship of the proletariat must operate on the basis of the full play of the role of the masses, the editorial said that the Stalin cult emerged because that principle was not fully practised during that period. There was an indirect criticism of the latest Soviet formulation in this editorial when it raised the theoretical issues of continuing contradictions in socialist society. It said: 'Some naive ideas seem to suggest that contradictions no longer exist in a socialist society. To deny the existence of contradictions is to deny dialectics.'[19]

The April 1956 editorial seems to represent the Maoist ideological line. However, even though the general point about the continuity of contradictions is stressed here, continuity of class contradictions between the bourgeoisie and the proletariat in the socialist society is not yet suggested.

After the Hungarian upheaval the debate on the Stalin issue was linked with these events. The *People's Daily* published a long editorial called, 'More on the Historical Experience of the Dictatorship of the Proletariat' on 29 December 1956. Taking up certain comments that the Yugoslav leaders Tito and Kardelj had made on the Hungarian events the editorial presented a clearly Maoist analysis of the situation. Anticipating Mao's famous speech of February 1957 the editorial made a distinction between antagonistic contradictions (between enemy and the people) and non-antagonistic contradiction (among people). The former is 'the fundamental type of contradiction, based on the clash of interests between antagonistic classes.'[20] In this emphasis on the *fundamental* Character of the antagonistic contradiction lies the root of the subsequent theory of continuing class struggle in socialist society.

However, at least two points made in the December editorial are not consistent with the subsequently formulated theory of continuous revolution. Talking about the role of the dictatorship of the proletariat the editorial says:

> After the elimination of the exploiting classes and the wiping out in the main of the counter-revolutionary forces, it was still necessary for the dictatorship of the proletariat to deal with counter-revolutionary remnants— these could not be wiped out completely so long as imperialism existed but by then its edge should have been mainly directed against the aggressive forces of foreign imperialism.[21]

Guarding against imperialist aggression has continued to be one of the functions of the dictatorship of the proletariat. But since the Cultural Revolution its main function has been described to be to continue the struggle against the bourgeoisie within. In other words, guarding against revisionism and capitalist restoration has become its main function.

On the question of class struggle the editorial says something that may be closer to Liu Shaoqi's notion of 'dying out of class struggle'. It says: 'After the elimination of classes, the class struggle should not continue to be stressed as though it was being intensified, as was done by Stalin with the result that the healthy development of socialist democracy was hampered.'[22] In recent years Liu Shaoqi has been severely criticised by the Maoists precisely because he spoke of the diminishing intensity of class struggle after 1955. However, this point may have been made in t he context of Stalin's arbitrary handling of inner-party contradictions.

By the end of 1956 the Chinese Communist leaders were exercised over several questions. Was the pace of socialist transformation in China too fast or too slow? Why does a phenomenon like Stalin's personality cult arise in a socialist system? Why do counter-revolutionary and revisionist tendencies appear in the socialist system? The Chinese leaders had differences among themselves while answering these questions. Mao's thinking crystallised his answers to these when he made his speech 'On the Correct Handling of Contradictions Among the People' on 27 February 1957 at the Eleventh Session of the Supreme State Conference.

The importance of this speech cannot be exaggerated. Mao's January 1940 essay 'On New Democracy' spelled out the theory and policies of the people's democratic revolution. In the same way, this speech elaborated the basic principles regarding socialist construction. This speech suggested a class-struggle perspective for socialist construction and defined the ways of handling the contradictions among the people. In this class-struggle perspective the Maoist find the origin of the theory of continuous revolution. In early 1957 the speech seemed to provide answer to why revisionism and counter-revolution appeared in socialist system like Hungary. Mao said that if class struggle continued under the dictatorship of the proletariat then it would be a major guarantee against counter-revolution.

Maoists generally refer to those passages from Mao's 1957 speech which speak of the continuing class struggle. A Chinese Communist writer, for example, says:

> Using the Marxist-Leninist law of the unity of opposites in observing socialist society. Chairman Mao has, in his great work comprehensively set forth the existence of contradictions, classes and class struggle under the conditions of the dictatorship of the proletariat, set forth the thesis of the existence of two different types of contradiction in socialist society—those between ourselves and the enemy and those among the people—and set forth the great theory of continuing the revolution under the dictatorship of the proletariat.[23]

The most quoted sentences from Mao's 1957 speech in this context are the following:

> The class struggle is by no means over. The class struggle between the proletariat and the bourgeoisie, the class struggle between different political forces and the class struggle in the ideological field between the proletariat and the bourgeoisie will continue to be long and tortuous and at times will even become very acute. The proletariat seeks to transform the world according to its own world outlook, and so does the bourgeoisie. In this respect, the question of which will win out, socialism or capitalism, is still not really settled.[24]

These words appear in the section of the speech dealing with the cultural question or the right and wrong ideas in arts and sciences. It is because the bourgeois stronghold at the cultural level continues longer than at the political and economic levels that the class struggle must continue during the socialist period. This is the basic premise on which the theory of continuing revolution has been constructed.

However, even though the contradiction speech of 1957 was the highest point of theorisation on this subject, there are many other statements in the speech which appear contradictory to the main thrust on continuing class struggle. At one point Mao says:

> Contradictions in a socialist society are fundamentally different from those in the old societies, such as capitalist society. In capitalist society contradictions find expression in acute antagonisms and conflicts, in

> sharp class struggle; they cannot be resolved by the capitalist system itself and can only be resolved by socialist revolution. On the contrary the case is different with contradictions in socialist society, *where they are not antagonistic* and can be resolved one after another by the socialist system itself.[25]

Actually the whole perspective of continuing the class struggle is based on the assumption of continuing *antagonistic* contradictions in the socialist society. However, in this paragraph Mao may have said this only to emphasise the difference between capitalist and socialist systems. Even then there seems to be some inconsistency in this.

After stressing the need to continue the struggle at the ideological level Mao said that, Ideological struggle is not like other forms of struggle. The only method to be used in this struggle is that of painstaking reasoning and not crude coercion.'[26] This was later developed to mean that ideological struggle was also a form of class struggle, therefore, needed revolutionary efforts to be resolved in favour of the proletariat. Several anti-rightist campaigns and even the Socialist Education Movement proved to be insufficient to effectively curb rightist tendencies inside and outside the CPC. Thus, in 1957 Mao seemed to have believed that persuasive educational campaigns at the ideological level were, perhaps, enough to accomplish socialist objectives. He had not yet quite integrated the ideological struggle with the general perspective of continuing the revolution.

In early 1957 Mao reviewed the experiences during the preceding years in his talks with provincial leaders and reflected his emergent perspective: 'In the reconstruction period we lacked experience in class struggle (which is partial) and internal struggle (which is primary). This is a science. It should be carefully studied. Even ten thousand years from now there will still be people making trouble. We should get experience in the three five year plans.'[27] This shows that Mao was already thinking along the line of ubiquity of class struggle.

In this context, the 1957 speech on contradictions, in spite of the minor inconsistencies, did lay down the main elements of the Basic Line though it was not described as such yet. This contributed to the intensified ideological debate inside the CPC. The meetings of the Communist and Workers' Parties held in Moscow in November 1957 were somewhat stormy. Even though a common declaration was adopted at these meetings, the Chinese had submitted a note of dissent on some ideological questions. This also had its impact on the situation inside the Chinese Party. Mao appeared to have gathered enough strength by early 1958, when he addressed several party meetings to argue his viewpoint. His speech at the Hankow Conference in April 1958 was primarily devoted to the theme of class struggle. But the orientation in this speech was almost the same as in the contradictions speech of the previous year. On the one hand he stressed that the class struggle was 'protracted, repetitious and complex' and that they must have a strategy of 'cooling off for a while and then letting loose (the struggle)'. At the same time he spoke of the necessity of only 'a few more rounds in the struggle between the two roads.' He also said that 'the fundamental battle of the class struggle has been fought and a victory has been basically won.'[28] Thus the later-day insistence on continuing the revolutionary class struggle throughout the period of socialism was still not evident. However, one can notice the slow emergence of this perspective. It was in this context that the Eighth Party Congress of the CPC was called for a Second Session in May 1958 to launch a new line.

The Eighth Congress Communique described the Session in words that are quite meaningful:

> The Session reflected the victory of the rectification campaign and the struggle against the rightists, and the big leap forward in socialist construction. It was itself a session for rectifying style in work, opposing international revisionism and the rightists, and localists and nationalist elements who had infiltrated into the Party, a session which itself signified a big leap forward.[29]

This description which was echoed again at the time of the Tenth Congress makes the anti-revisionism perspective of the Eighth Congress clear. It signifies the defeat of the 1956 line.

The Resolution of this Session on the 'Report on the Work of the Central Committee' said: 'The Congress unanimously endorses the general line put forward by the Party's Central Committee on the proposal of Comrade Mao Zedong, i.e., to build socialism by exerting our utmost efforts and pressing ahead consistently to achieve greater, faster, better and more economical results.'[30] This clearly links the new General Line with Mao's initiative and proclaims its inauguration.

Presenting the 'Report on the Work of the Central Committee' Liu Shaoqi explained the main points of the General Line. He pointed out how Mao had developed the ideas from the time of the speech on cooperativisation in mid-1955 and had summed up the ideas in early 1956 in the slogan of building socialism by achieving 'greater, faster, better and more economical results'. Liu revealed that in April 1956 Mao had made a report to an enlarged meeting of the Politbureau in which he pleaded for the correct handling of 'Ten Sets of Relationship'. These were the relationships between (1) industry and agriculture and heavy and light industries, (2) coastal industries and inland industries, (3) economic construction and national defence, (4) the State, the cooperative, and the individual, (5) the central and local authorities, (6) the Han people and the national minorities, (7) the party and non-party people, (8) revolution and counter-revolution, (9) the right and wrong inside the party, and (10) international relations.[31] Mao dealt with most of these questions in his contradictions speech in February 1957. These ten relationships, in a way, crudely synthesise three trends in Mao's thought at that time—the desire for accelerating socialist construction in the economy, the question of counter-revolutionary trends inside the party and searching for a new economic model that would resolve those dichotomies between the industry and agriculture, and so on. The important thing to note here is that Mao's suggestions on these lines were ignored in the 1956 Congress of the CPC and now in 1958 those very suggestions became the basis of the policies of the great leap forward.

The Liu Shaoqi Report to the 1958 Congress which elaborated the Maoist General Line went beyond the Ten Sets of Relationships in a major way. It put them within the perspective of class struggle. Liu's Report says:

> Marx, Engels and Lenin often pointed out that the watchword of the working class should be uninterrupted revolution... the Central Committee of the Communist Party and Comrade Mao Zedong have always guided the Chinese revolution by this Marxist-Leninist theory of uninterrupted revolution... After the socialist revolution in the ownership of the means of production had been basically won, the Central Committee launched the socialist revolution on the ideological and political fronts. All this has enabled the revolution to advance at the

opportune moment from one stage to another, scoring one victory after another.[32]

The Resolution on the Report also spoke of 'continuing with the socialist revolution on the economic, political and ideological fronts'.[33] This was in sharp contrast to the Resolution of the 1956 Congress which had declared that 'the contradiction between the proletariat and the bourgeoisie in our country has been basically resolved... and that the social system of socialism has in the main been established in our country.'[34]

The decisions of the Eighth Congress in 1958 demonstrate the links between the CPCs strategy to prevent revisionist tendencies and its search for a new model for economic development. The policies of the great leap forward and the establishment of the people's communes were the major steps to implement the new GLSC. Thus the elements of the emerging Basic Line were integrated with the General line. Three elements of the developing theory of continuing the revolution had been put together by then. These were the perspective of class struggle, the urge for rapid movement in socialist construction, and the adoption of mass line approach to development.

IV. BASIC LINE AND THE THEORY OF CONTINUOUS REVOLUTION

The period of the great leap forward from mid-1958 till the end of 1960 saw both successes and setbacks for the Maoist line. The enthusiastic mass upsurge of 1958 confirmed the popularity of the new line. But severe economic difficulties had begun to appear by the end of 1958. The first step in moderating the policies of the great leap was taken in December 1958. The Central Committee in its Sixth Plenum passed a 'Resolution on Some Questions Concerning the People's Communes' which made cautious references to theory of 'uninterrupted revolution' where it said: 'We hold that no "Great Wall" exists or can be allowed to exist between the democratic revolution and socialist revolution and between socialism and communism. We are at the same time advocates of the Marxist-Leninist theory of the development of revolution by stages; we hold that these stages, different in quality, should not be confused.'[35]

Read by itself this passage appears to be a reiteration of the line stated in the Report to the Second Session of the Eighth Congress. But the totality of this Commune Resolution of December 1958 stresses the need for developing production—an idea reminiscent of the 1956 Congress. At several places the prolonged nature of the socialist period is underlined and the hasty steps of radical character are disapproved. At one place the Resolution states that:

> Both the transition from socialist collective ownership to socialist ownership by the whole people and the transition from socialism to communism must depend on a certain *level of development of the productive forces.* Only when the productive forces develop to a certain stage will certain changes be brought about in production relations. This is a fundamental principle of Marxism.[36]

This was a clear criticism of the establishment of the communes as the unit of collective ownership and distribution. The Central Committee, therefore, decided to declare Production Brigade as the unit of collective ownership in the same session of December 1958.

The 1959-60 period saw great economic difficulties causing more moderation of the 1958 strategy. In 1959 the CPC experienced an intense inner-party struggle with Defence Minister Pong Dehuai attacking the 1958 line and policies frontally. However, in the Eighth Plenum of the Central Committee in August 1959 Mao carried the majority with him in removing Peng from his position and reaffirming the CPC's commitment to the 1958 GLSC. The Communique of the Plenum pointed out that 'The imperialists and their lackeys have, from the outset, viciously slandered and attacked our country's general line for building socialism.'[37] This Plenum indirectly criticised all hostile comments on the 1958 policies including those made in the Soviet Union. It declared that the General Line was product of 'the creative integration of the universal truths of Marxism-Leninism with the practical situation in China achieved by Comrade Mao Zedong, great leader of our Party....'[38]

In the international communist movement 1959 was a crucial year. The Chinese press became more eloquent in its criticism of modern revisionism. Letters exchanged between the CPC and the CPSU were gradually taking more rigid ideological positions. The relations between China and the Soviet Union reached a very low ebb. Symbolic of the situation was the repudiation by the Soviet Union of its agreement to assist China in development of new technology—the nuclear weapon technology—in June 1959.

According to Mao the internal and international struggles against revisionism were closely related. Yet the economic crisis at home kept him sober during this period. Therefore, the next step in ideological development was slightly delayed.

There were two parallel tendencies again after 1959. Lin Biao, after taking over as the Defence Minister in November 1959, started rebuilding the PLA as a political organisation to carry out revolutionary tasks. The 'Resolution of the Enlarged Meeting of the Military Affairs Commission of the Central Authorities of the CPC on Strengthening Political and Ideological Work in the Army' passed on 20 October 1960 reads like a programme chalked out for the whole country during the Cultural Revolution that came six years later.

The other dominant trend in the national scene was the cautious programme of economic recovery carried out under the direction of Liu Shaoqi. In this process the GLSC was not formally abandoned, but practically became ineffectual. In an important speech at the meeting to celebrate the 40th anniversary of the founding of the CPC on 30 June 1961 Liu Shaoqi reiterated the GLSC describing it 'absolutely right and entirely necessary'. At the same time he said that 'the general line is developed and perfected through practice, and the various specific policies and specific measures essential for its realisation have also to be developed and perfected gradually through practice.'[39]

These two tendencies further demonstrated the conflicting lines operating within the CPC. After the Chinese economy fully recovered from the setbacks of 1959-60 the leadership faced a new situation in 1962. The Tenth Plenum of the Central Committee meeting in September 1962 once again took up the question of line. This was held before the Cuban missiles crisis and the China-India war.

The Political Report which Lin Biao presented to the Ninth Party Congress in 1969 said that Mao developed the theory of continuing the revolution in course of his talks on three occasions in 1962. At two working conferences of the Central Committee in January and August Mao spoke on the subject and at the Tenth Plenum he 'put forward more comprehensively the basic line of our Party for the whole historical period of socialism.' Mao's all-important speech at the Tenth Plenum has not yet been published. Only paragraphs have been quoted from it. However, the communique of the Tenth Plenum deals with the question almost in the language of Mao.

The Communique declared that 'modern revisionism is the main danger in the international communist movement'[40] at present. It noted that 'the imperialists, the reactionaries of various countries and modern revisionists gloated over the temporary difficulties encountered by the Chinese people, and they vilified China's general line for socialist construction...' Thus the Plenum stated its opposition to revisionism more firmly than before and reaffirmed the GLSC. Then the Communique went on to state the basic line without using that term yet:

> ...throughout the historical period of proletarian revolution and proletarian dictatorship, throughout the historical period of transition from capitalism to communism (which will last scores of years or even longer), there is class struggle between the proletariat and the bourgeoisie and struggle between the socialist road and the capitalist road. The reactionary ruling classes which have been overthrown are not reconciled to their doom. They always attempt to stage a come-back...this class struggle is complicated, tortuous, with ups and downs and sometimes it is very sharp. This class struggle inevitably finds expression within the Party. Pressure of foreign imperialism and the existence of bourgeois influence at home constitute the social source of revisionist ideas in the Party.[41]

This statement which contained most of the ideas of the published passages from Mao's speech at this Plenum is another high point in the development of Mao's theory of continuing revolution. It stressed the possibility of capitalist restoration in a socialist system for the first time. 'Thus far revisionism was the target of the attack; but the magnitude of its dangerous power was not kept in view. Secondly, even though opportunist tendencies inside the CPC were attacked before, now it was stated that the class struggle between the bourgeoisie and the proletariat finds its expression inside the party. By implication, it was pointed out that there may be antagonistic contradictions even inside the party. Thirdly, the intensity of the class struggle during the entire period of socialism was underlined for the first time. This is why 'revolution' was to continue. These constituted the party's basic line for the whole period of socialism.'[42]

The Basic Line and the theory of continuing the revolution were more sharpened in course of the intensified ideological debate between the CPC and the CPSU. In several of the polemical documents the CPC refuted the CPSU's notions of 'State of all people', 'Party of all people', and 'peaceful transition to socialism' by spelling out the notion of continuing class struggle under the dictatorship of the proletariat. The CPC's proposal concerning the General Line of the International Communist Movement published on 14 June 1963 affirmed that 'For a very long historical period after the proletariat takes power, class struggle continues as an objective law independent of man's will.'[43] Point 18 of the same document says that the 'entire period before the advent of the higher state of communist society is... the period of the dictatorship of the proletariat'. In this transition period, ...the proletarian State, goes through the dialectical process of establishment, consolidation, strengthening and withering away.'[44] Incidentally, the Chinese communists described their current task as 'consolidating the dictatorship of the proletariat.'

The Socialist Education Movement (SEM) was launched in late 1962 to educate the party and the masses in the anti-revisionist perspective. In 1963 the question of the orientation of the SEM was debated again and on Mao's initiative the 'Decision of the CCP Central Committee on Certain Problems in the Present Rural Work (Draft)' was circulated. This document identified the three main elements in social practice, namely, 'the struggle for production, the class struggle and scientific experiment.' These were advanced within the perspective of continuing class struggle in socialist society which was reiterated in this document.

This document did not succeed in reorienting the SEM along Maoist lines. In September 1963 the Maoist drafted another document on behalf of the Central Committee on the SEM in the rural areas which went a step further in consolidating the Maoist ideological line. It says that certain tests were conducted in selected places to examine the implementation of the SEM and in the light of the findings this document had been formulated. The document says that

'According to Comrade Mao Zedong's instruction, this movement should grasp five important points, viz, class struggle, socialist education, organising the class ranks of the poor and lower middle peasants, four clean-ups, and cadres' participation in collective labour. Among these five questions, class struggle is the most fundamental.'[45] This document charted out a programme which is very close to the subsequently launched Cultural Revolution. At that time, however, the policies of the 1961-62 period of economic stabilisation were continuing and the class-struggle-oriented-educational campaign did not get under way as a concerted effort.

Within the framework of the SEM Mao made another attempt in 1964 to broaden and deepen the class-struggle orientation. On 10 September 1964 a revised draft on 'Stipulations of Some Concrete Policies on the SEM in the Rural Areas' was circulated in which the Maoist Basic Line was sought to be made more effective. According to this document 'To study Comrade Mao Zedong's thought concerning the question of classes, class contradictions, and class struggle in socialist society...is the key premise to correctly developing and leading the socialist education movement.' The document lays down twelve specific tasks for developing the SEM further. These include specific tasks like holding cadre conferences and cadres participating in collective labour, and general tasks like education in class struggle.

As the disclosures during the Culture Revolution show, the experiences during the SEM were not altogether favourable either to Mao or to Liu Shaoqi. There was simultaneous practice of Liu Shaoqi's economic and administrative policies and Mao's educational policies. The two were not yet integrated. However, the SEM highlighted one dimension of ideological development, i.e., the dimension of political education. It demonstrated the need for mass education in the Basic Line and the General Line within the perspective of continuing class struggle.

The practice of the SEM had two additional lessons for Mao. One was that the leadership at all levels must be firmly based on the correct perspective, otherwise the implementation of correct polices, may take place along mistaken lines. The perspective of the SEM did not percolate down to the grassroot level because of the lack of firm commitment on the part of the leadership to the class-struggle perspective. The second lesson related to the cadres, the mainstay of the party's organisation. The cadres were mainly responsible for the failure of the SEM. Therefore, Mao wanted first of all to create alternative instruments for reaching the masses and at the same time wanted to develop ways of bridging the gap between the cadres and the masses. Beginnings were made on both fronts during the SEM. 'Work teams' were formed to carry out the SEM and cadres were directed to do manual labour along with the masses. However, the magnitude was not high enough to achieve the Maoist goals. This is why a Cultural Revolution was needed.

The Cultural Revolution

The Cultural Revolution provided the form and the focus to the idea of continuing revolution. It established the need for revolutionary class struggle involving the masses to uphold proletarian line. The focus was now on the struggle against revisionism with unprecedented stress.

The Central Committee Circular of 16 May 1966 which launched an attack on the 'Outline Report on the Current Academic Discussion of the Group of Five in charge of the Cultural Revolution',[46] initiated the Great Proletarian Cultural Revolution (GPCR). The 16 May Circular clearly states that the Report of the Group of Five 'runs counter to the line of the socialist cultural revolution set forth by the Central Committee and Comrade Mao Zedong and the guiding principles formulated at the Tenth Plenary Session of the Eighth Central Committee of the Party in 1962 on the question of classes and class struggle in socialist society'.[47] Thus, the perspective of the GPCR was made clear right at the start. On the question of the academic debate on the play 'Dismissal of Hai Jui' the Group of Five had primarilly dealt with it as an academic debate and not as a reflection of class struggle. The 16 May Circular emphasised the perspective of class struggle as the basis of the GPCR.

The Eleventh Plenum of the Central Committee passed the 16-Point Decision concerning the GPCR on 8 August 1966 which laid down the theory, strategy, and policies of the GPCR. It explicitly links the new campaign to the Basic Line. This document declares that a new stage has been reached in socialist revolution. This stage can be described as the stage of 'consolidation of the socialist system'.[48] The document clearly identifies the focus of the new movement as 'the work in the ideological sphere'. It quotes from Mao's speech at the Tenth Plenum that 'To overthrow a political power, it is always necessary, first of all, to create public opinion, to do work in the ideological sphere. This is true for the revolutionary class as well as for the counter-revolutionary class.'[49] The Maoists believed that revisionists like Liu Shaoqi and Peng Zhen had used their high offices to support anti-proletarian ideas. Therefore, it was necessary to create a revolutionary public opinion to counter that. That is why the Political Report ot the Ninth Congress described the GPCR as 'a great political revolution personally initiated and led by our great leader Chairman Mao under the conditions of the dictatorship of the proletariat, a great revolution in the realm of superstructure.'[50]

The main concern of the Maoists during the GPCR was anti-revisionist struggle at the superstructure level or mainly at the level of ideology and politics. This struggle was different from the SEM in a major way. Now it was linked with class struggle not in an analytical sense, but in concrete ways of revolutionary struggle. This time the ideological struggle was also a power struggle with the objective of seizing political power back from the revisionists. This is why it was called a 'revolution in the first place and more often a 'political revolution'. The Ninth Congress Political Report quotes Mao to have said (in January 1965) that 'The main target of the present movement is those Party persons in power taking the capitalist road.'[51]

This revolutionary struggle at the superstructure level was described in terms of the perspective of continuing class struggle between the proletariat and the bourgeoisie. That is how the new ideological struggle against revisionism became different from the similar struggles earlier. The Ninth Congress Report quoted Mao to the effect that the GPCR is a 'continuation of the class struggle between the proletariat and the bourgeoisie.' The Report described the aim of the GPCR as 'to smash revisionism, seize back that portion of power usurped by the bourgeoisie, exercise all-round dictatorship of the proletariat in the superstructure, including all spheres of culture, and strengthen and consolidate the economic base of socialism so as to advance in giant strides along the road of socialism.'[52] This statement very well summed up the dimensions of the political, ideological, and the class struggle which the GPCR attempted to realise.

The form that the GPCR represented was extremely important in the development of the theory of continuing revolution. The Ninth Congress Report quoted Mao from a speech of February 1967 that, 'in the past we waged struggle in rural areas, in factories, in the cultural field, and we carried out the socialist education movement. But all this failed to solve the problem because we did not find a form, a method to arouse the broad masses to expose our dark aspect openly, in an all-around way and from below.'[53] Herein lies an important feature of the CPC's approach to carrying out political campaigns. Firstly it must be *open.* If persons alleged to be revisionists are secretly eliminated then there is no permanent guarantee against the recurrence of such tendencies. Moreover, the campaign must be conducted in an all-round way. This means that all levels of activity and thinking must be integrated. The class-struggle perspective must percolate through the policies in specific spheres and ideological and political aspects should be linked. That is why ever since the GPCR, the Chinese communists talk about the two lines at every level. At the same time such campaigns should be from *below* and not from above. If determinate ideological formulations are announced from above there may not be proper understanding of the formulations at lower levels. This is why Mao denounced Peng Zhen and others for their 'refusal to follow the mass line.'[54]

Several questions may be raised as to whether the principles embodied in the description above have been implemented in China. It may be said for example, that the Maoist gradually made things 'open' as and when they found them suitable. The 'all-round' perspective is broad enough to cover variety of tendencies, as indeed, it covered both Mao's and in Piao's approaches. About the mass initiative, it may be said that, as has been clearly stated, both the GPCR and the latter campaign against Lin Biao were personally initiated by Mao. In other words, GPCR was a centrally initiated mass upheaval and therefore, did not necessarily emerge from below.

In spite of these limitations, the new form, i.e., the GPCR had significant implications. It meant that the leadership could straight away appeal to the masses in case the organisation degenerated. Thus the main force of the revolution were the masses and they were capable of overcoming the incorrect lines of the leadership. This way the new form adopted the CPC's traditional notion of mass line to the new perspective of continuing the revolutionary class struggle during the socialist period. This aspect did make it possible to completely undermine the role of the CPC and Lin Biao took advantage of the mass upsurge to increase the dominance of the PLA. However, the principle of mass line which became an integral part of the theory of continuing revolution during the GPCR continues to be important.

Since the Cultural Revolution was primarily a large-scale practical demonstration of the theory of continuing revolutionary class struggle, it was natural that the theory itself acquired more sophistication during this period. In June 1967 the CPC's theoretical journal *Hong Qi* (Red Flag) republished Mao's 1957 speech on contradictions and wrote an important editorial entitled 'A Theoretical Weapon for Making Revolution under the Dictatorship of the Proletariat.' Until then the Chinese communist writings had spoken of Mao's 'thought' concerning class struggle or his 'thesis'. This editorial spoke of it as 'theory' and discussed the context of its development: 'It was precisely in the course of struggle against international and domestic revisionism that Chairman Mao developed his theory of contradictions, classes and class struggle in a socialist society and of making revolution under the dictatorship of the proletariat.'[55] Later on 6 November 1967, on the eve of the 50th anniversary of the October Revolution, a joint editorial of *Hong-qi*, *Ren-min-ri-bao* and *Jie-fang-jun-bao* entitled 'Advance along the Road Opened up by the October Socialist Revolution' proclaimed and summed up what it called 'Chairman Mao Zedong's theory of continuing the revolution under the dictatorship of the proletariat.'[56]

The Communique of the 12th Plenum of the Central Committee, which was held in October 1968, stressed the 'profound and far-reaching significance of Comrade Mao Zedong's theory on continuing the revolution under the dictatorship of the proletariat'. Thereafter references to and discussions of the theory rapidly multiplied. The Ninth Congress Political Report as well as the Constitution clearly stated the Basic Line and the theory. Ever since then these concepts have become an essential part of the Maoist parlance.[57]

Even after the theory was stated, explained, and defended it continued to develop further. The GPCR added two dimensions to the theory. One was the 'cultural' dimension and the other was the 'revolutionary' dimension. One referred to the class struggle at the superstructure level and the other to the revolutionary power struggle. The proletarian perspective emphasised the class character of the revolution. However, the experiences of the GPCR while effectively demonstrating the validity of the theory also showed anti-proletarian tendencies. Mao found that the PLA while performing a political role during the GPCR was being used by a group led by Lin Biao for the ascendancy of their faction to supreme power. He also found his personal role and his ideas having become absolute and all-powerful, a situation also used by the Lin Biao group to its advantage. In the name of Mao they exercised all power. In this process the party as a concept and as an organisation had lost its leading position. As to how should one respond to such deviations, became Mao's latest worry.

Lin Biao who had emerged as the hero of the GPCR, next only to Mao, had now been denigrated as a revisionist. His understanding of the theory of continuing revolution was, perhaps, based on different assumptions. A revolution in terms of Maoist outlook was a revolutionary war. Therefore, the role of a people's army in such revolutions was political. That, after all was the legacy of the Chinese communists' struggle against the Japanese imperialists and the Kuomintang reactionaries. So when Mao launched a cultural revolution and formed 'Revolutionary Committees' in place of the Party Committee, the PLA did have an appropriate role. Moreover, the PLA intervened in the GPCR only in January 1967 on Mao's explicit instructions. Lin Biao's efforts, similarly, in raising Mao and his ideas to the level of a highly inspiring symbol for purposes of mass mobilisation were by themselves not counter-revolutionary.

However, it is possible that Lin Biao had a crude understanding of the Cultural Revolution. Perhaps he wanted people to find out the Maoist line on a particular thing from the 'Quotations' and apply them, so that the correct line or the proletarian line would be implemented. That was perhaps Lin Biao's approach to the cultural work or ideological struggle. He, probably, took revolution too literally as a military take-over or forcible seizure of power. In this contest the Maoists criticising Lin Biao cite Lin Biao's speech at the Politbureau meeting on 18 May 1966. Lin had said that:

> Here the greatest problem is the prevention of subversion, and the prevention of coup d'etat. The fundamental problem of revolution is the problem of political power. Once they obtain political power, the proletarian class and labouring people will have everything. Once they lose it, they will lose all. Production is undoubtedly the basis; however, it relies upon the changes, consolidation, and development resulting from the seizure of political power.[58]

It is true that Mao has said similar things on 'political power'. But the stress on coup d'etat and interpreting revolution less in terms of class struggle and more in terms of coup d'etat was something to bother about. Mao took a serious note of this and remembered it all the way until Lin himself planned a coup.[59] Whether actually Lin Biao was guilty of these deviations is less important than the fact that such deviations were possible. Therefore, the theory should take precautions against such tendencies.

The Second Plenum of the Ninth Central Committee initiated a further development of the theory keeping in view the latest problems. Mao presented a document called 'My Views' to this Plenum which called upon the party to 'study seriously' and 'strengthen party leadership'. During this Plenum Lin Biao's attempt to be nominated as the Chairman of the Republic had failed. Thereafter, it is now known that Mao decided to 'rise against the tide', i.e., rise against Lin Biao when the latter had enormous support on his side. Several campaigns were launched one after another. The campaign to study the classics of Marx, Engels, Lenin, Stalin, and Mao reversed the trend which had limited the knowledge of Marxism of the Red Guards to the 'Quotations' from Mao. The campaign to sing the International which rejects the belief in saviors and prophets reversed the trend that had raised Mao to the level of a 'genius'. Complementing this campaign was the widespread criticism of 'idealism and metaphysics' which indirectly included Liu and Lin in the same category.[60] The new critical writings said that Liu Shao-ch'i had followed absolutely Marxism-Leninism and ignored the importance of Mao's Thought to achieve his objectives and the new revisionists (meaning Lin Biao) followed only Mao Zedong Thought and delinked it from Marxism-Leninism for similar reasons.[61]

Another set of campaign called for re-establishing the party's centralised leadership in all sectors. Mao's 'Views' had also initiated the process of putting the PLA under the party command. This campaign was intensified in 1971 when party groups in the Revolutionary Committees were asked to exercise leadership over them. The success of this campaign was announced in a special joint editorial on 1 December 1971. Ever since 1971 this aspect has been reiterated on all occasions to say that the Communist Party must always exercise its vanguard role over all the seven sectors of the society—industry, agriculture. Commerce, culture and education, army, government, and party. The party's leadership role in continuing the revolution under the dictatorship was compromised during the GPCR. During the recent years that deviation has been sought to be corrected.

The joint editorial of 1 December 1971 also announced that Mao had directed a campaign to 'carry out education in ideology and political line.'[62] There had been reports in the Chinese press about meetings on line education. This editorial focussed on the question of line. The quotations from Mao like 'The correctness or the incorrectness of the political and ideological line decides everything' were frequently used in 1971. The emphasis on line and the struggle between two lines continued to be the main theme in the campaigns during 1971-73 and the Tenth Congress identified the line as the main issue describing the anti-Lin Biao campaign as the last of the ten great struggles between the two lines inside the party.[63]

The campaigns after the Second Plenum of 1970 were put within the general framework of 'criticise revisionism and rectify the style of work' (*Pi-xiu zheng-feng*). The perspective that integrated these campaign with the GPCR was the theory of continuous revolution. The GPCR had stressed the ideological dimensions of the struggle against revisionism. The recent campaigns stressed the organisational dimensions. The CPC now combined the two dimensions to consolidate the socialist system.

The organisational mistakes which led to the PLA's dominance, rise of the genius theory, decline of the vanguard role of the party, and many other mistakes like arrogance, splittism, careerism and conspiracy were all attributed by Mao to poor understanding of the ideology and line. This is why he called upon the party to study seriously and grasp the correct proletarian line. Then proletarian line could be grasped only by distinguishing it from the bourgeois line. Therefore, the perspective of the struggle between two lines within the party must be kept in view. This dimension was not absent during the GPCR. But the recent campaigns stressed it as a major dimensions of the theory of continuing revolution.

The Tenth Party Congress in August 1973 was the culmination of these campaigns. Besides denouncing Lin Biao and Chen Boda the documents of the Congress reiterated the theory of continuous revolution as the CPC's Basic Line. In the Preamble to the party Constitution the necessary of the Cultural Revolution was emphasised and a new statement was added which said that 'revolutions like this will have to be carried out many times in the future'. In Article 12 of the Constitution, which dealt with the tasks of primary organisations of the party, the phrase 'criticising revisionism' was inserted symbolising the new orientation. In addition to this, the two-line struggle was extolled as an inevitable element throughout the socialist period and a new Maoist slogan— 'Going against the tide is a Marxist-Leninist principle'—was put into the Constitution. That was inner-party struggle was a reflection of the contradictions in socialist society was now formally acknowledged by the party. Zhou Enlai's Political Report to the Congress summed up the lessons of the 'ten major struggles in the history of the Party' and asserted the ubiquity of class struggle in socialist society.

The Tenth Congress intensified the campaign to 'criticise Lin Biao and rectify the style of work' which went on in full swing in 1973. In January 1974 another dimension was added to this campaign by linking the criticism of Lin Piao with the criticism of China's ancient philosopher Confucius. The thrust of this campaign (*Pi-Lin Pi-Kong*) was on the necessity of continuing political campaign against old ideas—a point which had provided the rationale for the Cultural Revolution. At the level of decadent ideas Confucius and Lin Biao belonged to one category. This campaign pointed out glaringly—also in an exaggerated manner—how feudal and bourgeois ideas continued actively in a socialist society.

The first session of the Fourth National People's Congress (NPC) in January 1975 was another landmark in the history of the PRC for it drastically revised the State Constitution. But in terms of theoretical development the NPC only put together the principles which had gradually crystallised since the Cultural Revolution. The preamble of the new State Constitution stated the theory of continuous revolution in the same way as the new constitution of the CPC had done in 1973. The new State Constitution also embodied the perspective and policies of the GPCR. Article 12, for example, declared that the 'proletariat must exercise all-around dictatorship over the bourgeoisie in the superstructure, including all spheres of culture.'

What followed the Fourth NPC session was of enormous significance to the development of the theory of continuous revolution. On 9 February 1975 the *People's Daily* published an editorial entitled, 'Conscientiously Study the Theory of Dictatorship of the Proletariat.' Of course, ever since the Cultural Revolution the statement of the theory of continuous revolution always meant continuing the revolution *under the dictatorship of the proletariat.* But this only implied that throughout the period of socialism there was a dictatorship of the proletariat and the proletariat had to continue its class struggle against the bourgeoisie till the completion of the socialist stage. Now the emphasis was on the understanding of the nature of the proletarian state. It was pointed out by the *People's Daily* editorial that many 'bourgeois rights' continued to exist in the socialist society and their existence must first recognised and then be gradually restricted.

Until 1975 the Maoists had talked about the theory of continuous revolution only in terms of cultural struggle or the struggle against bourgeois ideas. They were thus far open to the criticism that unless material basis for the old ideas remained how could the power of old ideas continue? To this the Maoists now came forward with a reply and Politbureau member Yao Wenyuan wrote an essay, 'On the Social Basis of the Lin Biao Anti-Party Clique' in the March 1975 issue of *Red Flag.* He quoted from Mao's recent instructions which said that 'China is a socialist country. Before liberation, she was more or less like capitalism. Even now she practises an eight-grade wage system, distribution to each according to his work and exchange by means of money, which are scarcely different from those in the old society. What is different is that the system of ownership has changed.' Again: 'Our country at present practised a commodity system, and the wage system is unequal to.... They can only be restricted under the dictatorship of the proletariat.' Mao also quoted Lenin and pointed out that since 'small production' was continuing extensively in agriculture and handicrafts, capitalist mentality had a social basis. Moreover, the vast dichotomies between workers and peasants, mental and manual labour, city and countryside continued to exist.

Vice-Premier Zhang Chunqiao explained this further in an article entitled, 'On Exercising All-Round Dictatorship over the Bourgeoisie' in April 1975. Undertaking a statistical analysis of some rural people's communes on the outskirts of Shanghai he pointed out that the lowest unit, namely the production team was the accounting unit and it accounted for more than 50 per cent of the fixed assets owned at all three levels of the commune. Therefore, until the commune became the accounting unit— and this would take 'a fairly long time'—the collective ownership would still be undeveloped. The ownership by the whole people is the most developed form of socialist ownership and it will take a lot more time to accomplish it for all production activities. Thus at the current stage some elements of the capitalist system of production still continued. Besides, there is the phenomenon of the emergence of the 'new bourgeoisie', a strata of newly privileged people among state and party functionaries whose motivation and style of life are anti-socialist in character. As the *People's Daily* editorial of 9 February 1975 put it, 'These differences mean that certain people can gain more than others because of certain acquired knowledge or skill of simply because they are born into certain localities.'

Actually as the recently available writings of Mao show he had advocated the correct handling of the bourgeois rights as early as 1958. Discussing the necessity of continuing commodity production and commodity exchange even after bourgeois legal power was abolished Mao said that this was necessary because commodity production was still not developed in China. Similarly, the grade level wage system was still necessary and should only be gradually reduced. On these points Mao severely criticised Stalin and the later Soviet economic thinking of the fifties which had either confused the transitional character of socialism with communism or had not charted out a line of steady development.[64] However, such a mass campaign to restrict bourgeois rights was not conducted before in China.

The campaign against bourgeois rights in 1975 appeared to be fairly balanced. In certain articles the dogmatism of those who wanted an immediate abolition of the bourgeois rights was criticised. As Zhang Chunqiao explained, the level of production in China was still far too low to allow a communist type distribution according to need among eight hundred million people and therefore, the present practices involving bourgeois rights had to continue for many more years. In fact, in 1975 the State Constitution legalised the principle of 'each according to his work' leading to differentiated wage system (Article 9), the provision 'to engage in individual labour' (Article 5), the designation of production team as the basic accounting unit and existence of private plots (Article 7). At the same time those who only favoured the continuation of these practices without trying to gradually restrict them were criticised for their rightist mistakes. It was stressed that they must be restricted because bourgeois right, as Lenin said, 'gives to unequal individual in return for unequal (really unequal) amount of labour, equal amounts of products.' Thus the 'wind of communisation' (dogmatism) was as bitterly criticised in China as the 'bourgeois wind' (revisionism).

As the campaign to study the dictatorship of the proletariat gathered momentum a study the dictatorship of the proletariat gathered momentum a debate started in late 1975 regarding the policies in education and scientific research. The issue was whether to continue the GPCR policies and give a worker-peasant orientation to education and research. Also during this time the central authorities issued three directives: 'Study the theory of the Dictatorship of the Proletariat and Oppose Revisionism; promote Stability and Unity; and Promote National Economy.' By the New Years' Day of 1976 it was clear that the three directives attributed to Mao wee used by some important leaders to undermine the Basic Line of the party, namely, the perspective of continuing class struggle and all its attendant policies. By February a campaign was on against 'the unrepentant capitalist-roader' (clearly implying Deng Xiaoping) who was allegedly trying hard to 'reverse correct verdicts'.

Teng Hsiao-p'ing, the Vice-Premier who was described as the number two capitalist-roader during the Cultural Revolution was rehabilitated in March 1973. It was presumed that he had repented of his past mistakes and had accepted the Basic Line. In 1974-75 Deng emerged as the most important political leader of China after Mao and Zhou. However, in early 1976 allegations floated in the Chinese press that he was trying to reverse the policies upheld by the GPCR. About the three directives it was asserted that Chairman Mao wanted the three directives to be promulgated taking 'class struggle as the key link' (*Jie-ji dou-zheng shi gang*). In other words, the Maoists wanted the drive for stability and production within the broad perspective of class struggle. But Deng Xiaoping apparently asked people to 'take the three directives as the key link' (yi *san xiang zhi-shi wei gang*) and thereby he undermined the Basic Line.

After the struggle between the two lines intensified and riots took place on the Tiananmen Square in Peking on 5 April 1976 Deng was removed from the State and party posts. This experience once again reaffirmed the class-struggle perspective of the dominant section of the CPC. It was not only a question of theoretical commitment to the Basic Line, but whether Teng had accepted its policy implications. A *People's Daily* editorial of 27 March 1976 criticised Deng for his attempts.

> to oppose independence and self-reliance and advocate the slavish comprador philosophy and the doctrine of trailing behind at a snail's pace; to oppose the activation of both the central as well as local initiatives and re-impose the practice of 'direct and exclusive control of enterprises by the ministry concerned': to oppose the policy of *walking on two legs* and lay one-sides stress on things big and foreign; and to oppose the *Charter of the Anshan Iron and Steel Company* and advocate the rules and regulations of the Magnitogorsk Iron and Steel Combine of the Soviet Union.'

Thus the struggle against Deng Xiaoping once again demonstrated the Maoists' determination to build socialism in China only along the road implied by their Basic Line.

In May 1976 the tenth anniversary of the launching of the Cultural Revolution was celebrated in China. A joint editorial on that occasion described how correct was the CPC Central Committee Circular of 16 May 1966 and quoted the following from a new statement of Mao: 'You are making the socialist revolution, and yet don't know where the bourgeoisie is. It is right in the Communist Party—those in power taking the capitalist road. The capitalist-roaders are still on the capitalist road.' In this joint editorial and in many other articles which followed, the 'bourgeois essence' of the revisionists within the party was emphasised. An article by Fang Kang in the June 1976 issue of *Red Flag* explained that since the bourgeoisie finds it hard to achieve success outside the party it attempts to subvert the socialist system from inside the party. The capitalist-roaders try hard to safeguard the bourgeois rights or 'those very parts of the superstructure and relations of production that hinder the development of the socialist economic base and productive forces in an attempt to restore capitalism.' Thus the 1976 struggle against Deng Xiaoping emphasised the fact that the two-line struggle in the party is a serious type of class struggle and will continue throughout the socialist period. When this ideological campaign was going on in China Mao Zedong passed away in September 1976. One of the key ideas extolled during the memorial rallies was none else than the theory of continuing revolution under the dictatorship of the proletariat.

V. THE THEORY STATED

Put in the form of deductive logic the theory of continuing revolution can be stated in the following manner:

1. (*i*) All bougeoisie resort to political, economic as well as cultural means to hold on to power.
   (*ii*) The politically overthrown bourgeoisie is still a bourgeois force in some sphere in the socialist society.
   (*iii*) Therefore, it is bound to use every available means to hold on to power.
2. (*i*) Class struggle is a revolutionary struggle.
   (*ii*) Proletariat's struggle against bourgeoisie even after the latter's political overthrow is a class struggle.

Chart 2
Development of the Theory of Continuing Revolution

1. Phases of development	Accelerating agricultural cooperativisation 1955-56	Early reaction to revisionism, the CPSU's 20th Congress; counter-revolution in Hungary	New General Line for socialist construction; the Great Leap Forward; Communes, 1958-60	Intensified struggle against revisionism—international and internal, 1962-63	Socialist Education Movement, 1963-65
2. Events of importance	1. Sixth Plenum of the Central Committee on cooperativisation, October 1955 2. Politbureau considers ten year plan on agricultural development, January 1956	1. 20th Congress of the CPSU, February 1956 2. 8th Party Congress adopts Liu's line, September 1956 3. Counter-revolution in Hungary, October 1956	1. Second Session of the 8th Party Congress, May 1958 2.Eighth Plenum of Central Committee, August 1959 3. Soviet withdrawal of personnel from China, 1960	1. Tenth Plenum of the Central Committee, September 1962 2. China-India war, October 1962 3. Cuban missile crissis, October 1962	Attempts to reorient the SEM in May 1963, September 1963, and September 1964
3. Relevant decuments	1. Mao: On Agricultural Co-operativisation, July 1955 2. Preface to *Socialist Usurge in China's Countryside,* December 1955	1. On the Ten Great Relationships' April 1956 2. On the historical experiences of the dictatorship of the proletariat, April 1956 3. More on the historical experiences of the dictatorship of the proletariat, December 1956, 4. Mao: 'On the correct handling of contradictions among the people', February 1957 Published in June	1. Report to the second session of the Eighth Congress, May 1958 2.Gentral Committee Resolution on Communes, December 1958	1. Communique of the Tenth Plenum 1962 2. CPC's proposal concerning General Line for the international communist movement, 14 June 1963	1. Central Committee Policies on SEM (draft), May 1963, September 1963, and September 1964
4. Dimension of the theory	Rapid movement toward socialist construction	Class contradictions continue to exist	Mass Line model of development added	Continuing the revolutionary class struggle between the bourgeoisie and the proletariat	Intensive ideological education

Continued...

1. Phases of development	Great Proletarian Cultural Revolution (GPCR)	Campaign to criticise revisionism and rectify style of work	Campaign against bourgeois rights	Campaign against reversing correct verdicts	Campaign against the 'Gang of Four'
2. Events of importance	1. Politbureau meeting on 16 May 1966 overthrows the P'eng Chen led Group of Five in charge of the Cultural Revolution 2. Central Committee 11th Plenum, Aughust 1966 3. Central Committee 12th Plenum, October 1966 4. Ninth Congress of the CPC, April 1969	1. Second Plenum of the Ninth Central Committee, August-September 1970 2. Lin Biao's escape and air-crash, 13 September 1971 3. Tenth Party Congress, August 1973	1. Fourth NPC, January 1975	1. Politbureau Meeting of 8 April 1976 which dismissed Deng Xiaoping.	1. Overthrow of Wang Hong-wen, Zhang Chunqiao, Jiang Qing, and Yao Wenyuan on 7 October 1976 2. Third Plenum of Tenth Central Committee rehabilitates Deng in July 1977 3. Eleventh Pary Congress, August 1977
3. Relevant decuments	1. May 16 circular 2. 16-point decisions on the GPCR 3. Documents of the Ninth Congress	1. Communique of the Second Plenum 2. Joint editorial on the CPC's 50th anniversary, 1 July 1971 3. Joint editorial on the Centenary of the Paris Commune, 19 March 1971	1. *People's Daily* editorial of 9 February 1975 2. Yao Wenyuan's article in *Red Flag* of March 1975 3. Zhang Chunqiao's article in *Red Flag* of April 1975	1. *People's Daily* editorial of 27 March 1976 2. Joint editorial of 16 May 1976 celebrating the Tenth anniversary of the GPCR	1. Joint editorial. 'A Great, Historic Victory, of 24 October 1976 2. Documents of the Eleventh Party Congress
4. Dimension of the theory	Class struggle at the super-structure level Revolutionary power struggle	Struggle between the two lines. Party's leadership role in dictatorship of the proletariat	Capitalist elements still exist in socialist economic structure	Take class struggle as key link, Bourgeois essence of the revisionists within the party	Curbing idealism and splitism. Strengthning the economic base by allout modernisation call for 'great order'

(*iii*) Therefore, it is a revolutionary struggle.

3. (*i*) Continuous revolutionary struggle can prevent bourgeois restoration.
   (*ii*) Some communist parties are continuing revolutionary struggle.
   (*iii*) Those communist parties can prevent bourgeois restoration.

Part in the frame of inductive logic the theory can be stated as follows:

1. (*i*) Bourgeoisie attempted to overthrow the socialist systems in Hungary and Czechoslovakia.
   (*ii*) Bourgeois trends in political and economic policies have been operating in the USSR.
   (*iii*) Bourgeois policies were propounded and practised by some leaders of the CPC.
   (*iv*) Therefore, even after the overthrow of the bourgeoisie from political and economic power, it uses the cultural realm and transitional economic forms to stage a comeback.
2. (*i*) Under Lenin's leadership the revolution continued from democratic to the socialist stage through revolutionary class struggle.
   (*ii*) Under Mao's leadership the proletarian-led democratic revolution continued to the socialist stage through revolutionary class struggle.
   (*iii*) Therefore, the proletariat must continue the revolutionary class struggle until the onset of the communist stage when the political, economic, and cultural power of the bourgeoisie would have been fully replaced by socialism.

The theory of continuing revolution which is reflected in the statement of the CPC's Basic Line has been summed up in the latest Constitution of the CPC thus:

> Socialist society covers a considerably long historical period. Throughout this historical period, there are classes, class contradiction and class struggle; there is the struggle between the socialist road and the capitalist road; there is the danger of capitalist restoration; and there is the threat of subversion and aggression by imperialism and social imperialism.

> These contradictions can be resolved only by depending on the theory of continued revolution under the dictatorship of the proletariat and on practice under its guidance.

The first two sentences are taken from Mao's Tenth Plenum speech which, however, spoke only of 'the danger of capitalist restoration'. To that has been added 'subversion and aggression by imperialism and social-imperialism'. Besides, the Ninth Congress Constitution April, 1969 used the phrase 'modern revisionism' whereas in 1973 it was replaced by 'social-imperialism'.

A clarification regarding the terms, Basic Line and the theory of continuing revolution, is necessary here. After stating the theory of continuing revolution in 1967 the Chinese communists have gradually expanded the spectrum of its relevance to include all epochs and stages of revolution from democratic to socialist and to communist.[65] The Ninth Congress Political Report spoke of Mao's theory of continuity revolution under the dictatorship of the proletariat and identified it as his 'historic contribution'. Later writings in the Chinese press have however been cautious on this. While the general theory of continued revolution is attributed to Marx, Engels and Lenin, the theory of continuing revolution under the dictatorship of the proletariat, i.e., in the socialist phase, is attributed to Mao. The contents of this particular theory and the Basic Line for the socialist period worked out by Mao are the same. According to an important article in *Hong Qi*:

> The Party's Basic Line, which is determined by Marxism-Leninism-Mao Zedong Thought, demonstrates the objective laws of class struggle in the historical period of socialism, points out the principal contradiction in socialist society and the way to resolve it, sets forth the strategic task of continuing the revolution under the dictatorship of the proletariat, and lays down a general policy with regard to distinguishing the contradictions between ourselves and the enemy from those among the people and handling them correctly.[66]

The basic motivation behind the theory of continuing revolution is the fear of regression. This can take place in two ways. Firstly, because bourgeois ideas live beyond the phase of political and economic overthrow and because they die hard, the bourgeois remnants can strengthen themselves and begin to initiate bourgeois policies under the garb of socialism. This is capitalist restoration which is brought about by revisionists. Secondly, imperialists and other anti-socialist forces outside the socialist country can intervene, invade, subvert, and attack the socialist system in various ways. They did this in the early years of the Soviet Union and later when opportunities arose. In the modern times this danger is even greater with nuclear armaments at their disposal and sophisticated technology of communication and control. Therefore, the proletariat must continue the revolutionary class struggle throughout the socialist period to defeat the bourgeois power at home and abroad.

The theory of continuing revolution has two positive motivations which are related to the foregoing considerations. One is related to mobilisation and preparedness and the other is related to the nature and strategy of development. Both consideration emanate from the CPC's commitment to the mass line. The Maoists believe that the best guarantee against the bourgeois restoration is alertness on the part of the masses. Therefore, there must be continuous political education of the masses in proletarian ideology. This education must involve harmonious mental and manual work. Therefore, education, production, and politics must be integrated. The Maoists talk about three revolutionary movements of 'class struggle, the struggle for production and scientific experiment'. All these must go on with the participation of masses and with their initiative under the party's leadership. This is a pattern of self-mobilisation by the masses which is not only meant for education and production, but also for preparedness against war and natural disasters. The orientation of continuing revolutionary class struggle sharply focusses on the need for mobilisation and preparedness, and facilitates it.

The nature and strategy of development also emerge from the same perspective. In order to facilitate the improvement of the conditions of living of all sections of the people—workers, peasants, and the intelligentsia—a poor and backward country must mobilise maximum resources. Human energy which is the greatest resource for production can be best activised if people are aroused and committed to their common goals. The General Line of 1958 for socialist construction was conceived precisely with this objective. The

Basic Line and the theory of continuing revolution only put that approach in perspective. Thus the mass line strategy of development can be fully implemented if the masses, namely, the proletariat and the peasantry are fully aroused to ensure the further development of the productive forces in their country so that the bourgeoisie is further weakened internally and externally.

It is appropriate, therefore, that the Constitution of the CPC should reiterate these aspects in the General Programme just after stating the Basic Line.

The perspective of continuing revolutionary class struggle has been gradually operationalised in course of the development of the theory. The three main forms that this struggle has taken are: (1) the struggle in the realm of politics and ideology, (2) the struggle between the two lines within the party, and (3) the struggle for socialist construction. The first struggle encompasses the whole society with emphasis on ideological and educational activities. The second form is confined to the party and the third is carried out in concrete spheres of economic policies and their implementation.

The struggle at the political and ideological levels must continue so that the proletariat spreads its ideology constantly and steadily consolidates its power. As indicated before, the bourgeoisie uses its last 'hereditary domains', i.e., the cultural domains to regain its power in other fields.[67] Moreover, the superstructure which has been built over the socialist base has many imperfect aspects. The existence of bourgeois ideology, certain unhealthy tendencies in state organs and defects in some links of the state systems stand in contradiction to the economic base of socialism.[68] That is why continuous revolutionary struggle is needed to make the superstructure harmonious with the economic base.

The struggle within the party is the reflection of the class struggle in the whole society. The bourgeoisie always tries to infiltrate into the party so that it becomes capable of taking over political power by occupying crucial positions in the party. That is why revisionism has always been defined by Marxists as an expression of the bourgeois ideology under the cover of Marxism. As the Political Report to the Tenth Congress put it, 'Class enemies at home and abroad all understand that the easiest way to capture a fortress is from within. It is much more convenient to have the capitalist-roaders in power who have sneaked into the Party do the job of subverting the dictatorship of the proletariat than for the landlords and capitalists to come to the fore themselves...' This two-line struggle that continues throughout the socialist period is caused by two sources. The existence of the influences of the landlords and the bourgeoisie in the country is its domestic source, while surrender to imperialist pressure is the external source.[69] As long as these sources exist the possibility of two-line struggles exists. The campaign against Lin Biao was the tenth major inner-party struggle and Zhou Enlai's Political Report declared that, 'For a long time to come, there will still be two-line struggles within the Party, reflecting these contradictions, and such struggles will occur 10, 20 or 30 times.'

The CPC's approach to the question of inner-party struggle has gradually developed from the level of ideological struggle to the political struggle and culminated in the recent perspective of class struggle. During the *Zheng-feng* Campaign of 1942-44 (the rectification campaign) the primary method of dealing with inner-party differences was democratic discussions. Though revisionism within the party was identified as a bourgeois tendency incorrect tendencies were continued to be called 'deviations'.[70] The Gao Gang controversy in 1954 culminated in the expulsion of the members of the 'anti-Party clique'. Even then the general policy of the party continued to be that of 1942. The contradictions speech of Mao in 1957 which has been discussed earlier took care to distinguish ideological struggle from other struggles. The Peng Dehuai controversy in 1959 added a new dimension to the policy towards inner-party struggles. While denouncing the 'right opportunist anti-Party cliques headed by Peng Dehuai' the Eighth Plenum of 1959 linked his opposition with the widening context of revisionism. Now not only persons but also tendencies were to be tackled. The inner-party ideological struggle thus became more explicitly a political struggle.[71] The Cultural Revolution took the inner-party struggle as struggle against the bourgeois representatives in power. Mao's call to 'Bombard the Headquarters' was as recognition of this new dimension. While the GPCR made the inner-party struggle a revolutionary class struggle between two lines the campaign against Lin Biao made it more meaningful by stressing the importance of the *Line.* The inner-party struggle now is a struggle between two lines, the correct and the incorrect, the proletarian and the bourgeois lines.

In the economic realm the class struggle goes on several fronts. On the question of the General Line for Socialist Construction the Maoists have denounced the 'Theory of Productive Forces' which was exclusively concerned with increasing production with little regard for qualitative question of socialism. In 1975 the programme of 'four modernisations' (in agriculture, industry, defence and science and technology—which Zhou Enlai had announced in the NPC in January 1975) was put forward as the new perspective for China's development the Maoists emphatically pointed out and said that the four modernisations must go on within the basic orientation of class struggle. At more specific levels this perspective has implied gradually restricting 'bourgeois rights' in the wage structure in factories and communes, ensuring 'red and expert' approach to training at all levels, and advocating a new management system in the enterprises to curb bureaucratism of managers. Above all the work ethic of the workers has to be based on class struggle rather than material incentives.

A range of strategies, policies, and tactics have been evolved and are still evolving to continue the revolutionary class struggle both at the superstructure level in general and inside the party in particular. The most important strategy is that of GPCR which is also a form of the continued revolution. In order to consolidate the dictatorship of the proletariat, the new Constitution of the CPC declared that 'Revolutions like this will have to be carried out many times in the future.' Mao wrote in 1966: 'Great disorder across the land leads to great order and so once again every seven or eight years monsters and demons will jump out themselves. Determined by their own class nature, they are bound to jump out.'[72] The Cultural Revolution is, therefore, a major strategy for carrying out the revolutionary struggle against the bourgeoisie inside and outside the party.

The policies and tactics arising out of this perspective are many. From time to time the emphasis on these has changed. The contradictions speech of 1957 spoke of six political criteria for judging words and actions in the political life. The campaigns since the fall of Lin Biao have highlighted some new policies which appear more pertinent at this point of time. The most widely publicised statement in this context is, 'Practice Marxism and not revisionism, unite and do not split, be open an above-board and do not intrigue and conspire.' This summarises a set of principles arising out of the experience, both positive and negative, since the beginning of the Cultural Revolution. One old principle has been restated recently: 'Learn from past mistakes to avoid future ones, save the patient by curing the sickness.' This contrasts with Stalin's method of dealing with political opposition. Within the framework of the CPC, a revisionist can reform himself by undergoing education in the 'May 7 Cadre Schools' and can be rehabilitated. The return of the 'Number two Capitalist-Roader' of the days of the GPCR, Deng Xiaoping in March 1973 was symbolic of this approach.

Two important methods evolved by the CPC to handle contradictions are: Unity-Criticisim-Unity and Struggle-Criticism-Transformation. Generally speaking, the first method applies to handling contradictions among people. As was explained in the non-contradictions speech of Mao in 1957 the resolution of non-antagonistic contradictions like the differences among the workers and peasants should start from the stand-point of unity, carry on criticism of erroneous ideas, and finally re-establish a new and well-grounded unity. On the other hand, the second method applies to the handling of antagonistic contradictions. These contradictions involve conflicts of greater intensity and reflect the relationship between exploiting and exploited classes. The first step in resolving these contradictions is for the oppressed classes to struggle against the representatives of the exploiting classes and overthrow them from the positions of power. The second step is that of ideological criticism of such persons and their class outlook which means that they are not treated merely as a law and order problem. The final step is an attempt to transform the minds of such people who may include the mistaken comrades in the Party as well. The 'May 7 Cadre Schools' have become the places for political education for people with mistaken ideas.

An important lesson that Mao had drawn from the inner-party struggles is that 'One tendency covers another'. In the Political Report to the Tenth Congress, Zhou Enlai discussed all the major struggles within the CPC to point out how a campaign against 'left' deviation allowed right opportunism to grow at the same time and vice-versa. The policy advocated therefore is to guard against the opposite tendency while fighting against one tendency.

Thus, the theory of continuing the socialist revolution under the dictatorship of the proletariat starts with identifying the nature and forms of class struggle during the socialist period and suggests a number of principles of strategy, policy, and tactics to carry out the revolution. In recent years all specific policies are linked directly with the main theory and the Basic Line. Specific lines and policies in every sphere from economy to diplomacy are to be based on the Basic Line. The Political Report to the Tenth Congress quoted Mao that 'we should attach importance not only to the Party's line and policies for specific work but, in particular, to its Basic Line'.

VI. THE THEORY DISCUSSED

The three main philosophical premises supporting the theory are: (1) The major contradiction in the entire socialist period is that between the proletariat and the bourgeoisie; (2) while matter determines the nature of consciousness, the consciousness can also be transformed into matter; and (3) 'One divided into two'. Of these the first premise is the important one.

Debate on the Theory of Productive Forces

The first philosophical premise has acquired enormous significance because this has been advanced to refute an alternative proposition associated with Chen Boda. In his Political Report to the Tenth Congress, Zhou Enlai referred to 'the revisionist trash that Liu Shaoqi and Chen Boda had smuggled into the resolution of the Eighth Congress, which alleged that the major contradiction in our country was not the contradiction between the proletariat and the bourgeoisie, but that between the advanced socialist system and the backward productive forces.'

The references to this debate can be found in the literature published during the Cultural Revolution. But the debate assumed a major proportion in public in early September 1971 when Ch'en's position (without mentioning his name) was described as one which was opposed to the theory of continued revolution.[73] After the open reference at the Tenth Congress the discussion on this issue grew steadily.

As discussed earlier, the Eighth Congress of 1956 had laid down a General Line that was abandoned in 1958. It had passed a resolution which spelled out the theoretical character of the then prevailing situation. After saying that 'the contradiction between the proletariat and the bourgeoisie has been basically resolved', the Resolution of the Eight Congress declared that:

> the major contradiction in our country is already that between the people's demand for the building of an advanced industrial country and the realities of a backward agricultural country.... Under the condition of a socialist system having been established in our country, the essence of this contradiction between the advanced socialist system and the backward social productive forces.[74]

This position has been attributed to Chen and Liu. The Chen Boda view argues that according to the law of historical materialism the basic contradiction in all societies is that between the relations of production and the forces of production, between the superstructure and the economic base. Therefore, the advanced superstructure cannot be sustained without a correspondingly advanced base. When socialist transformation was completed in 1956, Chen argued, the production base should be further advanced to fulfil the aspirations of even more hopeful party members and the people whom the advanced superstructure represented.

Maoist writings use two terms in this context. One is 'basic contradiction' (*ji-ben mao-dun*) and the other is 'major or principal contradiction'. Till now Maoist writings have maintained what Mao had said in his 1957 contradictions speech: 'The basic contradictions in socialist society are still those between the relations of production and the productive forces and between the superstructure and the economic base.'[75] After stating this the Maoists go on to define the contradictions in class terms. In the 1957 speech, even though Mao said that the struggle between the bourgeoisie and the proletariat was still going on and who would win was still undecided, he had not quite developed the thesis that the *major contradiction* in the socialist period was that between the bourgeoisie and the proletariat. In fact, he said things that conform to Chen's position. As Mao put it, 'Socialist society also develops through contradictions between the productive forces and the relations of production. In a socialist or communist society, technical innovations and improvement in the social system inevitably continue to take place; otherwise the development of society would come to a standstill and society could no longer advance.'

Only after 1962 Mao seems to have decided to stress the dimension of continuing class struggle and ever since the notion of the *major contradiction* has been advanced. In retrospect, however, the Maoists refer to Mao's 1949 speech on 'People's Democratic dictatorship' where he said that the principal contradiction would be one between the proletariat and the bourgeoisie.

At the conceptual level if Chen was only advancing the well-known Marxist notion of *basic contradiction* and Mao was suggesting *the major contradiction* then the debate over this question would not have become so vindictive, as both positions are correct in Marxist theory. But the controversy actually related to the role that the superstructure plays in social development and whether continuous class struggle in the form of mass upheavals helps or hinders production. Mao would say that it helps the development of production on the socialist path.

Lin Biao is said to have advocated that the main task after the GPCR was the development of production and Mao wanted continuous revolution. This is where the difference is borne out. Maoists advance two arguments to support the view that superstructure is capable of strengthening or subverting the base. Firstly, while it is true that productive forces are primary, it is also true that the workers are the most important productive force. The tools are made by men and can be used by the proletariat and the bourgeoisie for political and ideological organisation and movements which enthuse and orient men influence the productive forces in a major way. Secondly, there is a dialectical relationship between the relations of production and the forces of production. A certain level of productive forces demands corresponding relations of production. At the same time, 'tremendous growth of the productive forces always takes place after the establishment of new relations of production which correspond to the development of productive forces.'[76] The Maoist writings quote from 'On Contradiction' where Mao had said that though the productive forces 'generally play the decisive role' 'in certain conditions' the relations of productions 'in turn manifest themselves in the principal and decisive role.'

This approach of the Maoists which manifested in the Great Leap Forward and the GPCR has been criticised by the Soviet writers as 'subjectivist approach' and 'voluntarism' typical of 'Mao's petty bourgeois outlook'.[77] They say that Mao believes in the subjective factor of human will performing miracles independently rather than relying on the objective development of the productive forces. They point out at the failure of the 1958 policies for this. To this the Maoists retort that leaving the productive forces to develop spontaneously would be like allowing the capitalist economic forces 'to peacefully evolve' into socialist economy. The Maoists say that just as conscious mass organisation is needed to bring about a socialist revolution, conscious political struggles at the level of the superstructure are needed to develop the productive forces. That is why the Maoists have coined the slogan, 'grasp revolution, promote production' which means 'firmly grasp class struggle as the key link, give prominence to proletarian politics and use revolutionisation to lead mechanisation.'[78] Thus the Maoists far from giving up the production orientation want to conduct it along the proper path.

In this debate if one accepts the perspective of anti-revisionism then the important role of superstructure as advocated by the Maoists cannot be denied. However, the debate is not yet conclusive as to the 'decisive' role of the superstructure. Mao had said that 'in certain conditions' the relations of production would play the decisive role. Maoists have not yet elaborated these conditions. If these conditions are as pervasive as the threat of capitalist restoration covering the entire socialist period then it would amount to a reversal of the Marxist proposition on the decisive role of the forces of production. But every time the Maoists state their position on the important role of the superstructure they also state the original Marxist proposition. That does not seem to be enough. They have to identify within the framework of the theory of continued revolution the conditions and ways when the generally decisive role of the forces of production and the base is punctuated by the periodically decisive role of the relations of production and superstructure.

Is it Consistent with Dialectical Materialism?

The second philosophical premise is related to the first. Even though we will return to this question for a more detailed examination in a later chapter it is necessary to briefly take it up here insofar as its relevance to the theory of continued revolution is concerned. Maoists argue, as Mao put it in May 1963 in 'Where do Correct Ideas come from?', 'Matter can be transformed into consciousness and consciousness into matter.' Without denying the primacy of matter and being, they stress the importance of consciousness and thinking which in turn reflect themselves in the base. This philosophical statement is related to the first premise and the perspective of continuing revolutionary class struggle because the Maoists believe that intense political awareness and education in Marxist theory and line would result in workers working still harder and production going up. This is also basic to the recent campaigns for grasping the Basic Line. Once people's thinking is based on true Marxism, they believe, mistakes would be avoided.

After Mao's 1963 essay a debate started inside China on the question of 'Identity of Thinking and Being'. The eminent philosopher Yang Hsien-chen criticised Mao's formulation as idealist deviation from dialectical materialism which gives primacy to material foces.[79] This debate acquired major proportions in the 1960s as the inner-party struggle intensified. Lin Biao upheld Mao's formulation and unleashed the campaign to study Mao's thought within the PLA. In 1960 he set forth the 'Four Firsts' which emphasised the role of revolutionary theory and ideological education. The GPCR further popularised the Maoist position by basing the ideological education movement on Mao's thought and advancing the all-important slogan of 'Putting Politics in Command'. In 1971 this trend took a new turn when idealism was attacked by the Maoists. Lin Biao's 'Four Firsts' and his responsibility for building a genius cult were criticised as apriori idealism and were bracketed with Liu Shaoqi's idealist fallacies propounded in his book *Self-Cultivation*. In the new campaign, however, the theory of reflection of consciousness, or consciousness transforming into matter was not attacked. It was the genius theory of history which was attacked.

The Maoists argue that their position is derived from the dialectical materialist theory of knowledge. Knowledge comes from practice and continuously develops through practice. Revolutionary theory which is tested already becomes the basis for practice. Therefore, Marx said that the task now was to remake the world. This is why knowledge has an active function which 'manifests itself not only in the leap from perceptual knowledge to rational knowledge, but—and this is more important—it also manifests itself in the leap from rational knowledge to revolution and practice.... The second leap is of greater significance than the first.'[80] This is how consciousness also transforms itself into matter when practice creates new material force.

It is not the capacity of matter and consciousness to influence each other mutually that is criticised by the Soviet writers but the question of primacy. Can matter and consciousness 'change places'? The Maoists seem to say yes, they can. Here they seem to allow equal claims to primacy for both matter and consciousness. However, the Soviet writers criticising Mao go to another fallacious position in denying the important role of consciousness. Their definition of matter 'as the objective reality existing outside our consciousness' is closer to the position of mechanical materialists.[81] So also is their assertion that matter and spirit 'are two independent phenomena.'[82]

The third philosophical premise 'One Divides into Two' was advanced by Maoists in course of the criticisms against Yang Hsien-chen's proposition that 'Also Two Unite into One'. Maoists take their stand on this premise to justify that there is struggle between two contending classes everywhere. The socialist system is divided into two contending forces, i.e., the proletariat and the bourgeoisie engaged in class struggle. The Communist Party is also divided into those taking the correct line and those opposing it. According to the Maoists this position is based on the Marxist notion of dialectics as the doctrine of unity of opposites. Maoists quote Lenin to say that 'the splitting of a single whole and the cognition of its contradictory parts is the essence of dialectics.'

Maoist writings criticised Yang's 'Also Two Unite into One' proposition saying that Yang did not stress the contradictory or struggle aspect of things. They accused him of supporting Liu's theory of 'dying out of class struggle.' The Maoists charge that Yang's view would lead to a theory of class collaboration in socialist systems and collaboration between socialist States and imperialist States in world politics.[83]

The Maoists criticism of Yang's position holds good if the unity aspect of the contradiction is regarded as more important than the struggle aspect by the latter and if Yang's theory is meant to justify 'revisionism' and 'peaceful coexistence with imperialism' etc. But by itself the 'Also Two Unite into One' concept put forth as a subsidiary and supplementary concept is evidently consistent with Marxist theory. Mao said in the contradictions speech in 1957:

> Between opposites in a contradiction there is at once unity and struggle, and it is this that impels things to move and change. Contradictions exist everywhere, but they differ in accordance with the different nature of different things. In any given phenomenon or thing, the unity of opposite is conditional, temporary and transitory, and hence relative, whereas the struggle of opposites is absolute.[84]

Mao has restated here the basic Marxist notion that it is the primacy of struggle in a relationship that makes it a contradiction even though the unity aspect cannot be ignored.

Mao and Trotsky

Mao's theory of continuous revolution has often compelled writers to draw parallels with Trotsky's theory of permanent revolution. In fact, there are certain followers of Trotsky today who believe that Mao had developed Trotsky's theory further in the light of present day situations in the world, as well as in China. Their comparison is generally based on three arguments. They point out that Mao ensured working class leadership of the democratic revolution so that there was no need for another armed revolution to establish a dictatorship of the proletariat. After all, Trotsky had advocated this in effect when in his 1906 pamphlet, *Results and Prospects*, he pointed out how in a backward country the bourgeoisie was unable to lead its own revolution. In 1928 he developed this further to say that in a backward country the bourgeois-democratic revolution would lead directly to the dictatorship of the proletariat which in turn would seek to accomplish socialist aims. This is why Trotsky had opposed the CPC joining the KMT in united front in 1924. This approach to Trotsky which unites the democratic and socialist stages into one permanent revolution is compared to the actual experience of the Chinese revolution which made a smooth and swift transition from the democratic to the socialist stage.

Another point of comparison is that like Mao, Trotsky had advocated pervasive effect of revolutionary class struggle in all spheres of social activity. In his *Permanent Revolution* Trotsky said that the proletariat would try to bring about transformations in the fields of economy, technology, science, family, morality, etc. and thus the society would never reach an equilibrium and socialist revolution will acquire a permanent nature.

A third level of this comparison is related to Trotsky's notion of world revolution. In the course of the celebrated debate between Stalin and Trotsky the former argued the thesis of 'socialism in one country' and the latter said that 'world revolution is the pre-requisite for the victory of revolution in one country.' Trotsky advocated his thesis on the ground that as long as advanced capitalist countries existed they would attempt to destroy the fruits of revolution. Therefore, revolution must spread from country to country and should become permanent to complete the world revolution. Mao also regarded Chinese revolution as a part of world revolution. His formulations that 'revolution is the main trend in history' and 'countries want independence, nations want liberation and people want revolution' are expressions of a similar orientation as Trotsky's. The advocacy of the CPC of a world-wide united front against imperialism and social-imperialism is a part of the process of world revolution.

These comparison, however interesting they may appear, are superficial if we take into account the totality of their respective ideological frameworks. Mao's theory is concerned with the nature of the socialist period and the fact that classes and class struggle exist even after the elimination of bourgeois ownership of the means of production. On the other hand, Trotsky's theory was a general formulation encompassing the entire process of revolution from feudalism to communism. Mao's theory of people's democratic revolution was an agrarian revolution with peasantry as its main force and where the countryside surrounded the cities. Trotsky consistently distrusted the revolutionary potentiality of the peasantry. Moreover, the united front policies of the CPC during the early years of the PRC were not merely a bundle of formalities. The national bourgeoisie was a partner in economic construction and it was slowly transformed.

As to the pervasive impact of class struggle it is doubtful if Trotsky would have condoned Mao's emphasis on the role of superstructure. Trotsky's philosophical writings convey the impression that he believed in an exclusive over-determining role of the economic base. It is not surprising that the majority of the Trotskyites and the leaders of the Fourth International have denounced the Cultural Revolution as idealistic deviation.

Mao's pronouncements on the world revolution are sharply different from those of Trotsky. The consolidation of fruits of revolutions is clearly put in primary place in the world-view of the CPC. Revolutions are essentially the business of the people of the respective countries. With this as the basis the CPC has advocated proletarian internationalism and anti-imperialist unity. Thus China's path to world revolution is through the strengthening of national revolutions and not by relying on stirring revolutions elsewhere. Even though the Chinese have assisted revolutionary movements abroad in various degrees, their main orientation has been essentially different from that of Trotsky.

This is why in his speech at the Supreme State Conference on 28 January, 1958 Mao said:

> I stand for the theory of permanent revolution. Do not mistake this for Trotsky's theory of permanent revolution. In making revolution one must strike while the iron is hot—one revolution must follow another, the revolution must continually advance... Trotsky believed that the socialist revolution should be launched even before the democratic revolution is complete. We are not like that.[85]

In fact the Chinese communists used the same expression 'permanent revolution' (*bu-duan ge-ming*) to convey both Trotsky's theory as well as their theory from 1958 onwards. Sometimes they translated this as 'uninterrupted' (literally the meaning of *bu-duan*) revolution. But after they claimed a new theoretical status for this formulation of Mao in 1967 the Chinese started using the term 'continuous revolution' (*ji-xü ge-ming*). Now they leave no opportunity to point out that there is absolutely no similarity between Trotsky's theory and Mao's theory.

The operational problems that appear while practising the theory of continuous revolution in China are not few if only we take the admissions of the Chinese communists themselves into account. The inner-party struggle, the mass campaigns, and the mass line work-style which form the core of the theory of continuous revolution rely heavily on 'correct leadership'. Whether the absence of Mao will create a void and make this whole perspective only an idealised faith only future will show. But interestingly enough this whole theory and the Basic Line along with its policies were primarily developed to prepare China to carry on the business without Mao. If ideological commitment to the Basic Line becomes pervasive then Mao's fears of regression would be allayed. If the quality of socialist construction envisaged in the class struggle perspective is guaranteed Mao's dream would have been fulfilled. The operational principles of struggles and campaigns would keep various sections within the party and outside always in guard against degeneration. All this involves costs, but the cost-benefit analysis of all kinds depends on what value one puts on what. Mao clearly thought that no cost was great enough for building the socialist society of his dream. Thus the most important problem facing the CPC is how to accomplish three things simultaneously. One is to maintain the revolutionary character of polices with the initiative in the hands of the party. The perspective of total transformation at a faster speed while not allowing capitalist trends to appear sustains the revolutionary character of Chinese politics. The second is to steer the development process in the communist direction. This requires progressively quantitative as well as qualitative changes in the forces and relations of production. The third is an organisational problem. The party must continue to steadily develop its commitment and work-style in course of mass upheavals and internal struggles to perform the leadership role.

Slackening of the first task would make China a routinised bureaucratic society, much against Mao's wishes to prevent revisionism. Lin Biao thought Mao did not seriously believe in the second task. So he thought that Mao's continuous revolution was not different from Trotsky's 'theory of incessant revolution'.[86] Interestingly enough, at the Tenth Congress the Maoists criticised Chen Boda who is supposed to have criticised Mao's theory of continuous revolution among other things, as 'Trotskyite'. If the task of developing production is not fulfilled in a major way Mao would be open to the Soviet charge that his theory is likely to keep Chinese economy backward. Mao's successors have already shown determination to develop China into the front ranks of the world. The third task is an arduous task riddled with many uncertainties. How to effectively counter forces like P'eng Teh-huai, Liu Shaoqi's, and Lin Biao? Here the Maoists rely on their optimism and on faith in masses and history while at the same time taking elaborate steps to continue their progress on the socialist path.

NOTES

1. Joint editorial celebrating the 50th anniversary of Boslhevik Revolution *Peking Review* (hereafter *PR*), No. 46, 10 November 1967. For earlier discussions of this theory see Stuart Schram, 'Mao Tse-tung and the Theory of permanent revolution'. *China Quarterly*, No. 46. 1971; John B. Starr, 'Conceptional Foundations of Mao Tse-tung's Theory of Continuous Revolution', *Asian Survey*, Vol. 11, No. 6, June 1971; and Manoranjan Mohanty. 'Theory of Continued Revolution and the CPC's Line', *The Institute for Defence studies and Analyses Journal,* Vol, VI, No.2, October 1973. (this article was an earlier version of the present chapter).
2. For example, the Constitution of the CPC describes the 'basic programme' as 'The complete overthrow of the bourgeoisie and all other exploiting class, the establishment of the dictatorship of the proletariat in place of dictatorship of the bourgeoisie and the triumph of socialism over capitalism'.
3. A study of stratification of these concepts can be found in Manoranjan Mohanty 'Maoist Revolutionary Strategy—A Reinterpretation', *Institute for Defence Studies and Analyses Journal*, Vol. 2, No. 3, January 1970.
4. However, after the death of Mao it is now possible that enthusiastic Maoists might use the term *Mao Zhu-yi*, because, Mao's theories have the potentiality for further universalisation.
5. See Chapter 4 for a discussion on this.
6. Not all mistakes are attributed to incorrect line. Some might take place while *applying* a correct line because of unfavourable natural conditions and other adverse factors. The line of the Great Leap Forward was correct, but, nevertheless mistakes were committed in its application.

7. See an important article that discusses this question, 'Persist in Education in Party's Correct Line', *Hong Qi* No. 7 in *Xin Hua selected News Items*, No. 29, 17 July 1972.
8. 'Constitution of the PRC' in Theodore Chen (ed.), *Chinese Communist Regime: Documents and Commentary*, New York: Praeger, 1967, p. 75. Also Constitution of the CPC adopted on 26 September 1956 in *Documents of Chinese Communist Party Central Committee* September 1956-April 1969 (Hereafter *Document* 1956-1969), Hongkong: Union Research Institute, 1971, p. 2.
9. 'Liu Shao-ch'i's Political Report to the Eighth Congress' in R.R. Bowie and J.K. Fairbank (eds.), *Communist China* 1955-1959, Cambridge, Mass: Harvard University Press, 1962, p. 165.
10. Ibid., p. 186.
11. Ibid., p. 197.
12. Some Soviet scholars at the Institute of Far East informed me in Moscow in 1973 that the practice of paying the five per cent compensatory interest on the capital to the erstwhile capitalists which was to be abolished in 1965 had still not been discontinued.
13. Bowie and Fairbank, op. cit., p. 177.
14. Zhou prefaces his proposals with the same list of fundamental tasks.
15. See G. Dmitriev, 'Lenin on Socialist Economic Development: The Practice of Socialist Construction in China' in M. I. Sladkovsky (ed.), *Leninism and Modern China's Problems,* Moscow: Progress Publishers, 1972, p. 127. He describes how the Central Committee criticised Mao's 'Leftist' line in 1956. He also refers to the 'extremely important task set by the 8th Congress'.
16. 'Talk at the Third Plenum of the 8th Central Committee' (7 October 1957), *Miscellany of Mao Tse-tung Thought* (translations of Mao Tse-tung Ssuhsiang Wan-sui), *JPRS,* No. 61269-1, February 1974, p. 72.
17. Bowie and Fairbank, op. cit., p. 118.
18. G. Dmitriev, op. cit., p. 126.
19. Bowie and Fairbank, op. cit., p. 148.
20. Ibid., p. 258.
21. Ibid., p. 267.
22. Ibid., p. 267.
23. Chao Yang, 'Conscientiously Study Chairman Mao's theory of Continuing the Revolution under the Dictatorship of the proletariat', *PR,* No. 5, 30 January 1970.
24. 'On the Correct Handling of Contradictions Among People' reprinted in *PR,* No. 26, 23 June 1967, p. 21.

25. Ibid., p. 13, emphasis mine.
26. Ibid., p. 21.
27. 'Summary of Conference of Provincial and Municipal Committee Secretaries' (January 1957), *Miscellany of Mao Tse-tung Thought*, op. cit., p. 61.
28. 'Speech at the Hankow Conference' (6 April 1958), *Miscellany of Mao Tse-tung Thought*, op. cit., pp. 85-8.
29. *Documents* 1956-1959, p. 77.
30. Ibid., p. 87.
31. Bowie and Fairbank, op. cit., p. 426. In December 1976 the full text of Mao's 'On the Ten Great Relationships' was officially published in China. The fact that Mao delivered the speech to sum up the experiences of the Soviet Union and draw lessons for China confirms its anti-revisionist orientation. The class struggle perspective is implicit in the document.
32. Ibid., p. 427. Later English translations of this passage in Chinese communist writings use the terms *continuous* for *uninterrupted* to make it distinct from Trotsky's *permanent revolution.*
33. *Document* 1956-1969, p. 87.
34. Ibid., p. 32.
35. Ibid., p. 132.
36. Ibid., p. 131.
37. Ibid., p. 154.
38. Ibid., p. 164.
39. Ibid., p. 96.
40. Ibid., p. 187.
41. Ibid., p. 190.
42. It is interesting to note that the Maoist writings on this subject quote Mao's unpublished speech and not the Communique of the Tenth Plenum. This is, perhaps, because of the fact that the Communique also praise the implementation of the economic policy of adjustment carried out under Liu's direction.
43. *More on the Great Debate,* Bombay: People's Publishing House, 1964, pp. 1-50.
44. Ibid., p. 30.
45. *Documents* 1956-1969, pp. 754-5.
46. 'Cicular of the Central Committee of the Chinese Communist Party,' *CCP Documents of the Great Proletarian Cultural Revolution 1966-1967*, Hongkong: Union Research Institute, 1968, p. 20.
47. Ibid.

48. The first point ends with this statement of purpose, *Documents* 1956-1969, p. 208.
49. Ibid., p. 207.
50. *PR,* No. 18, 30 April 1969, p. 21.
51. How important was the power struggle dimension of the GPCR can be seen from Mao's 'Conversation with Premier Chou on Power Struggle' in Jerome Ch'en (ed.), Mao Papers, Bombay: Oxford University Press, 1971, pp. 48-50.
52. *PR,* No. 18, 30 April 1969, p. 21.
53. Ibid.
54. Jerome Ch'en, op. cit., p. 34.
55. *PR,* No. 26, 23 June 1967, p. 28.
56. *PR,* No. 46, 10 November 1967.
57. Interestingly enough, after stating the Basic Line the 1969 constitution said: 'These contradiction can be resolved only by depending on the Marxis theory of continued revolution and on practice under its guidance.' The Tenth Congress Constitution omitted the word 'Marxist' from this sentence and retained the rest.
58. 'Informal Address at Politbureau Meeting' 18 May 1966 included in Martin Ebon, *Lin Piao,* New York: Stein and Day, 1970, p. 253.
59. Mao wrote in his letter to Chiang Ch'ing on 8 July 1966 as follows: 'His address was devoted entirely to a political coup—There has never been any address like this before. I was quite uneasy at some of his thinking.' *Issues and Studies,* Vol. IX, No. 4, January 1973, p. 95.
60. The Second Plenum Communique had called upon the party to 'oppose idealism and metaphysics', *Ta Kung Pao,* No. 228, 10-16 September 1970, p. 1.
61. See for example an article by Wang Che, 'How Engels criticised Duehring's Theory of Apriorism', *Summary of World Broadcasts,* 2 February 1972, p. 1.
62. *Ta Kung Pao,* No. 291, 2-8 December 1971.
63. For a discussion of the campaign against Lin Piao from the perspective of political consolidation see Manoranjan Mohanty 'Problems of Political Consolidation on China', *China Report,* Vol. IX, No. 5, September-October 1973.
64. See 'Speech on the book *Economic Problems of Socialism*', November 1958. Also 'Reading Notes on the Soviet Union's Political Economics' (1961-1962) in *Miscellany of Mao Tse-tung's Thought,* op. cit.
65. Chao Yang, op. cit. 'The Theory of continued revolution was first advanced by Marx and Engels...Using this brilliant concept of continued

revolution, the Bolsheviks led by Lenin developed the Russian bourgeois democratic revolution into the October Socialist Revolution.'

66. Ch'i Yung-hung, 'It is Necessary to Attach Importance to the Party's Basic Line', *Hong Qi,* No. 10, 1 October 1973, *SCMM,* No. 761, 29 October 1973.
67. 'They are bound to use the exploiting classes' old ideology, old culture, and old customs and habits—the remains of thousands of years in society and in men's minds—as their spiritual "capital" to corrupt the masses and win the people's hearts, thereby paving the way for the restoration of capitalism. This being the case, it is therefore insufficient to carry out socialist revolution on the economic front alone, and such revolution cannot be secured by itself', (Chao Yang, op. cit.).
68. Li Chen, 'Attach Importance to the Revolution in Superstructure', *Hong Qi,* No. 8, 1973, *SCMM,* No. 758, 20 August 1973.
69. Yi Piao, 'Two-Line Struggles in the Party will Exist for a Long Time to Come', *PR,* No. 46, 16 November 1973.
70. Two important documents of the *Zheng Feng* are the Central Committee Resolution on the Methods of Leadership drawn on Mao's *initiative* and adopted on 1 June 1943 and Liu Shao-ch'i's 'On the Intra-Party Struggle'. See Boyd Comptom (ed.), *Mao's China: Party Reform Documents,* 1942-44, Seattle: University of Washington Press, 1952. Also the 'Resolution on Some Questions Concerning the History of our Party' of April 1945 critically discusses deviations.
71. In retrospect, however, all inner-party struggles have been redefined as class struggle. A recent article in Chinese press quotes Mao from his unpublished speech at Lushan. 'The struggle at Lushan was a class struggle and a continuation of the life-and-death struggle between the two major hostile classes—the bourgeoisie and the proletariat...', Ch'i Yung-hung, op. cit.
72. Letter to Chiang Ch'ing, in *Issues and Studies,* Vol. IX, No. 4, January 1973.
73. Writing Group of the State Planning Commission, 'Continuing the Revolution or Restoring Capitalism'? Criticising the 'Theory of Productive Forces of Liu Shao-ch'i and other Political Swindlers', *PR,* No. 37, 10 September 1971. This was clearly hurled against Ch'en, because, Lin Piao is quoted here in support of the Maoist position.
74. *Documents* 1956-1969, p. 32.
75. *PR,* No. 26, p. 13. Restated in 'Continuing the Revolution or Restoring Capitalism?', op. cit., p. 7 and the *People's Daily* article 'Lin Piao's Theory of Productive Force Refuted', *Ta Kung Pao,* No. 392, 22-28 November 1973.

76. 'Continuing the Revolution or Restoring Capitalism?', op. cit., p. 7.
77. 'Man, they say, is society's chief productive force, and without him the implements of labour are dead. Therefore, if man is armed with revolutionary ideas he can, regardless of the level reached by material production, achieve anything he wishes... Any attempt to counterpose man to material production, to accentuate attention on man generally and ignore the role played by implements of labour in social development is a departure from Marxism-Leninism and leads directly to subjectivism and idealism.' See F.Y. Sidikhmenov, 'Against Distortions of the Leninist Philosophical Heritage' in M.I. Sladkovsky, op. cit., p. 49.
78. 'Continuing the Revolution or Restoring Capitalism?', op. cit., pp. 10-11.
79. A critical discussion on Yang's views is in 'Momentous Struggle on the Question of Indentity of Thinking and Being', *PR*, No. 15, 19 April 1971. For a detailed discussion see Chapter 4.
80. 'Guiding Principle for Knowing and Changing the World', *PR* No. 25, 18 June 1971, p. 9.
81. See Sidikhmenov in M.I. Sladkovsky, op. cit., p.56.
82. Ibid., p. 56.
83. 'Theory of "Combining Two Into One" is a Reactionary Philosophy for Restoring Capitalism', *PR*, No. 17, 23 April 1971.
84. Reprinted in *PR*, No. 26, 1967, p. 13.
85. Stuart Schram, *Mao Tse-tung Unrehearsed*, Penguin Books, 1974, p. 94.
86. The allegedly Lin Piao coup document also compares Mao's theory with Trotsky's theory. 'The 517 Engineering Outline', *Issues and Studies*, Vol. VIII, No. 8, May 1972.

3

Contradictions in the Modern World

The Maoist World-View

1. WORLD-VIEW

It is argued in the following that the contemporary world-view of the CPC represents an essential continuity from the time of its Seventh Congress in 1945. World-view does not mean the periodic strategic assessment in the course of a movement. World-view is a much wider concept that tries to grasp the essential aspects of a historical epoch. It involves identification of the main historical current and acknowledgement of the considerations governing the period. Strategy of international politics, on the other hand, is tied to specific periods of a process and one strategy can be replaced by another when significant changes take place in the international environment. However, the statement of the world-view is like the statement of the other theories. In fact, as we will see in this chapter, this is a theory of anti-imperialist struggle in the present historical epoch.

The CPC has formulated its world-view using the dialectical materialist method. This method, as we will see in detail in Chapter 4, identifies the fundamental contradictions of the epoch and then for strategic purposes finds out which is the 'principal contradiction' during a particular stage of the epoch. Grasping the principal contradiction is important because its 'existence and development determine or influence the existence and development of the other contradictions.'[1] According to this viewpoint when there is a qualitative change in the situation and a new stage of development emerges, a new principal contradiction will come to the fore. In addition to this, the Maoist explication of this method puts forth the notion of the 'principal aspect' of the contradiction which plays the leading role in the contradictory relationship. It is the principal aspect which determines the nature of a thing at a particular point of time. In the process of movement of the forces a formerly non-principal aspect becomes principal. Another relevant dimension of this method is the notion of antagonistic relationship. This refers to the relationship between the exploiting forces and the exploited forces. The principal contradiction is necessarily an antagonistic contradiction and can only be resolved by resort to force. Non-antagonistic contradictions can be resolved by non-coercive means.

Applying this method to the understanding of the present epoch the CPC has gradually formulated its ideas on the contradictions in the modern world. It continues to regard the present epoch as Lenin viewed it, namely, that of 'imperialism and proletarian revolution.' The CPC's articulation of fundamental contradictions is derived from this starting point. Based on its experiences in course of the people's democratic revolution in China, the CPC has formulated its world-view that sees the world situation in terms of (1) increasing *struggle against imperialism* (2) conducted through the strategies and tactics of an *international united front* (3) with reliance on *armed struggled* as the main form of struggle. Each one of these aspects was an essential element of the theory of new-democratic revolution. They have continued to be the guiding ideological considerations for the Chinese international behaviour. Even though the principles of new democracy have been superseded by the principles of socialist revolution within China, in the international arena, however, anti-imperialist revolution is yet to be completed.

Anti-Imperialist Revolution

If we piece together the foreign policy pronouncements of the CPC since its Seventh Congress in April 1945, it is possible to see the most important component of its world-view. This component was the assertion that China's people's democratic revolution was a part of the world revolutionary process. As Mao stated in his 1940 essay 'On New Democracy', since the revolution in China was meant to overthrow imperialism, feudalism and comprador bourgeoisie, internationally it was a part of the revolutionary struggle against imperialism. When the Second World War was drawing to a close, Mao told the Seventh Party Congress that

> ... the remnant forces of fascism which are still widespread will certainly continue to make trouble; while within the camp now fighting fascist aggression there are forces which oppose democracy and oppress other nations, and they will continue to oppress the people in various countries and in the colonies and semi-colonies. Therefore, after international peace is established, there will still be numerous struggles over the greater part of the world—between the anti-fascist masses and the remnants of fascism, between democracy and anti-democracy, between national liberation and national oppression.

International United Front

Not only the Chinese revolution was regarded as part of the world-wide anti-imperialist revolution and a continuation of the process initiated by the Bolshevik revolution of 1917, the CPC also stressed the importance of Lenin's concept of united front which equally applied to national as well as international struggles. As discussed in an earlier chapter, for the CPC the united front was one of the main strategic principles of the Chinese revolution. All classes opposed to the enemy were to be united both from above and from below. This concept of united front, according to the CPC viewpoint, applied to the international sphere as well. In November 1948 Mao said that

> since the victory of World War II, U.S. imperialism and its running dogs in various countries have taken the place of fascist Germany, Italy and Japan and are frantically preparing (for) a new world war and menacing the whole world; this reflects the utter decay of the capitalist world and its fear of imminent doom. This enemy still has strength; therefore, all the revolutionary forces of each country must unite, and the revolutionary forces of all countries must like-wise unite, must form *an anti-imperialist united front headed by the Soviet Union* and follow correct policies; otherwise, victory will be impossible.[2]

This idea was reaffirmed in Mao's article 'On the People's Democratic Dictatorship' wherein he emphasised the need to lean to the side of socialism and ally with the 'Soviet Union, with the People's

Democracies and with the proletariat and the broad masses of the people in all other countries and form and international united front.'[3]

Subsequently, the unity of Asian and African nations in their common struggle against colonialism and imperialism prominently figured in Zhou Enlai's speeches in Bandung in April 1955. China's foreign policy actions around this time, which advocated the principle of peaceful coexistence in the relations of countries having different social systems were conscious measures to strengthen the anti-imperialist forces in the Afro-Asian world. Thereafter, in the course of the Sino-Soviet ideological debates the concept of anti-imperialist united front was defended frequently by the CPC. Later still the most emphatic statement of this aspect of China's world-view came in Lin Piao's essay 'Long Live the Victory of the People's War' in September 1965. Another high point of Chinese thinking at this time was Mao's statement of 20 May 1970 entitled 'People of the World, Unite and Defeat the US Aggressors and All their Running Dogs'. This aspect also prominently figured in Hua Guofeng's memorial speech of 18 September 1976 on Mao's death when he stressed the need 'to form the broadest possible united front against imperialism, in particular against the hegemonism of the two superpowers...' Who belonged to the united front and who did not is a question we shall return to later. That at any given point of time there exists a united front against imperialism and colonialism, has always been an essential aspect of the world-view of the CPC.

Revolutionary Armed Struggle

Besides taking the current period of world history as an era of anti-imperialism and dividing the world in terms of a united front against a principal enemy, the CPC has also conceived the main form of this anti-imperialist struggle as a revolutionary war against counter-revolutionary war. This was based not only on their own experience in China against the Japanese and then the Kuomintang, but also on their analysis of the developments in the world situation which they witnessed. In his 1948 speech cited earlier Mao spoke of 'US imperialism...preparing (for) a new world war'. The Korean war and the subsequent military developments reinforced this idea in the mind of the Chinese leaders. Besides, the Chinese have always regarded armed struggle as one of the 'three magic weapons' (united front and party-building being the other two) of their people's democratic revolution. Hence, in their view, armed struggle against imperialism and colonialism is inevitable. They explain it further on the basis of Lenin's thesis that imperialism always resorts to war to defend its interests and, therefore, the revolutionaries are left with no alternative but to defend themselves through revolutionary war. According to the CPC, armed struggle is the main form of struggle against imperialism, though not the only form of struggle. This is true of internal as well as international revolutionary movements. This viewpoint has continued to mould China's outlook right up to the present time. The Sino-Soviet debate on the question of war and peace in the early 1960s further clarified the Chinese position. Ever since the Tenth Congress of the CPC in 1973, the Chinese have talked loudly about the threat of a new world war arising from the contention between the two superpowers.

These are the main aspects of the CPC's world-view determined primarily by the Chinese communists' own revolutionary experience. It was consistent with the nationalist goals of all Chinese revolutionaries from the time of Sun Yat-sen, insofar as it was a concrete response to China's humiliating experiences of the past century at the hands of imperialist powers. At the same time, the CPC maintained the principle of international solidarity with CPSU for a long time and with revolutionary forces elsewhere in order to participate in the international anti-imperialist movement.

This world-view was implicit in the CPC's international policies and actions until the late 1950s. The CPC had not spelt out the ideological view for all these years mainly because it largely coincided with the world-view of the CPSU at least until the Korean war. The Seventh Congress of the Comintern in 1935 had charted out the united front line for the international communist movement which suited the Chinese eminently. The Soviet recommendation of the 'China path' for revolution in the colonial societies for the brief period of 1949-50 confirmed the viability of the world-view of the CPC. But after the Korean war the Soviet leaders took a new initiative to win friends amongst the Afro-Asian nations. The Chinese seemed to pursue the same line as was evident in Bandung. But while bandung convinced the Chinese about the need to continue their quest for an anti-imperialist united front as implied in their world-view, the Soviets decided to inaugurate a new approach to imperialism, the line of peaceful competition and peaceful coexistence with it. The new ideological formulations at the Twentieth Congress of the CPSU in 1956 and the subsequent ideological exchanges between the CPC and the CPSU called for an explicit statement of the world-view of the CPC. In these circumstances the CPC Central Committee sent a letter to the CPSU on 14 June 1963 entitled, 'Proposal Concerning a General Line for the International Communist Movement' (1963 Proposal, for short) in which it stated its understanding of the modern world situation.

II. THEORETICAL STATEMENTS OF THE WORLD-VIEW

Fundamental Contradictions

The 1963 Proposal of the CPC said that the following were the 'fundamental contradictions in the contemporary world':

> the contradiction between the socialist camp and the imperialist camp;
>
> the contradiction between the proletariat and the bourgeoisie in the capitalist countries;
>
> the contradiction between the oppressed nations and imperialism;
>
> the contradiction among imperialist countries and among monopoly capitalist groups.

These were the fundamental contradictions of the 'epoch of imperialism and proletarian revolution' according to Lenin, and the CPC thought that they still held good for the contemporary world.

The CPSU, on the other hand, gave a new definition of the epoch in 1956 which was reiterated by the Moscow meetings of communist parties in 1957 and 1960. In the words of the Statement of the 81 parties in 1960:

> Our time, whose content is the transition from capitalism to socialism initiated by the Great Socialist Revolution, is a time of struggle between the two opposite social systems... *It is the principal characteristic of our*

> *time that the world socialist system is becoming the decisive factor* in the development of society ... (emphasis added).

The recognition of the principal characteristic of the epoch was the issue which sharply divided the CPSU and the CPC. In the view of the CPSU, because the world socialist system had become powerful and indestructible it did not need to risk a destructive nuclear war. It should engage in peaceful competition with imperialism and demonstrate the superiority of the socialist system in rest of the world. According to them, national liberation movements in Asia, Africa and Latin America (ASAFLA) could derive strength from this principal force and contribute to the advancement of mankind towards socialism.

The CPC viewed the situation differently. It recognised the fact that imperialism was on the decline. As the 1963 Proposal put it, 'The international balance of forces has changed and has become increasingly favourable to socialism and to all the oppressed peoples and nations of the world, and most unfavourable to imperialism and reactionaries of all countries.' Actually, even earlier Mao had declared in Moscow in 1957 that 'a new turning point' had been reached in the international situation and that 'the characteristic of the situation today is the East wind prevailing over the West wind, that is to say, the socialist forces are overwhelmingly superior to the imperialist forces'.[4] This implied that imperialism had creased to be the principal aspect of the contradiction between it and the oppressed nation.

While the CPC acknowledged the new balance of forces, it did not accept the formulation that the world socialist system had become the decisive force in the sense in which the CPSU meant it. The 1963 Proposal insisted that all the four fundamental contradictions existed; they were interrelated and influenced one another. It said that the 'Marxist-Leninists must not regard the contradictions in the world as consisting solely and simply of the contradiction between the socialist camp and the imperialist camp.'

Focus of Contradictions

The CPC declared that the movement in the colonial areas was the main arena of the international struggle imperialism. The 1963 Proposal said:

> The various types of contradictions in the contemporary world are *concentrated* in the vast areas of Asia, Africa and Latin America, these are the most vulnerable areas under imperialist rule and the storm-centres of world revolution. The national democratic revolutionary movements in these areas and the international socialist revolutionary movement are the two great historical currents of our time... The anti-imperialist revolutionary struggles of the people in Asia, Africa and Latin America are pounding and undermining the foundations of the rule of imperialism and colonialism, old and new, and are now a mighty force in defence of world peace.

In an earlier document entitled 'More on the Differences between Comrade Togliatti and Us', the CPC described these areas as an 'intermediate zone between the United States and Socialist countries' which had become 'the focus of all the contradictions of the capitalist world'. It described them as 'the weakest link in the imperialist chain and the storm centre of world revolution.'

These statements about the 'focus of all contradictions' or about their being 'concentrated' in the vast areas of ASAFLA did not imply any ordering of the fundamental contradictions. In fact, inspite of a requirement of the Maoist method of dialectical materialist analysis, the 1963 proposal did not use the term 'principal contradiction' to describe the contradiction between the oppressed nations and imperialism, nor did it use the term 'secondary contradiction' to describe the rest. However, by implication the anti-imperialist contradiction assumed the principal character.

This exercise in defining ideologically the contradictions of this epoch essentially reaffirmed the world-view of the CPC implicitly held for nearly two decades. The world situation was seen in terms of imperialism as the principal enemy and the rest of the world including China forming a united front against imperialism. The unity of the socialist States with the oppressed nations is stressed in all the ideological documents of the CPC. There is also a link between the CPC's understanding of the main form of struggle in the people's democratic revolution and its differences with the CPSU on the question of war and peace. Since this is relevant to their present talk about a new world war, its implication needs to be underlined.

On War and Peaceful Coexistence

While formulating the line of peaceful coexistence and peaceful competition between socialism and imperialism at the Twentieth Congress, the CPSU leaders pointed out two qualitative developments since the time of Lenin. One was that the emergence of the world socialist system had launched a powerful movement for peace all over the world. Secondly, nuclear weapons had threatened the very existence of human civilisation. The CPSU declared in 1956 that 'In these circumstances, certainly the Leninist precept that as long as imperialism exists, the economic basis giving rise to wars will also be preserved. That is why we must display the greatest vigilance.... But war is not fatalistically inevitable.'

The CPC position is that until the imperialist system and the exploiting classes come to an end, wars of one kind and another will continue. As it pointed out in 'Long Live Leninism.'

> Imperialism always has two tactics: the tactics of war and the tactics of peace; therefore, the proletariat and the people must also use two tactics to deal with imperialism: the tactics of exposing imperialism's peace fraud and striving energetically for genuine world peace and the tactics of being prepared to use a just war to end the imperialist unjust war if and when imperialism should unleash it.

The coming of the nuclear weapons did not change this thesis. The 1963 Proposal stressed that 'the people are the makers of history' and that 'it was wrong to exaggerate the role of technology.' It held 'that the emergence of nuclear weapons does not and cannot resolve the fundamental contradictions in the contemporary world, does not and cannot alter the law of class struggle, and does not and cannot change the nature or imperialism and reaction.' Besides reaffirming that peace was possible only after the defeat of imperialism, the CPC restated Mao's 1946 view that the 'imperialism and all reactionaries are paper tigers.' One of the strategic principles of the Chinese revolutionary war was to 'strategically despise the enemy and tactically take full account of him.' This applied to nuclear-armed enemy as well, and in 1958 the CPC declared that the atom bomb was also a paper tiger. Therefore, the people of the world should not be bullied by the nuclear powers. In recent years Mao has given an additional argument for this line. He has said that the superpowers wanted to control different parts of the world and the use of nuclear weapons would not leave many men and much wealth to be controlled. Therefore, the superpowers were developing their conventional weapons as speedily as the others.

On the question of the relationship between war and revolution, the Chinese stated that while both the world wars had created conditions leading to the victory of socialism in some countries, as the 1963 Proposal put it, 'on Marxist-Leninist ever has held or ever will hold that revolution must be made through world war'. As the CPC has articulated this later, either 'war will give rise to revolutions or revolution will prevent war'. The CPC has frequently stated that imperialism is the source of war.

This attitude also determined the CPC's and the CPSU's divergent approaches to the concept of peaceful coexistence. The CPSU proclaimed that 'peaceful coexistence of the socialist and capitalist countries is an objective necessity for the development of human society.' On the contrary, the CPC has said that the contradictions in the world should be correctly handled and the principle of peaceful coexistence should apply to relations between countries with different social systems. The 1963 Proposal stated that this principle 'should never be extended to apply to relations between the oppressed and the oppressor nations, between the oppressed and the oppressor countries or between the oppressed and the oppressor classes, and never be described as the main content of the transition from capitalism to socialism'. The documents of the CPC clearly gave precedence to revolutionary struggle over peaceful coexistence in a situation of antagonistic contradiction between the oppressed and the oppressor. Thus, in the dialectical materialist formulation, the struggle of the opposites was more important than their unity; one dividing into two was more significant than two uniting into one. The CPSU, on the other hand, declared peaceful coexistence and peaceful competition as its general line of foreign policy.

The debate with CPSU helped the CPC to articulate theoretically and ideologically its world-view within the framework of Marxism-Leninism. But all these formulations regarding the focus of the contradictions, the united front, war, and peaceful coexistence only crystallised the various aspects of an already existing world-view which the CPC had gradually evolved during the anti-Japanese war. This world-view consisted of principles relating to both internal revolution and international movement which they believed were inseparable.

People's War Against US Imperialism

The link between these formulations and the earlier experiences of the CPC was sharply asserted in September 1965 by Lin Biao in his essay entitled 'Long Live the Victory of the People's War', which has not yet been criticised in China.[5] In this essay the orientation and strategy of China's people's democratic revolution were generalised for the world anti-imperialist revolution. Lin Biao stressed the importance of the theory of revolution by stages which Mao Zedong had applied to China. According to Lin Biao, 'the national-democratic revolution is the necessary preparation for the socialist revolution is the inevitable sequel to the national-democratic revolution.'[6] The completion of the first stage was necessary before launching the socialist revolution. This is how the Chinese reaffirmed that the struggle against imperialism was the most crucial element of the contemporary world revolution for overthrowing the capitalist system.

Lin Biao clearly stated that 'in this stage of revolution, imperialism and its lackeys are the principal enemy'. He also identified the principal contradiction. According to him, 'the contradiction between the revolutionary peoples of Asia, Africa and Latin America and the imperialists headed by the United States is the principal contradiction in the contemporary world.' This was always inherent in China's foreign policy statements since 1948. But Lin Biao explicitly identified the principal contradiction because this is basic to the application of the Maoist dialectical materialist method to revolutionary struggle. This isolates the principal enemy and unites the rest. Speaking of the united front against imperialism Lin Biao said that 'the struggles waged by the different peoples against US imperialism reinforce each other and merge into a torrential worldwide tide of opposition to US imperialism.'

Lin Biao also proclaimed that 'people's war', which was the main form of struggle of the victorious Chinese revolution was also bound to be the main form of struggle against imperialism. He said that 'the theory of people's war.... has the characteristics of our epoch.' He especially recommended a strategic principle:

> Comrade Mao Zedong's theory of the establishment of rural revolutionary base areas and the encirclement of the cities from the countryside is of outstanding and universal practical importance for the present revolutionary struggle of all the oppressed nations and peoples and particularly for the revolutionary struggles of the oppressed nations and peoples in Asia, Africa and Latin America against imperialism and its lackeys.

Just as peasants constitute the main force of the national democratic revolution, the main battle fields of the fierce struggle against imperialism were the vast areas of ASAFLA. These constituted 'the rural areas of the world' as against North America and Western Europe which were 'the cities of the world'. Their struggle, like that of China, should be essentially self-reliant which at the same time assumes 'mutual sympathy and support on the part of revolutionary peoples'. This is how Lin Biao generalised the experiences of China's people's democratic revolution (he, however, used the term national democratic revolution which in this context means the same) for the entire world situation.

This restatement of the world-view was not a departure from the 1963 Proposal in any significant way. However, whereas the 1963 Proposal was polemical and had responded to the issues of the ideological debate, this article sharply suggested a line of anti-imperialist struggle with clearer strategic implications. Whereas the former was modest about integrating the lessons of the Chinese revolution with the basic issues of the Marxist debate, Lin Biao's essay went ahead and assimilated them into the Marxist formulations on world anti-imperialist revolution.

However, its parallel with the Chinese revolution was not drawn mechanically. First of all, Lin Biao did not discuss if the working class leadership in the new-democratic revolution suggested the parallel that the socialist States should exercise leadership in this international anti-imperialist united front. (He did not make any reference to the 'socialist camp'.) The more plausible formulation would be that each nation is the basic unit of anti-imperialist struggle while at the same time being a member of the united front. Because of the nature of the anti-imperialist epoch, and since achievement and consolidation of national independence is one of the primary goals, mutual assistance among revolutionary people is limited by that principle. Therefore, the question of leadership of the international united front is subordinated to the concepts of equality and sovereignty of nations. This seems to be the guiding formulation even now.

III. REDEFINITION OF THE WORLD-VIEW

Towards the end of the 1960s the Chinese leadership intensified the struggle against revisionism. This added a new emphasis to their internal as well as external policies. This resulted in an emphasis on revolutionary class struggles in all spheres. The GPCR proclaimed this perspective as the Basic Line of the CPC evolved by Mao Zedong keeping on view the dangers of capitalist restoration in socialist society. The CPC declared in 1967 that a capitalist restoration had taken place in the USSR and that a similar experience must be avoided in China at any cost. China's international struggle against revisionism was no longer confined to ideological debates. Now it was taking note of the 'anti-socialist restoration process' in the USSR. The Soviet leaders, in turn, denounced the GPCR as a petty bourgeois idealist campaign, led by the army, which would lead to the abandonment of the fruits of revolution. This conflict took a new turn in August 1968 when the Soviet and some other Warsaw Treaty forces invaded Czechoslovakia. The Chinese denounced this as a violation of sovereignty and national independence of Czechoslovakia by the Soviet Union. In March 1969 when armed clashes flared up on the Sino-Soviet border on the Ussuri river their confrontation was complete. The Chinese revived two terms to describe the USSR since the Czechoslovakia event. One was 'social-imperialism' which Lenin had used to denounce the revisionists of the Second International; the other was 'the new Tsars' recalling the Tsarist expansionism of the pre-revolutionary years. By 'social-imperialism' they meant, quoting Lenin, 'socialism in words, imperialism in deeds, the growth of opportunism into imperialism'. They argued that since capitalism was being increasingly restored in the Soviet Union, its international expression was imperialism. Soviet leaders, of course, returned these compliments with matching rancour and accused the Chinese of 'great nation chauvinism.'

Ninth Congress Formulation

Thus the class-struggle perspective in domestics politics manifested itself in the international campaign against revisionism and social-imperialism. This necessitated a redefinition of the Chinese world-view. The Political Report which Lin Biao presented to the Ninth Congress of the CPC in April 1969 stated the 'four major contradictions in the world today' (*Si da mao-dun* literally means four great contradictions), as follows:

> the contradiction between the oppressed nations on the one hand and imperialism and social-imperialism on the other;
> the contradiction between the proletariat and the bourgeoisie in the capitalist and revisionist countries;
> the contradiction between imperialist and social-imperialist countries;
> the contradiction between socialist countries on the one hand and imperialism and social-imperialism on the other.

These contradictions were of the same order as the 1963 statement of 'fundamental contradictions in the contemporary world' and not different from what have been often described as basic contradictions of this epoch. When this statement is compared with that of 1963 one notices first the change in the ordering. But as suggested earlier this ordering was not significant even in 1963. The contradiction between the oppressed nations and imperialism which was then listed third was virtually taken to be the principal contradiction. In 1969 this was at the top of the list. This time there was no reference to the 'socialist camp' and the contradiction between 'the socialist countries on the one hand and the imperialist and social-imperialist countries on the other' was listed last. The most important change, however, was the reference to 'social-imperialism'. The Soviet Union was pushed into the company of United States in all the four contradictions, whereas even in 1963 it was assumed to be in the 'socialist camp.'

This redefinition of the world-view, however, was not a departure from the basic characterisation of the epoch. The CPC still believed in an international united front to fight against imperialism with armed struggle as the main form of struggle. But it was a redefinition nevertheless, insofar as the understanding of the socialist camp was concerned. The legacy of the October Revolution and the belief in proletarian unity had brought into being a 'socialist camp'. Now, not only the camp was destroyed, its leader had also defected to the imperialist camp. The Chinese explained the social basis of social-imperialism in terms of capitalist restoration. Thus, this amounted to a redefinition of their world-view.

Contention between Superpower

The new formulation of the Ninth Congress referred to the 'collusion and contention by the US imperialism and Soviet revisionist social imperialism' without saying which was the more prominent aspect of their relationship. Lin Biao's Report (which, as was disclosed later, was drastically revised by Mao before being presented) said that,

> they (the USA and the USSR) collude and at the same time contend with each other in a vain attempt to redivide the world. *They act in coordination* and work hand in glove in opposing China, opposing communism and opposing the people, in suppressing the national liberation movement, and in launching wars of aggression. They scheme against each other and get locked in strife for raw materials, markets, dependencies, important strategic points and spheres of influence.[7]

This formulation was expressed also by describing the US and the USSR as the two superpowers constantly colluding and contending with each other. This view was put forth by China's representatives in international forums in which China was beginning to participate.

In 1971 with the announcement of the visit of Nixon to China and the restoration of the PRC's seat in the United Nations there began a new strategic phase in China's foreign policy. The efforts towards detente between the US and the USSR, and the latter's attempts to organise an all-European security network, introduced new elements in the world situation. The imminent defeat of the US forces in Vietnam was another significant factor. In this context, starting from late 1971 as shift of emphasis was noticed in China's description of the relationship between the superpowers. The Chinese now spoke more of their contention and less of collusion. Qiao Guanhua, the leader of the PRC delegation to the United Nations General Assembly, in November 1971 asserted that 'one or two superpowers are stepping up their arms expansion and war preparations and vigorously developing nuclear weapons, thus seriously threatening international peace.'[8]

This shift of emphasis became explicit at the time of the Tenth Congress of the CPC in August 1973. Chou En-lai in his Political Report said that the purpose of the USA and the USSR was to contend for world hegemony. According to him 'their collusion serves the purpose of more intensified contention. Contention is absolute and protracted, whereas collusion is relative is relative and temporary.'[9] Chou also declared that the 'key point' of their contention was Europe. According to him the Soviet revisionists were 'making a feint to the East while attacking in the West' and 'stepping up their contention in Europe, and their expansion in the Mediterranean, the Indian Ocean and every place their hands can reach'. This reference to Europe as the focus should not be interpreted as the 'focus of world contradictions'. Europe is the focus of superpower contention while ASAFLA continues to be the focus of the fundamental contradictions.

This contention thesis has been reiterated ever since on several occasions, Vice-Premier Deng Xiaoping addressing the Sixth Special Session of the United Nations General Assembly in April 1974 elaborated this further by saying that 'since the two superpowers are contending for World hegemony, the contradiction between them is irreconciliable.'[10] He said that the agreements reached between them were only 'a facade and a deception'. This was voiced further by Chou En-lai in his Report to the Fourth NPC in January 1975. He said that their fierce contention was bound to lead to world war some day. At present the Chinese vastly publicise this point about the superpowers' contention leading to a world war.

China's international campaign against the Soviet policies reached a new state in 1975 when the decline of US imperialism became even more visible with the victory of liberation forces in Vietnam. Now the Chinese leaders seem to point to the increasing Soviet activities around the globe. This is why Foreign Minister Qiao Guanhua announced in the United Nations General Assembly in September 1975 that 'the superpowers are the source of a new world war, and the danger of war comes mainly from the wildly ambitious social-imperialism.' He reiterated this in his speech at the United Nations on 5 October 1976. At one place Qiao described the two superpowers as 'the biggest international oppressors and exploiters of our time' and 'the sources of a new world war'. At another place he contended that the 'Soviet social-imperialism is the biggest peace swindler and the most dangerous source of war today.'

The contention thesis is not much of a new formulation. It is actually a manifestation of the basic contradiction 'between imperialist and social imperialist countries and among the imperialist countries' which the Ninth Congress had proclaimed, and the latter half of this formulation also figured in the 1963 Proposal. A question arises as to which is the *principal aspect* of this contradiction between the US and the USSR at present. Has the USSR become the principal aspect of the contradiction between the two superpowers? China's identification of the USSR as the main source of war seems to suggest that it was in the process of becoming the principal aspect. However, the Chinese have not yet clearly attributed the dominant position to the USSR. Of the superpowers they keep saying that 'one either overpowers the other, or is overpowered'. This implies that right now neither superpower is decisively stronger than the other. But according to the Chinese, if the present trends continue the USSR might well become the stronger power.

Principal Contradiction

The contradiction between the two superpowers, however, has not been specifically described as the principal contradiction. Leading Chinese spokesmen have spoken of this only next to the contradiction between the oppressed nations of the world on the one hand and imperialism and social-imperialism on the other. Even though the Chinese leaders lose no opportunity to stress the progressive intensification of the contention between the two superpowers, they give more prominence to the anti-imperialist struggle. Addressing the United Nations General Assembly in October 1974 Qiao Guanhua declared that 'all the basic contradictions in the world are further sharpening, particularly the contradiction between the two superpowers on the one hand and the people of all countries on the other and the contradiction between the two superpowers themselves.'[11]

By strictly applying the notion of principal contradiction we may say that within the Chinese world-view the anti-imperialist contradiction listed earlier continues to be the principal contradiction. But with changes in the objective environment, the principal and the secondary contradictions change places. It is possible that the trend of superpower contention may occupy the principal place in the not too distant future, indicating that the present situation is only a transitionary stage. If the contention between the superpowers became the principal contradiction, it would be like the situation during the Second World War which began essentially as a reflection of the contradiction among imperialists. The strategic implication of that situation will also be parallel. Since all other contradictions will be temporarily subordinated to the handling of the principal contradiction, there would be a programme of united front resistance against the principal enemy, that is, one of the superpowers. As during the Second World War, this resistance would be based on the principle of self-reliance, independence, and initiative which would be retained in the hands of the revolutionary people. This is how the Maoists believe, war would give rise to revolution.

The Maoists also believe that revolution can prevent war. Therefore, if the present united struggle against imperialism and social imperialism continues to make progress, and remains the principal contradiction, then imperialism will be steadily weakened. It is only with the elimination of imperialism that the main source of war will disappear.

IV. THREE WORLDS

With two features—people's struggle against the superpowers and their intensifying contention—in mind, Vice-Premier Deng Xiaoping explained China's view of the world in his address at the United Nations in April 1974. He defined a superpower as 'an imperialist country which everywhere subjects other countries to its aggression, interference, control, subversion or plunder and strives for world hegemony'. Thus, even though the term superpower was a new addition to the Marxist vocabulary, it was applicable only to an imperialist country. Teng designated the two superpowers, the USA and the USSR, as making up the first world. The developing countries in Asia, Africa, Latin America, and other regions make up the third world. The developed countries between the two make up the second world.[12]

The three-worlds analysis is clearly an innovation in the Marxist vocabulary. But it is not inconsistent with the world-view of the CPC. In fact, it has a parallel with the CPC's class analysis during the people's democratic revolution. After identifying the principal enemy on the one hand and the main revolutionary classes like the workers and peasants on the other, the CPC formulated a strategic line towards the intermediate classes like the patriotic landlords, rich peasants, and the national bourgeoisie. Without forgetting their reactionary class character the CPC persistently tried to win over these classes to join the united front. This is how the 'three-thirds system' of forming political councils was introduced in the early 1940s in the Border Region controlled by the CPC. The same approach applies now to the countries of the second world. Some countries of Europe like France who had demonstrated their independence of the big powers were considered to have belonged to the Second Intermediate Zone in the 1960s. But the concept of 'intermediate zone' was valid only insofar as there was a *socialist camp* and an *imperialist camp*. Teng said in his General Assembly speech that 'as a result of the emergence of social-imperialism, the socialist camp which existed for a time after World War II is no longer in existence.' He also said that the uneven development of capitalism had resulted in increasing disintegration of the Western imperialist bloc. Therefore, the old division of the world into an imperialist camp, a socialist camp, and an intermediate zone was no longer valid.

The new division of the world is based on the identification of the principal enemy in the world and the force struggling against that enemy. Among the struggling forces, Deng and Qiao Guanhua have described the third World as having become the 'main force'. (The Chinese spokesmen still do not speak of the leadership role in this struggle.) In between the superpowers and the developing countries are the countries of the second world. They are the developed countries and some of them still retain colonial relations with some countries of the third world. This refers to the remaining colonial possession of some of the West European nations and also their neo-colonial economic practices elsewhere. At the same time, members of the second world are in varying degrees controlled, threatened, or bullied by one superpower or the other and are trying to shake off these pressures and safeguard their national independence. This is why they are potential members of the united front against the two superpowers. It is this consideration which explains China's support to West European unity through the European Economic Community, so that the countries of Western Europe can face the challenge of the USA and the USSR collectively. This is why the Chinese are also trying hard to encourage the loosening of the Soviet grip over Eastern Europe.

The third world consists of the countries who still face the historic task of 'clearing out the remnant forces of colonialism, developing the national economy and consolidating national independence'. These countries are winning one victory after another against the superpowers. The liberation of Indo-China, the unity of these countries at the United Nations, their use of the oil weapon to fight against superpower politics, the winning of independence by the Portuguese colonies in Africa, the increasing coordination among the third world countries to achieve economic independence, and the progress of the non-aligned movement are some of the most glaring evidences of this trend. This is why Deng Xiaoping described them as 'a revolutionary motive force propelling the wheel of world history' and 'the main force combating colonialism, and particularly the superpowers'. The third world, therefore, plays the same role in the international anti-imperialist struggle which the peasants played in China's new democratic revolution.

These descriptions clearly convey the impression that the principal contradiction in today's world is still between imperialism and the oppressed nations, or between the superpowers on the one hand and the third and the second worlds on the other. As to the principal aspect of this contradiction, the Chinese statements are not very definitive. Mao's statement in Moscow in 1957 regarding 'the historic turning point in world situation' and 'East Wind prevailing over West Wind' had made the anti-imperialist front, including the socialist camp headed by the Soviet Union, the principal aspect of the principal contradiction. Lin Biao's 1965 essay gave a picture of the decaying

American imperialism and the rising wave of people's wars all over ASAFLA. According to the Chinese the emergence of social-imperialism inevitably arrested this trend. But people's struggles have continued to make progress. The lesson from Vietnam was that a small and militarily weak country can defeat a big and strong country by people's war. All this presents an optimistic picture. But whether at present the balance is in favour of the anti-superpower forces, or whether the turning point in the revolutionary struggle is yet to be achieved, is not clear from the Chinese statements. This may, therefore, be a period of transition not only from one principal contradiction to another, but from one principal aspect to another. This is why nearly equal prominence is now given to both the anti-imperialist and the contention contradictions. This situation is expressed in the Chinese statement: 'Either they (the two superpowers) will fight each other, or the people will rise in revolution.'

Revolution is the Trend

The Chinese statements, however, clear about the overall trend. They very often quote Mao's statement of 20 May 1970 that 'the danger of a world war still exists, and the peoples of all countries must get prepared. But revolution is the main trend in the world today.' Year after year the CPC spokesmen identify the new successes achieved by the third world. Deng Xiaoping said in the United Nations in 1974 that the special session of the General Assembly itself marked the beginning of a new phase of struggle for economic independence which alone can consolidate political independence. The intensification of two trends—the struggle against imperialism and social-imperialism and their mutual contradictions—has created what the Chinese call the 'great disorder under heaven'. This, however, is a positive sign of progress. As Mao said in his letter to Jiang Qing in 1966 'Great disorder across the land leads to great order'. This perspective of continuing revolutionary class struggle applies both to socialist construction at home and anti-imperialist struggle in the world. The 'great disorder' notion has been thrown against the Soviet talk of 'detente', just as the stress on class struggle in domestic affairs was contraposed to the idea of class conciliation embodied in the Soviet concepts of 'State of all people' and 'Party of all people'.

This overall trend has been outlined in more specific terms by the Chinese formulation that 'countries want independence, nations want liberation and people want revolution: this is the irresistible trend in history.' This formulation, besides reaffirming the optimistic course of history, stresses two things. One is the idea of stages of development, and the other is the essential links between these stages. Movement for national independence is the primary task of a distinct stage in the capitalist epoch. Next comes consolidating that independence economically and culturally against all pressures of colonialism and non-colonialism. The next historical stage is social revolution by overthrowing the exploiting classes. Each stage has a distinct character that is reflected in a corresponding strategy. Each stage has its principal enemy and a united front to oppose it. At the same time the CPC theory suggests that these are interrelated. Independence and liberation can be made fruitful only as part of an overall process of revolution.

In this struggle for independence, liberation, and revolution. China considers herself as a member of the third world which is the 'main force' in this struggle. Chinese representatives repeatedly point out to China's economic and military backwardness which make her a developing country. Referring to their nuclear programme, they say that it is basically defensive programme and is primarily intended to break the nuclear monopoly of the superpowers. Moreover, they have announced in their Party Congresses and in the forums of the United Nations that they would never be the first to use nuclear weapons. They have also challenged other nuclear powers to declare so. Announcing that China would never be a superpower Deng Xiaoping said in 1974 that, 'if one day China should change her colour and turn into a superpower, if she too should play the tyrant in the world, and everywhere subject others to her bullying, aggression and exploitation, the people of the world should identify her as social-imperialist, expose it, oppose it and work together with the Chinese people to overthrow it.' Whether all this is meant to generate support among the third world people or not, this is a major shift from the 'socialist camp' thesis of the 1950s. At that time the socialist camp with the Soviet Union and China in it was an important component of the anti-imperialist united front. Now, with the disappearance of the socialist camp, the situation has changed in the Chinese view.

V. HANDLING CONTRADICTIONS CORRECTLY

The world-view of the CPC, perceived in terms of a series of contradictions, is translated into a general line for each sphere of society, and into policies and specific lines for particular aspects of each sphere. Formulating these lines and carrying them out belong to the realm of practice. The most important question that arises here is to what extent practice conforms to theory, or to what extent the contradictions have been handled correctly. Without going into an exhaustive analysis of China's foreign policy performance, we can only raise some analytical problems.

Foreign Policy Line

The main principles of the foreign policy of the PRC have been stated in many official documents. In 1949 the united front document, called the Common Programme of the CPPCC, declared in its Preamble that the PRC would unite with the USSR, the people's democracies, and all oppressed nations (Article II). Article 54 said: 'The Foreign Policy of the People's Republic of China is based on the principle of protection of the independence, freedom, integrity of territory, and sovereignty of the country, upholding lasting international peace and friendly cooperation between the people of all countries, and opposing the imperialist policy of aggression and war.' This orientation was maintained in the 1954 Constitution which spoke of the 'indestructible friendship' with the USSR. Its Preamble also envisaged the establishment of diplomatic relations with 'all countries on the principles of equality, mutual benefit, and mutual respect for each other's sovereignty and territorial integrity'. It contained the two essential points of the 'five principles of peaceful coexistence' announced five months before. The 1975 Constitution, however, went a step further. It seeks to apply the class-struggle approach of the CPC more explicitly to international affairs and announced that the PRC will 'uphold proletarian internationalism' and 'will never be a superpower.' It also said that the PRC should strengthen 'unity with the socialist countries and all oppressed people and oppressed nations with each supporting the other, and striving for peaceful coexistence with countries having different social systems on the basis of the 'five principles'. It would also 'oppose the imperialist and social-imperialist policies of aggression and war and oppose the hegemonism of the superpowers.' This formulation accompanies several other constitutional changes signifying China's transition from the stage of people's democratic revolution to that of socialist revolution. At the same time, it seems to be consistent with the CPC's original world-view that saw China as a member of the anti-imperialist united front. In addition, it takes into account what the CPC considers the changed character of the Soviet Union.

These general policy statements and China's external policies in specific situations acquire more meaning only if they are put in the context of the Chinese world-view. It is also clear that this world-view, put in the form of Chairman Mao's proletarian revolutionary line in foreign policy, has a long-term relevance and as in the case of many other Maoist theories, it is up to the political leadership to apply it to the concrete situation. An understanding of the approach of the CPC will, therefore, help us not only to explain the actions of the PRC but also to some extent predict the future course of action.

Yet human minds have to apply this theory to the concrete conditions developing from time to time. Whatever process of democratic centralism or mass line decision-making may have been evolved in China, practice can never be mechanically derived from theory. Therefore, there can be aberrations in every country's experience. But if these aberrations are frequent and they build up a deviant pattern of action, then either the concerned theory is incorrect or it is invalidated by practice and a divergent, perhaps deviationist, line is being pursued by the leaders even though lip service is paid to the basic line.

Problem of Dialectics of Stage

There are two areas where a great deal of discretion is available to the Chinese policy-makers. One is regarding the application of the principle of peaceful coexistence, and the other is about the superpowers. The 1963 Proposal mentioned three 'interrelated and indivisible' aspects of what it called the '*general line of the foreign policy of the socialist countries*': proletarian internationalism, peaceful coexistence, and support to 'revolutionary struggles of all the oppressed peoples and nations.' Presumably, this is valid even today. Equal importance to all the three aspects, when translated into practice, implies sometimes mutually exclusive alternatives. Winning the friendship of the Gulf states implied the stoppage of Chinese material assistance to the revolutionaries of the Gulf area. Of course, revolution is the business of the concerned people. Still the first and the third aspects of a socialist foreign policy mentioned above seem to be limited by the second. In terms of the theory of contradictions it is the principal contradiction which should determine the priority of alternative. But even then the alternatives sometimes look hazy: Whether the victory of the Thai revolutionary struggle or friendly relations with the Thai government would help fight superpower domination in South-East Asia? The same dilemma was visible in Chile, Bangladesh, Sri Lanka and many other places. China's policy-makers appear to have lately upgraded the principle of peaceful coexistence to fight Soviet influence. But whether this shift from commitment to the 'indivisibility of all three aspects of socialist foreign policy' while handling the anti-imperialist contradictions, amounts to an effective strategy for the current period is not certain.

The room for uncertainty is even greater in relation to the handling of the contradiction between the two superpowers. As mentioned earlier, in China's current world-view both the superpowers, not one, constituted the principal enemy of the third world or the oppressed nations. It was also observed that the USSR had not yet become the principal aspect of contradiction between the two superpowers, even though the trend was in that direction. If this is a correct reading of the Chinese world-view, then one notices an increasing gap between this and the Chinese foreign policy behaviour. Instead of fighting both imperialism and social-imperialism the Chinese seem to have slackened their efforts against the former and hardened their efforts against the latter. In Western Europe, for example, the Chinese have not only condoned socio-political status quo strengthening their support for the European Economic Community for the sake of countering superpower domination, but also encouraged continued American presence in Western Europe for the time being. Talking about China's policy towards France, Qiao Guanhua said in a speech in an inner-party meeting in Tientsin in May 1975: 'We made known to the Americans that they should leave when we tell them to go and should not move when we tell them not to go... It should be made clear that we support them (the French) only for their anti-Soviet and anti-American stand, but not for their current system. On the contrary, we will overthrow their system in the future.'[13] This speech does have the correct orientation, but in practice there is little evidence to show that China's policy in Western Europe is both anti-Soviet and anti-US and linked to the social revolution in Europe.

The same overemphasis on fighting Soviet influence is also noticeable in South-East Asia. After the victory of the liberation forces in Vietnam, China has been greatly alarmed by the prospect of Soviet influence further spreading into the vacuum created by the American withdrawal. The Chinese leaders are unhappy with both North Korea and Vietnam for their continuing neutrality in the Sino-Soviet dispute. There is an interesting remark by Mao which was quoted by Jiang Qing in her speech at a meeting of the Chinese diplomatic cadres in Peking in March 1975. Mao said: 'Vietnam is a temple occupied by four chief monks who become masters of anyone who gives them food and clothing. To oppose imperialism without opposing revisionism will eventually lead to a second revolution.'[14] Qiao Guanhua's inner-party speech made a similar comment on North Korea. The Chinese are right in expecting this of the South East Asian countries if both imperialism and social-imperialism have to be opposed. But at the same time, a Korean or a Vietnamese might retort, paraphrasing Mao, that 'opposing social-imperialism without opposing imperialism will equally lead to a second revolution.'

This is the most crucial problem of revolution which can be called the 'problem of dialectics of the stage'. Each stage of revolution has its principal contradictions and, therefore, its principal task. All other tasks ought to be subordinated to this. But the principal contradiction must never be divorced from the fundamental contradictions of the epoch. No stage should be so handled as to be an impediment to further progress to the next higher stage. Both the Bolshevik revolution and the Chinese revolution solved the problem of the dialectics of stage by a fairly smooth transition from the democratic to the socialist stages. On the international plane however, we see both the Soviet Union and China seized by the problem of dialectics of the stage.

Like the Soviet Union, the Chinese also have begun showing signs of being over-preoccupied by the pressures of the present stage. In the case of Chinese foreign policy, this is very pronounced in the application of the principle of peaceful coexistence and handling the contradiction between the two superpowers. These problems arise within the theoretical framework of the CPC itself. Outside the framework a plethora of questions may be raised as to whether the USSR is indeed social-imperialist, and if it is revisionist why the model of relations with Yugoslavia does not apply to it, and so on.

This is however, not to say that the overall performance of China's foreign policy has already demonstrated the abandonment of the world-view of the CPC. China's role in the liberation struggles of Vietnam and her policy towards West Asia still weigh heavily in favour of her revolutionary image. But if these aberrations become more frequent, then this may suggest not only a deliberate shift in China's strategic line but also its departure from the world-view— a departure which theoretically should be justified only when world anti-imperialist revolution would have been successfully completed. These aberrations took place even when Mao was alive. Mao himself initiated dramatic policy shifts like normalisation of China's relations with the USA. Therefore, Mao's death does not necessarily imply change of policy orientations. All evidences indicate that in the immediate post-Mao era China is not likely to abandon its world-view as redefined during the past ten years. But the question remains whether the aberrations mentioned earlier are going to increase or decrease. The Chinese leaders have perhaps opted for limited withdrawal from revolutionary activism in world politics to pay more attention to socialist construction at home. This was indicated by Jiang Qing in her March 1975 speech when she referred to how the revolutionary movements all over the world were reciprocating the Chinese assistance to them by keeping the superpowers on their toes. According to her, 'neither US imperialism nor the Russian revisionists can raise their hands to cope with us. This has provided us with a peaceful environment not only for accelerating the construction of our country's industry, agriculture... also for satisfactorily completing the socialist revolution on the political, ideological and cultural front lines.'[15] However, one foreign policy strategy valid for one specific period, can be replaced by another when the balance of world forces changes. There was such a change of strategy around 1969 without changing the world-view. Similar strategic shifts can also take place in future. But whether such strategic shifts amount to the abandonment of the world-view would depend on how far the Chinese practice has compromised the world-view.

NOTES

1. Mao Zedong, 'On Contradiction', *Selected Works* (hereafter *SW*), Peking: Foreign Language Press, 1965, Vol. I, p. 331.
2. 'Revolutionary Forces of the World Unite', *SW* IV, pp. 284-5 (emphasis added).
3. *SW* IV, p. 415.
4. *Imperialism and All Reactionaries Are Paper Tigers,* Peking: Foreign Language Press, 1958, p. 28.
5. There are certain ideas in this essay which can be picked up for adverse comments by Lin Piao's critics. But, on the whole, it is one of the best elaborations of the Maoist principles of new-democratic revolution.
6. Lin Piao, 'Long Live the Victory of People's War', reproduced in Martin Ebon, *Lin Piao: The Life and Writings of China's New Ruler,* New York: Stein and Day, 1970, p. 230.
7. 'Report to the Ninth National Congress', reproduced in Ibid., p. 347.
8. *Irresistable Historical Trend,* Peking: Foreign Language Press, 1971, p. 13.
9. 'Report to the Tenth Congress', reprinted in *China Report,* Vol. IX, No. 5, September-October 1973, p. 90.
10. *Peking Review* (Supplement), Vol. 17, No. 15, 12 April 1974, p. 11.
11. *Peking Review,* Vol. 17, No. 41, 11 October 1974, p. 9.
12. Qiao Guanhua in his speech at the United Nations General Assembly on 5 October 1976 said as follows: 'Making a penetrating analysis of all the basic contradictions of our time and the division and realignment of all the political forces in the world, *Chairman Mao Tse-tung advanced his great strategic concept of the three worlds.* He pointed out: The United States and the Soviet Union make up the first world; the developing countries in Asia, Africa and Latin America and elsewhere constitute the third world; and in between the two is the second composed of Europe, Japan, Canada and other countries' (emphasis added). Mao may have assimilated the three-worlds concept into his framework. But the concept itself is by no means a Chinese innovation. When the two military blocs were engaged in a cold war in the 1950s the concept of the third world emerged in the developing countries.

13. An English version in *Issues and Studies,* Vol. XI, No. 12, December 1975, p. 96.
14. An English version in *Issues and Studies,* Vol. XI, No. 7, July 1975, p. 94.
15. Ibid., p. 93.

4

Four Laws of Materialist Dialectics

A Reconstruction of Mao Zedong's Theory of Cognition and Practice

I. THE PRESENT STATE OF MATERIALIST DIALECTICS

The gulf between certain streams of interpretation of Marxism in Europe and Marxist theoretical activity in Asia has steadily widened in recent years. Their divergence is particularly pronounced in their respective approaches to materialist dialectics. Important Marxist commentators of Europe like Cornforth have either raised dialectics to a super-abstract level with little action-relevance or reduced it to a set of loosely formulated formal laws muddled with ambiguities. On the other hand, the Chinese communists constantly publicise their efforts to apply materialist dialectics in handling all kinds of concrete problems. Mao Zedong, for example, said in 1959: 'We have to popularise dialectics and dialectics has to be developed. In a word, I ask that dialectics be popularised step by step so that we will have 600 million dialecticians.'[1] During the past five years or so a series of publications have appeared in China with titles like *Philosophy is No Mystery* and *Serving the People with Dialectics* giving multifaceted examples of the practice of the dialectical method in day-to-day life.

This essay will attempt to explore to what extent the theoretical problems raised by the European Marxists have been tackled by the Chinese communists and in what areas problems continue to remain in the application of the dialectical materialist method in real life.

The present essay seeks to make two points of departure. Firstly, while earlier all the exponents of the dialectical method presented it as a theory of knowledge, Mao Zedong took it as a theory of practice as well. Mao too initially seemed to have understood dialectics mainly as a mode of cognition. But his post-Liberation writings, some of which are available to us now in various forms, and the actual political practice in China have demonstrated that to Mao materialist dialectics is both a theory of knowledge and a theory of practice. Lenin who was essentially a philosopher of practice began the enquiry in this direction in his *Philosophical Notebooks,* but did not have an opportunity to develop it. It was Mao who developed the notion further in terms of the inseparability of knowledge from practice, cognition from action, and knowing from doing.

Some years ago Holubnychy made a very lucid exposition of Mao's ideas on dialectics, but he confined himself to the older tradition of taking dialectics, only as a theory of knowledge.[2] His textual analysis of the essays, 'On Practice', 'On Contradiction,' 'On Dialectical Materialism' (this is still unpublished in China), and other relevant writings of Mao primarily aimed at juxtaposing these ideas with those of Engels, Lenin, and Stalin identified the areas of comparability and innovation. This seemed adequate then. But now the very same writings of Mao read with the later materials and understood within the total framework of the theory and practice of the Chinese communists seem to suggest a different point of emphasis. It is that Mao's ideas on dialectics have evolved in the process of applying the dialectical method to day-to-day practice from the highest level of national decision-making to the concrete problems faced by individual citizens. By practice Mao Zedong means social practice in the form of class struggle. As Mao said, 'it is only with class struggle that there is philosophy—it being useless to discuss the theory of knowledge apart from practice.'[3] In fact, according to him the two outstanding characteristics (*liang-ge zui-xian-zhu de te-dian*) of dialectical materialism are its 'class nature' (*jie ji xing*) and its 'practicality' (*shi jian xing*).[4]

Besides analysing Maoist dialectics as a theory of practice, this essay also tries to reconstruct the body of Marxist ideas on dialectics into a set of four laws based on an understanding of Mao Zedong's writings and the Chinese communist experiences. In one of its established meanings a law is a generalised statement of relationships derived from empirical observations and verified through practice. A law therefore is a tool for comprehending reality and confronting it. The laws stated here are both helpful in understanding problems and solving them. Risking possible charges of oversimplifications or of sacrifice of scholastic sophistication (so compellingly evident in the writings of European Marxists), a modest attempt has been made here to reformulate the Marxist thoughts on materialist dialectics in terms of usable laws which can be applied in concrete situations. The four laws, *Law of unity of Knowing and Doing, Law of Analysis, Law of Synthesis,* and *Law of Particularity,* can guide both our understanding of reality and the practice of handling a contradiction to achieve a desired end.

It should be stressed that the four laws are a set of four tools for grasping reality and changing it. According to the first law, the Law of Unity of Knowing and Doing, knowledge is the product of continuous practice through struggle and knowledge in turn, can be transformed into material force. In social practice in class society, struggle takes the forms of class struggle. Thus, understanding the interdependence of knowledge and practice is the starting point. Next, according to the Law of Analysis a thing is a contradiction which is in constant movement. In other words, every phenomenon is to be analysed and 'to analyse' means to divide one into two and understand the internal and external relationships of the aspects of a contradiction. The third law, the Law of Synthesis, says that development of a process takes place through continuous negations or confrontations which causes the change of the positions between the contending aspects of a contradiction. Fourthly, accordingly to the Law of Particularity a contradiction is defined in terms of (1) the particular essence of its two aspects, (2) its relative position vis-a-vis other contradictions to determine the principal contradiction at a particular stage of development, and (3) whether its opposites are antagonistic or not at that stage. Each of these laws aims at understanding the *nature and strength of a problem* internally as well as externally and guiding its development towards a desired end.

It would be presumptuous for anyone to believe that these laws meet all the demands of a complete method of analysis and action. Far from it. It can be said that the dialectical method itself is also subject to the dialectical laws of development and, therefore, in course of further social practice these laws will necessarily be developed into still higher laws. However, the present formulation of the dialectical laws based on the Chinese communist practice does overcome some of the problems raised by some European Marxists. Three controversies are referred to briefly here as representative of the kinds of issues raised by some European Marxists.

Maurice Cornforth, the British Marxist known for his elaborate study of dialectical materialism, wrote an article in 1965 entitled 'some Questions about Laws of Dialectics',[5] which started a long controversy. Cornforth placed the laws of dialectics above the laws of nature, they being 'much more general, or universal' and said that the laws of dialectics, unlike the laws of nature, 'are not discovered and are not tested by any such investigations'. According to him the laws of dialectics are universal because of their 'absolute necessity'. Thus, Cornforth while claiming that these laws tell us 'how to think properly' suggested a complete rupture between thinking and being. Cornforth tried to negate what Engels tried to prove, namely that knowledge is acquired by the process of observation of relationships within and between material phenomena. By delinking dialectics from investigation and suggesting a series of subjective tests Cornforth made the practical use of dialectical method more difficult.'[6]

As against this Mao's very starting point is the interconnection between knowledge and practice. That knowledge arises through the process of perceptual experience informs the entire set of Mao Zedong's dialectical laws. Cornforth perhaps has an intense desire to allow enormous flexibility in the practice of Marxism—a desire in which his critics see elements of revisionism. Mao's formulation also ostensibly carries a similar purpose, i.e., to acquire the ability to be extremely flexibile in concrete situations. But the similarity is only superficial, because Mao is trying to render materialist dialectics into practical laws subjected to constant investigation, practice, and development.

Althusser, the French Marxist theoretician, has the opposite apprehension. In the name of contingencies of new situations and for overcoming Hegelian idealism dialectics has been misunderstood to such an extent that the overall direction of development of a process is often ignored and what causes a revolutionary situation is rarely explained. Therefore, in his famous essay 'Contradiction and Overdetermination' of 1962, Althussar says that dialectical materialism demands that in each period of history all the specific contradictions form an 'animating unity' and are 'overdetermined' (by the basic contradiction in the social structure). A revolutionary situation arises out of this active accumulation of contradictions. Thus their unity transcends their specificity and is the source of revolutionary development.[7] Althusser thus poses the problem very well. When revolutionaries undertake a dialectical analysis of the vast number of specific contradictions in their environment they are constantly confronted with the problem of ordering the hierarchy of the contradictions for overcoming the present situation. But in solving this problem Althusser does not go beyond reaffirming the idea of transcendence. His analysis does not clarify what determines what. Sometimes he suggests that the 'general contradiction' between the forces of production and the relations of production essentially embodied in the contradiction between two antagonistic classes is the one that determines the nature of the overall situation. But he also argues that this general contradiction has to become 'active through the process of accumulation or overdetermination.[8]

Mao Zedong dealt with this question of overall position of contradictions long before Althusser and suggested a distinction between the *process* of revolution and the *stage* of revolution. The process is characterised by *basic* contradictions, in the sense in which Marx used the concept, which determine the nature of the various stages while each stage has a *principal* contradiction. As we shall see later, Mao developed the Law of Particularity to solve this problem.

While Cornforth and Althusser tried to solve some problems of the dialectical method which arise in course of its application, the Italian Marxist scholar, Lucio Colletti, has raised a purely logical problem in Marxist dialectics.[9] His provocative essay in 1975 takes Engels, Lenin, and Mao to task by saying that in the name of dialectics they were actually talking about Kant's notion of 'real opposition' which is a relationship of mutual exclusion or contrariety of incompatible opposites. Colletti feels that the examples of dialectics that they give are actually examples of contrariety. According to him the only example of dialectical contradiction—a relationship of unity of opposites— is the capitalist system as Marx saw it. This 'supposedly tentative argument,' as Colletti calls it, 'attacks the Marxist notion of reality at its very root! Whether the nature of an object is defined in terms of a dialectical interconnection or it is to be understood as a monolithic entity identical or opposed to another entity—this has distinguished the dialectical viewpoint from the non-dialectical viewpoint. Moreover, Colletti seems to be concerned only with the external relationship of a phenomenon. Once the focus changes to the internal composition of a thing then he has to explain what holds a thing together and what also changes it. Therefore, what Colletti is questioning is not a certain logical formulation of dialectics but the dialectical materialist notion of reality itself. Here Mao's methods of analysis and synthesis specifically separate the relationship of struggle from the relationship of unity within and between things while stressing the point that the main source of development of a thing lies within itself and is essentially a function of the relationship of struggle.

Space does not permit either a full-scale discussion of these controversies nor a survey of the vast Marxist and non-Marxist literature on dialectical materialism. But the problems raised within the Marxist circles themselves are very basic and it is worth examining the Chinese communists' theoretical performance keeping them in mind.

II. LAW OF UNITY OF KNOWING AND DOING

The first step in the dialectical materialist method of knowing about reality is to understand what the 'process of knowing' is. This question is especially important now because in many discussions the link between dialectics and materialism is becoming weaker and weaker. Marxist theory advocates that matter is the basis of knowledge, therefore, the process of knowing necessarily involves the human mind's interaction with matter. This interaction is more in the nature of man's struggle against nature for the purposes of production for fulfilling the needs of man. Thus the mental process of man is interconnected with his interaction with nature. This is how knowing and doing are related.

Three Aspects of the Law

Mao Zedong's theory of cognition starts with the assertion that matter is the basis of the idea. But the idea is not merely a mechanical reflection of matter. Man's sense perception of material forces gathers what Mao calls perceptual knowledge. When man applies his earlier knowledge to understand the newly available perceptual knowledge the outcome is logical or rational knowledge. Now comes the more important point. The rational knowledge so formed (principles, theories, laws, etc.) is again subjected to testing, verification, refinement, and correction. The process of doing and knowing thus goes on. Their unity lies in their mutual dependence on each other. Knowledge guides man's senses in perceiving the objects while these very experiences determine the nature and content of our knowledge.

Interaction with material forces is the key aspect of the theory of cognition. This is practice. All knowledge arises through practice and develops through practice. Thus Mao shifts the discussion of materialist theory of knowledge from the level of matter and spirit to the level of practice and knowledge and stresses their interdependence. But he does not talk of practice in abstract terms. By practice he generally means carrying out struggle and especially carrying out class struggle in class society. Thus knowledge or scientific laws of social development arise and are tested constantly through the experiences of class struggle. This is how philosophy and class struggle are in unity.

The final and the most important aspect of this theory is the process of mutual transformation between idea and matter or thinking and being. Here Mao makes a distinction between the question of matter being the origin or basis of an idea on the one hand and the transformation of idea into matter on the other. The first is the characteristic of materialism which separates it from idealism. The second is the characteristic of dialectical materialism that distinguishes it from mechanical materialism. It is this which emphasises the role of human initiative in history. It is this understanding which guided the CPC's activities like the revolutionary people's war, the Great Leap Forward, and the Cultural Revolution. Thus the transformation of matter into idea (i.e., knowing what exists or more accurately, trying to know about the matter through investigation) and transformation of idea into matter (i.e., changing the material forces along the lines you know to be correct) also form a unity of knowing and doing. The latter transformation will succeed only if objective reality demands it. In other words, if there is conclusive failure in materialising an idea, then it is probably an incorrect idea that needs to be modified or the method of applying it may be wrong. Thus the main materialist argument overrides all other aspects. Yet the unity of idea and matter stands out.

These three aspects of the Law of Unity of Knowing and Doing, namely, interdependence of knowledge and practice, practice as class struggle, and mutual transformation of matter and idea form the essence of Mao's theory of cognition. Mao's 1937 essay 'On Practice' emphasised the first aspect. The recently available writings of Mao, especially those of between 1957 and 1964, stress class struggle and the question of transforming an idea into matter. Mao's controversy with a contemporary Chinese philosopher, Yang Xianzhen brought out the third aspect more sharply than before. Together they form the basic philosophical perspective underlying the strategies, policies, and work-methods of CPC.

Knowledge and Practice

Mao explains the interdependence of knowledge and practice by discussing the two steps in the process of knowing. As he says in 'On Practice':

> ...it can be seen that the first step in the process of cognition is contact with the objects of the external words: this belongs to the stage of perception. The second step is to synthesise the data of perception by arranging and reconstructing them: this belongs to the stage of conception, judgement and inference. It is only when the data of perception are very rich (not fragmentary) and correspond to reality (are not illusory) that they can be basis for forming correct concepts and theories.[10]

Mao here puts stress on two points. One is the dependence of rational knowledge upon perceptual knowledge and the other is that perceptual knowledge always needs to be developed into rational knowledge. The absence of the first point leads to idealism and the error on the second point brings in empiricism. This is how knowledge and social practice are interconnected, with practice in the primary position.

Man's pursuit of knowledge guided by his social practice undergoes a continuous process of development. This process of development further illustrates the nature of interaction between knowledge and practice. Mao also says in 'On Practice':

> Discover the truth through practice, and again through practice verify and develop truth...Practice, knowledge, again practice, and against knowledge. This form repeats itself endless cycles, and with each cycle the content of practice and knowledge rises to a higher level. Such is the whole of the dialectical-materialist theory of knowledge and such is the dialectical-materialist theory of the unity of knowing and doing.[11]

It is important to remember that 'On Practice' was written in order to expose, as the official introduction puts it, 'the dogmatist kind of subjectivism, which belittles practice'. The objective was to counter the opponents of the united front line in the middle of 1930s and to argue that the strategic line of the Chinese revolution must arise out of the practical experiences of the Chinese revolutionary movement itself. However, in the 1960s the same philosophical argument was hurled against the right deviationists or revisionists. The Maoists pointed out at this time that Chinese conditions demanded a development strategy different from that of the Soviet Union and criticised leaders like Liu Shaoqi and Peng Dehuai who apparently advocated the Soviet pattern of development for China.

Practice as Class Struggle

The second aspect, namely, practice as class struggle was also evident in the essay 'On Practice', in which social practice was referred to as 'material production, class struggle or scientific experiment.'[12] These three have since become 'the three great revolutionary movements of class struggle, the struggle for production and scientific experiment' which have found place in the recent Constitutions of the CPC and the PRC. However, of the three, the stress on class struggle and the class character of all forms of practice has become evident since the late 1950s. As the debate on the question of continuing class struggle in socialist society became sharper and sharper, the Maoists have upheld the ubiquity of class struggle throughout the period of socialism. The 1976 controversy in which Deng Xiaoping allegedly played down

Mao's instruction to take class struggle as the 'key link' was yet another point of reaffirmation of the class perspective. This perspective underlies the whole range of policies of the CPC meant to prevent the growth of revisionist tendencies in the country.

Transforming Idea into Matter

The third aspect regarding the transformation of idea into matter became an acute controversy in China around the time of the Great Leap Forward.[13] Yang Xianzhen, a philosophy teacher, argued that the relationship between thinking and being is primarily a relationship between opposites and secondarily one of identity. On the face of it, this formulation does not sound un-Marxist if it is accepted that both thinking and being are always in the process of becoming the other. But if it means denying the identity relationship absolutely, it amounts to reducing dialectical materialism to mechanical materialism. Since the Great Leap Forward strategy was a political initiative to advance the productive forces, Yang accused Mao of idealism and of having subordinated matter to idea.

As against Yang's theory, the Maoists put forth what they called 'the active and revolutionary theory of reflection' according to which idea is not a mechanical reflection of matter, but also has the capacity to mould matter. Yang compared Mao's notion of identity between thinking and being with the Machist notion of sameness between thinking and being which Lenin had so strongly criticised in his *Materialism and Empirio-Criticism.* The Maoists refuted this by saying that by identity Mao means the capacity of man's ideas to correctly reflect reality and act upon it. But the reflection of reality has to be 'active and revolutionary' in order to be correct. An official Chinese article accused Yang that, 'in denying the identity between thinking and being he totally denied the great role of revolutionary theory, negated the conscious dynamic role of the masses, and twisted the active and revolutionary theory of reflection into the mechanical theory of reflection.'[14]

The debate with Yang Xianzhen reached its climax in 1963-64. At that time Mao dealt with this question in an essay entitled, 'Where Do Correct Ideas Come From?' He restated his earlier ideas on practice and said that correct ideas came only from social practice. He wondered at his critics' inability to 'comprehend that matter can be transformed into consciousness and consciousness into matter, although such leaps are phenomena of everyday life'.[15] He explained how it happens: 'Once the correct ideas characteristic of the advanced class are grasped by the masses, these ideas turn into a material force which changes society and changes the world.'[16] This viewpoint linked itself up with Mao's famous statement in his essay, 'On Contradiction' that 'in certain conditions, such aspects as the relations of production, theory and the superstructure in turn manifest themselves in the principal and decisive role.'[17]

Ever since the beginning of the GPCR, greater stress has been placed on this aspect. Human will, politics, and mass enthusiasm all cultivated in the course of productive labour as well as 'study' and participation in mass campaigns are themselves sought to be transformed into material forces. It is believed that a motivated worker produces more for the socialist revolution. The preference for revolutionary incentive for hard work instead of material incentives, 'red and expert' combination, mass study of 'theory',—in fact all the notable features of China's political process are based on this philosophical premise of mutual transformation of matter and idea.

The Law of Unity of Knowing and Doing can be now stated in the following words: *Knowledge is the product of practice through struggle and it can also be transformed into material force.*

The Law in Marxist Tradition

The Chinese claim that 'Chairman Mao inherited, defended and *developed* the dialectical-materialist theory of reflection and raised the Marxist theory of knowledge to a *higher, completely new stage.*'[18] Whether the formulation of the Law of Unity of Knowing and Doing justifies this statement is open to debate.

Each one of the three aspects of this Law can be traced back to Marx, Engels, and Lenin. On the relationship between knowledge and practice, for example, Marx's second and third theses on Feuerbach are well known.[19] Engels has said that, 'It is no longer a question anywhere of inventing interconnections from out of our brains, but discovering them in facts.'[20] For Engels the task was to settle the epistemological question by refuting both the idealists as well as the mechanical materialists. For Lenin it was a slightly different kind of polemic. He found the influence of Machism among many social democrats and took up issue with them in his *Materialism and Empirio-Criticism.* In his discussion of 'The Criterion of Practice in the Theory of Knowledge' Lenin attacked Mach for divorcing practice from knowledge.[21] Mao's contention that the advance of human knowledge is never completed and that the knowledge-practice-knowledge cycle of development is endless even though in respect of a particular process the movement of knowledge may be considered completed[22] is not original either. Lenin, following Engels, emphasised the infinite scope for knowledge and unlimited possibility for comprehension of reality while at the same time rejecting reductionist relativism, a relativism that denies 'any objective measure or model existing independently of mankind to which our relative knowledge approximate.'[23] In other words, Lenin rejected reducing the relativity of our knowledge or the historical conditioning of our knowledge to empiricism and agnosticism which cannot guide practice.[24]

In spite of this exercise in tracing the origin of ideas to the earlier Marxist texts one is struck by the way Mao communicated these ideas to his party men. His was not an epistemological undertaking of settling scores with the idealists and perverse materialists. He was applying these concepts to the 'practical question' of Chinese revolutionary strategy in the 1930s. It is the total framework of continuous practice of revolutionary class struggle which has added more meaning to the epistemological question of the relationship between matter and idea. Whether these precepts were carefully reformulated by Mao to find philosophical justification for his strategic innovations will always be debated. But the Law of Unity of Knowing and Doing did simplify the basic philosophical concept of dialectical materialism for day-to-day practice.

III. LAW OF ANALYSIS

Once we realise how knowing and doing are interconnected, the next step is to try to understand the nature of objects or things and their development. The dialectical comprehension of things has often been attempted in terms of Hegel's three famous laws, the unity of opposites, negation of negation, and transformation of quantity into quality. This problem will however be approached differently here. The question is how to analyse a thing so that we know its essential character and its relationship with other things. Dialectics is primarily the science of interconnections. It is not a combination of 'on-the-one-hand' and 'on-the-other-hand' arguments, or 'positive' and 'negative' aspects nor it is an 'either-or' formulation in the popular parlance.[25]

Mao Zedong regards dialectics as a world outlook (*yu-zhou-guan*) which 'teaches us primarily how to observe and analyse the movement of opposites in different things and, on the basis of such analysis, to indicate the method for resolving contradictions.'[26] In order to comprehend the nature of things, we undertake dialectical analysis, and it necessarily involves dialectical synthesis. To Mao there is nothing like analysis for its own sake; it must be for the purpose of resolving contradictions or solving problems in practice which is what synthesis is all about.[27]

Two Aspects

In order to understand the nature of reality first it is necessary to understand in what state things exist. Things are in constant movement. This is the discovery of natural sciences. Thus, the starting point of scientific enquiry is to realise that matter is in continous motion. This applies to all forms of matter, non-living and living. To the question what causes the motion or movement of things, the answer is, its contradictory character. A thing itself is a contradiction, i.e., there are forces within it which are struggling against each other. At the same time, a thing exists in contradiction with other things. Both the internal and the external contradictions cause the movement of the thing. But the internal contradiction is the primary cause of movement because primarily the victory of one of the internal contradictory forces transforms that things and causes a significant movement. The external forces can only create conditions favourable to one or the other internal force.

Thus comprehension of the nature of an object means *analysing* it and the first aspect of analysis is to regard an object as a contradiction. Every contradiction is a set of internal and external relationships. Internally we must see the main contending forces which in unity give the essential definition of the thing. Externally we have to follow the same procedure by identifying the main opposite of the object under analysis. This is how the specific object is put in the context of the whole system. Philosophies which do not see the part and the whole together tend to observe the essential characteristics of the part. Philosophies which only talk of the whole with no regard for the specific characteristics of its parts obscure the crucial properties of the whole. Therefore, a dialectical materialist views a thing as a contradiction in order to comprehend both its specificity as well as its overall character.

The second aspect of the law of Analysis is actually a restatement of the first. But as a method of analysis it deserves special treatment. How to identify the contradictory aspects? The Chinese communist answer is : 'One Divides into Two' (*fen-yi-wei-er*). This means that everything can be split into its two main contending forces internally and externally. Only then can one realise which aspect is weak and to what extent it needs better attention. This is how observation of reality and transformation of reality are linked.

Thing as Contradiction

Mao Zedong's 1937 essay, 'On Contradiction' begins thus: 'The law of contradiction in things, that is, the law of the unity of opposites, is the basic law of materialist dialectics.' This echoes the traditional Marxist notion of dialectics. Mao has emphasised this law so much that he is on record as having said that he did not believe in the two other Hegelian laws of dialectics, namely, the negation of negation and the transformation of quantity into quality.[28] In several places, as can be seen in the recently available speeches, Mao stressed that the unity of opposites is the essence of dialectics.

The idea that every thing has an essence which reflects its internal composition and it is this essence which undergoes change, appears again and again in Mao. He wrote in 1937 that,

> ...in order to understand the development of a thing we should study it internally and in its relations with other things; in other words, the development of things should be seen as their internal and necessary self-movement, while each thing in its movement is interrelated with and interacts on the things around it. The fundamental cause of the

> development of a thing is not external but internal; it lies in the contradictoriness within the thing.[29]

Such stress on grasping the essence of a problem or an object of analysis has pervaded the Chinese communist outlook so much that the concepts of 'principal contradiction', 'main enemy', 'primary task' and so on have come to govern the strategic activities of the CPC. Giving an example of 'serving the people with dialectics', a crew of a 150-ton trailer-truck from Shanghai have recounted how they carried out investigations applying the laws of dialectics and grasped the essence of the problem of passing a mountain curve called Hell's Gate.[30] This is only a minor instance from day-to-day practice. But at all levels this seems to have become a part of the Chinese communist outlook.

That the internal contradictory structure is the decisive source of change is another important implication of the notion of 'grasping the essence'. According to Mao it is only the advocates of 'metaphysical mechanical materialism and vulgar evolutionism' who attribute the primary cause of change to external forces. Empirical observation has proved that the basic cause of development of a thing lies within the thing. Changes in nature as well as society take place primarily as a result of the development of internal contradictions. As Mao said: 'External causes are the condition of change and internal causes are the basis of change.'[31] According to this law, contradictions in the society can be resolved mainly with in the society. A revolutionary movement in a country can succeed only if it is backed by the masses of that country and if it is self-reliant. The principle of self-reliance in China's revolutionary people's war was a manifestation of this law. In recent decades China's essentially self-reliant strategy of economic development and particularly policies related to the Great Leap Forward which seek to generate resources within each sector, reflect the same approach.[32]

As mentioned earlier, the notion of contradiction integrates the parts with the whole while identifying their peculiarities. This is how dialectics helps us analyse things in a comprehensive way. Each objective thing is actually interconnected with other things. Therefore, it is important to understand the nature of development of a thing both in its long-term interconnections as-well-as in specific time periods. Here, Mao makes a distinction between the process (*guo-*

cheng) of development which covers a long period of time and the various stages (*jie-duan*) within a process. Process is characterised by 'fundamental contradictions' (*gen-ben mao-dun*) which will not disappear until the process is completed. But since process extends over a lengthy time-span, conditions vary from stage to stage. 'Among the numerous major and minor contradictions which are determined or influenced by the fundamental contradiction, some become intensified, some are temporarily or partially resolved or mitigated, and some new ones emerge; hence the process is marked by stages.'[33] While the process as a whole has 'fundamental contradictions', each stage has its 'principal contradiction' (*zhu-yao-mao-dun*). For example, throughout the 'process' of capitalism the 'fundamental contradiction' between the forces of production and relations of production expresses itself as the contradiction between proletariat and the bourgeoisie.[34] In the 'stage' of imperialism the contradiction between the colonial powers and the colonies was intensified and became the principal contradiction.[35]

Thus the first aspect of the Law of Analysis is to comprehend the nature of a thing by identifying its essence in terms of its fundamental internal contradiction and understand how all other contradictions, external as well as internal, interact with the fundamental contradiction.

One Divided into Two

If the dialectical Law of Analysis regards a thing as a contradiction, how does one go about identifying its contradictory aspects? How does one concretely understand the nature of an object as a unity of opposites? Here the Chinese communists have put forth the notion of 'One Divides into Two' as the essential meaning of 'unity and struggle of opposites'. According to Mao 'the interdependence of the contradictory aspects present in all things and the struggle between these aspects determine the life of all things and push their development forward.'[36] But the question is which of these two relationship is primary?

The unity relationship between two contradictory aspects is the interconnection between them that gives the object a relative stability. But the struggle relationship is of absolute nature and pushes the development of a thing. The notion of unity here is the same as 'identity' or 'complementarity' of opposites. According to Mao 'identity' refers to firstly, that existence of one aspect presupposes the existence of the other and secondly, that in given conditions the two contradictory aspects transform into their opposites.[37] While the unity aspect defines the relatively static character of an object, the struggle aspect explains the process of development of the object and the latter is the more important one since all things are in motion. Mao dealt with this when he pointed out 'there are two states of motion in all things, that of relative rest and that of conspicuous change. Both are caused by the struggle between the two contradictory elements contained in a thing.'[38] This is why 'the struggle between opposites permeates a process from beginning to end and makes one process transform itself into another...it is ubiquitous, and struggle is therefore unconditional and absolute.'[39]

This notion of 'unity of opposites' was explained in terms of an old Chinese philosophers like Yang Xianzhen in 1964. They pointed out that the 'indivisible link between two opposites makes up a thing'. They said, for example, that the action and reaction of things are the process of 'two combining into one' to form the mechanical movement of things. The attraction and repulsion among molecules within matter, the productive forces and productive relations, economic foundation and superstructure were some other instances of the same. This alone, they claimed, could explain the interconnection between contradictory aspects.[40]

Inspired by Mao, some other philosophers like Shao Huaze pointed out that 'One Divides into Two' and not 'Two Unite into One' was the correct representation of the 'Unity of Opposites.' They said that all objective things have two contradictory aspects which are interconnected yet struggling against each other. All things in the world, from the atom to the universe, and all forms of matter are divided from one into two. That is how contradiction is universal. They accused Yang's group of denying dialectics, engaging in metaphysics, and advocating mechanical reconciliation.

As against this the Yang Xianzhen school argued that 'Two Unite into One' was a conception of the world as it explained the objective reality dialectically, whereas 'One Divides into Two' was a 'method of cognition'. This also invited criticism from the pro-Mao philosophers because it made an artificial division between 'world outlook' and 'method of cognition'. They also pointed out that the 'Two United into One' viewpoint undermined the fact that the two aspects of a contradiction must transform themselves into each other and that is the essential question in dialectics.[41]

During the GPCR and later this debate was integrated with the broad perspective of continuing revolutionary class struggle and the 'Two Unite into One' view was regarded as a revisionist view favouring class collaboration between exploiters and exploited and peaceful transition to socialism. In recent times 'One Divides into Two' has been stressed as an important dialectical law. As one article puts it: 'From the viewpoint of one dividing into two, we must be good at making concrete analysis of the movement of opposites in different things and learn to look at all sides of the problems and their mutual transformation under given conditions. This is to say that we must practice the two-point theory instead of one-point theory.'[42] In a situation of success, there must be problems in certain respects and in a situation of failure there must be strength in certain other respects. The Great Leap Forward strategy in 1958 for example, met with severe setbacks, but by dividing this into two, its positive aspects were upheld and the basic approach underlying the strategy continued in China. The nature of socialist society is also understood by applying the same method. In a socialist society, socialist ownership develops while bourgeois rights still exist. The two-class struggle, the two-road struggle, and the struggle between two lines go on in socialist society. These are all explained in terms of the principle of 'One Divides into Two'.[43]

Thus according to the Law of Analysis *the thing is a contradiction and its nature is comprehended by dividing it into two.*

Marxist Debate on Contradiction

Mao's discussion of contradiction is profusely loaded with quotations from Engels, Lenin and Stalin. Mao accept Engels' assertion that 'motion itself is a contradiction'.[44] Engels said that if the contradictory nature was true of simple forms of motion it was even more true of the higher forms of motion of matter. Mao elaborated this in terms of the universality of contradiction.

Mao repeats Lenin's examples of unity of opposites given in Lenin's *Philosophical Notebooks*. Mao seems to have picked up Lenin's stress on the *transformation* of contradictory aspects and developed it further in his treatment of synthesis. This is where Lucio Colletti's problem looks very artificial. Commenting on Kant, Lenin had pointed out the identity relationship between dynamic opposites.[45] Mao explained this clearly by defining the *identity* relationship in terms of complementarity. As we have seen, the aspects of the nature of the identity and struggle explain what contradiction is. If the identity aspect is ignored then contradiction becomes a relationship of *real opposition*. Colletti seems to have undermined the identity relationship among the opposites. Without this the opposites cannot move into each other's positions through struggle.

If identity relationship is a crucial aspect of contradiction why do the Maoists reject the concept of 'Two Unite into One'? The accusation against the Maoists that they undermine the identity aspect may have some truth in it. For Mao himself wrote in 1937 that 'The combination of conditional, relative identity and unconditional, absolute struggle constitutes the movement of opposites in all things.'[46] And as we know, the Maoists stress the *identity* of thinking and being. Therefore, 'Two Unite into One' cannot be easily dismissed as metaphysical. But its advocates seemed to have implied the primacy of the unity relationship over the struggle relationship. In the context of the CPC's struggle against revisionism this implied preference for policies of compromise, class reconciliation, and stability. Moreover, the Yang Xianzhen group adopted a wrong tactic by describing it as explaining the world outlook and 'One Divides into Two' as a methodology for comprehending reality. Yet the debate regarding the practical ramification of the identity and struggle relationship between the opposites in a contradiction is bound to go on.

IV. LAW OF SYNTHESIS

'There should be synthesis when one analyses; there should be analysis when one synthesises.'[47] Cognition of a contradiction must be inherently linked with resolution of the contradiction. In Marxist theory understanding a problem and solving it are indissolubly linked.

'Mystification' of problems arises only when 'interpreting the world' and 'changing the world' are arbitrarily put apart. This, in fact, links up 'knowing' and 'doing' and raises the problem of the distinction between objective reality on the one hand and our knowledge of it on the other. That the process of synthesis goes on is a law which is empirically verifiable but what we know to be the extent of synthesis of a particular process and what we can do to accelerate the process is conditional upon practice. The Law of Synthesis is an important tool both for comprehending reality and guiding its development.

The commonsense notion of dialectics as the process of thesis, anti-thesis, and synthesis often implies conciliation of opposing forces. But in Hegel as well as in Marx and Engels, synthesis is not conciliation but the victorious development of one of the contending forces. This is why the meaning of dialectical synthesis, so central to both 'knowing' and 'doing' cannot be isolated from 'analysis' of things in terms of contradictions.

Two Points

As we saw earlier, the starting point of the dialectical notion is to see a thing as being in perpetual movement. What is the nature of this movement? Is there ever an end to this movement? Is it possible to direct and guide this process of movement? These questions have engaged the attention of the philosophers of dialectics for a long time. Mao's writings suggest two points by way of answering these questions. Firstly, Mao holds that the development of a thing takes place through a process of continuous negation; this process never ends. Opposites continue to arise to face all the active forces. All development takes place through struggle. Secondly, Mao holds that at any point of time, there is a principle or dominant aspect of a contradiction and there is a non-principal or weaker aspect. In the process of development these aspects change their places. This takes place spontaneously, but it can also be accelerated by correctly handling the contradiction. In order to promote the development of a contradiction in the desired direction it is necessary for an organisation and its leadership to master the Law of Synthesis and apply it to the concrete conditions correctly.

'Development through negation' complements the principle that the struggle between the opposing forces is the primary cause of development. Negation does not mean absolute destruction even though some destruction is involved in the process of development. This is why there is no construction without destruction. Negation and affirmation are dialectically related, each necessitating the other. Thus understood together with the concept of the 'unity of opposites', 'negation of negation' means struggle leading to development. According to Mao, the process of struggle is wave-like. There are periods of 'great disorder' (*da-luan*) followed by periods of relative peace. But the overall process is a process of struggle or repeated negation of negations. And this process goes on and on. There is no end to the process of synthesis. Everything, every social system, every ideology including Marxism, even mankind will undergo dialectical transformation and be negated in the sense that *something better will replace it.*

The other point is related to the nature of the opposing forces in a contradiction. The process of synthesis involves changing the balance of these opposing forces. Mao Zedong has introduced the concept of the 'principal aspect' (*zhu-yao fang-mian*) of a contradiction to describe the stronger and the more powerful force within a contradiction. This is an important concept for formulating a strategy of action because only thus can the balance of forces be measured and the temporarily weaker but potentially progressive force be developed to become the leading force. Only thus can one avoid one-sidedness and see the relative positions of both the aspects. In fact, an understanding of the unity and struggle between the opposing aspects, their existing relative position, and their potential for development and decay differentiates dialectical logic from formal logic.

Development Through Negation

Mao asks: 'One eats one and the big fish devours the smaller; this is synthesis ... How does one synthesise?' He then answers:

> The Kuomintang and the Communist Party being two opposites, you have seen how they have been synthesised on the mainland (the synthesis has been the establishment of the People's Republic of China); and it went like this: when their troops came, we swallowed them up, piece by piece. This is not Yang Xianzhen's theory of combining two into one; nor is it a synthesis of peaceful coexistence.[48]

Mao again and again asserts that synthesis is not peaceful co-existence; struggle is the norm of the process of development. What he means by big fish devouring the smaller is that at any given moment there is a stronger aspect and a weaker aspect. An important implication of the notion of contradiction is that even a smaller fish in unity with other small fishes can grow big and devour the big fish

It was Hegel who first described this process as negation of negation; Mao has integrated it in his dialectics. At one place Mao has said that he did not believe in the category of 'negation of negation'. This should not be read literally because what Mao most probably meant was that negation should not be equated with absolute destruction. He has further said that,

> There is no such as the negation of negation. Affirmation (*ken-ding*), negation (*fou-ding*), affirmation, negation... In the development of things, there is in each phase both affirmation and negation. When slave society negated primitive society; it was affirmation in regard to feudal society. Feudal society was a negation of slave society, and affirmation of capitalist society. Capitalist society was a negation of feudal society, and also an affirmation of socialist society.[49]

This is essentially similar to Engel's understanding of negation. As Engels says in *Anti-Duhring*, 'Negation in dialectics does not mean simply saying no, or declaring that something does not exist, or destroying it in any way one likes.'[50] Engels' example of a grain of barley which in specific conditions gives rise to the plant which grows, produces and decays, is indeed what Mao means by the process of negation, affirmation, and negation. Engels further adds that 'each repetition of this process, each fresh negation of the negation, enhances this process of perfection.'[51] The same, Engels says, is true of the development of philosophy:

> The old materialism was, therefore, negated by idealism. But in the course of the further development of philosophy, idealism, too, became untenable and was negated by modern materialism. Modern materialism, the negation of the negation, is not the mere re-establishment of the old, but adds to the permanent foundations of this old materialism the whole thought-content of two thousand years of development of philosophy and natural science, as well as of the history of these two thousand years.[52]

To Lenin, the concept of negation inhered in it a definite element of affirmation. He took Hegel's statement that 'Negation is to an equal extent positive' and explained that 'Negation is something definite, has a definite content, the inner contradictions lead to the replacement of the old content by a new, higher one.'[53]

This approach also pervades Mao's speeches and writings. But Mao's discussion of negation of negation was more frequent in the post-1957 writings than those of the pre-Liberation period. The new emphasis went hand in hand with the evolving class-struggle perspective.

Mao has made the perspective of 'struggle between two opposites' a basic principle of guidance for the CPC. Discussing the dialectical process Mao has even suggested that if in certain spheres there are no established opposites which are visible, then one should take the initiative in establishing opposites.[54] In other words, if the opposite forces are not clearly discernable then one must make an attempt to make them clear. This is so because the objective process of negation of negation requires it. The two-line struggle in the CPC in recent years may be an example of establishing opposites within the party in order to bring to the open anti-socialist tendencies.

Among the numerous examples of Mao's use of the concept of negation of negation, one can cite the following: 'Stalin made mistake in dialectics. "Negation of negation." The October Revolution negated capitalism but it refused to admit that socialism may be negated too. We believe that the world is both stable and unstable. Even socialism may cease to exist one day.'[55] 'Lenin's dialectics, Stalin's partial metaphysics, and today's dialectics are also the negation of negation.'[56]

Just as Mao did not discard negation of negation, neither did he abandon the other Hegelian category of quantity and quality. He said that he believed in only one category, namely, the unity of opposites. The crucial sentence of his in the same paragraph where he said so is 'Transmutation between quality and quantity is unity of opposites between quantity and quality' (*zhi-liang hu-bian jiu shi liang yu zhi de dui li tong-yi*).[57] The suggestion of a two-way transmutation can cause confusion because the notion of progressive movement implies only a qualitative change. From the dialectical materialist view point the accumulation of quantities of material forces leads to qualitative change. In other words, qualitative change does not regress into quantitative backwardness. Mao's quotation cited above tells us that a new form of matter immediately starts creating quantities whose accumulation and internal struggle lead to a new quality of matter. Thus the process, quantity-quality-quantity-quality...quantity goes on. In *Dialectics of Nature,* Engels explained this process of transformation essentially in the same way.[58]

Engels, however, defined the level at which qualitative transformation takes place. We do not see any clear discussion of this in Mao. Discussing the process in physics, Engels said: '...a definite minimum current strength is required to cause the platinum wire of an electric incandescent lamp to glow; and everly metal has its temperature of incandescence and fusion...'[59] In Mao's analysis, perhaps, the completion of a 'stage' by the resolution of the 'principal contradiction' and completion of a 'process' by the resolution of the 'fundamental contradiction' implies that level of development which brings about corresponding qualitative transformation.

That the process of dialectical development is endless is stressed again and again by Mao. As was mentioned earlier an interesting aspect of this notion of endless development is that 'change takes place in a wave-like fashion'. 'Everything happens in wave-like or spiral motion. Taking a walk, holding a meeting, an electric current, a sound wave, a dramatic performance, talking and writing are all wave-like motion. I support the study of dialectics.'[60] The periodic campaigns and upheavals in China in recent decades can be understood in this perspective. Every stage in the process of development of a things has periods of momentum and accelerated movement. In the overall sense this is always a change for the better or as Mao puts it everything is 'from small into big'. In one of his speeches Mao gives a long list of cases to illustrate the process of development; these pertain to great discoveries made by the youth. In this process human initiative is seen to be very important. He concludes: 'Our, method is to lift the lid, breakdown superstition, and let the initiative and creativity of the laboring people explode.'[61]

Mao explains how development takes place through negation, 'All individuals and all specific things have their birth, development, and death... Mankind is born and therefore mankind must also die.

The earth was born, and so the earth must also die... (by this) we mean that something more advanced than mankind will come to replace it, and this is a higher stage in the development of things.'[62]

Changing Aspects of a Contradiction

If synthesis, involves development through negation, what does it imply in terms of the specific aspects of a contradiction? Mao deals with this question in the following way:

> In any contradiction the development of the contradictory aspects is uneven. Sometimes they seem to be in equilibrium, which is however only temporary and relative, while unevenness is basic. Of the two contradictory aspects, one must be principal and the other secondary. The principal aspect is the one playing the leading role in the contradiction. The nature of a thing is determined mainly by the principal aspect of a contradiction, the aspect which has gained the dominant position.[63]

The principal aspect of a contradiction is not identical to the principal contradiction. The latter is the dominant contradiction among many contradictions and it determines the nature of a stage of development. The principal aspect on the other hand is an aspect of a contradiction. For example, in the imperialist stage of capitalism, the contradiction between the imperialist power and a colonised nation is the principal contradiction which influences all other contradictions of the process of capitalism. The principal aspect of this principal contradiction, however, is the imperialist power. But as the national liberation movement develops the imperialists lose this position and the national liberation movement become the principal aspect. This is how 'the principal and the non-principal aspects of a contradiction transform themselves into each other and the nature of the thing changes accordingly.'[64]

This process is never smooth, the contradiction between the new and the old aspects gives rise to many twists and turns. But on the whole the movement of opposites takes place through leaps— an idea that both Engels and Lenin had emphasised to demonstrate the swift spread of revolution. The Chinese communist concepts can also be put in the perspective of the dialectics of changing aspects. The fact that through protracted guerilla war a weak aspect like the CPC could grow into a dominant force (the principal aspect) can thus be explained. The contradiction between industry and agriculture has been so handled in the PRC that their positions have been constantly changed from one Five Year Plan to the other. The new synthesis giving priority to agriculture followed by light industry and then heavy industry thus does not become a permanent arrangement, according to this principle.

To summarise, according to the Law of Synthesis *development of a process takes place through continuous negations and change of the principle aspects.*

The Question of Synthesis

Mao Zedong's treatment of synthesis especially in the post-1956 writings draws heavily on Engels and Lenin. But as in other cases he has successfully clarified some of these aspects for purposes of concrete practice. The stress on perpetual struggle, the idea of wave like advance, and the strategic concept of the principal aspect and its transformation are examples of this. The most important dynamics of the process leadings to synthesis is struggle. The experience of the last decade in the PRC shows that class struggle in all spheres is the main instrument of synthesis. The post-1956 writings of Mao are full of references to struggle, negation, and synthesis.

It should once again be underlined that analysis and synthesis are closely related. The 'unity of opposites' and 'one dividing into two' hold that development of a thing can only take place through struggle; and development means that the emergent weak force of today can become full-grown and strong tomorrow. But the process does not stop there and further new forces emerge to negate the victorious force.

The role of human initiative guiding the development of the contradiction still remains crucial and perhaps the decisive factor in the process of development. Do the contending aspects change automatically or do they have to be directed in a definite direction? Marxist theory says that in the ultimate analysis the objective course of the process will inevitably change the position of the aspects. But practice shows that there are twists and turns and they can last for decades, even centuries. Therefore, grasping the Laws of Analysis and

Synthesis and applying them correctly cannot be reduced to mechanical formulas. Perhaps one intervenes in history on the side of history. One does not wait for the inevitable to happen but makes it happen knowing that it is inevitable. In any case, as we have seen, 'knowing' and 'doing' cannot be separated. Only through practice can we have a better grasp over the laws and the ability to handle the contradictions correctly.

V. LAW OF PARTICULARITY

Since development takes place through the aspects of a contradiction changing their places, we must know the specific character of each aspect, so that we can analyse the contradiction better and guide the process of synthesis. This calls for an understanding of the particularity of a contradiction. In this area of handling concrete problems by grasping their particularity, Mao's thoretical—therefore, practical—contribution is widely acknowledged. This is also an area where Mao's innovations have been subjected to severe attacks by his critics. Whenever Mao spoke or wrote about the question of particularity he was fighting against 'dogmatists' or the mechanical followers of Marxism. During the period of the war against Japan, Mao fought against Zhang Guotao's opposition to the strategy of a united front with the KMT. After Liberation Mao took up issues with Gao Gang, Peng Dehuai, and Liu Shaoqi who wanted China to adopt the Soviet path of development. Was this fight against dogmatism based on a feeling of national pride and cultural self-assertion or did it arise from the problems of combining Marxist theory with Chinese practice? Mao's present-day critics say that it was the former and that all talk of Marxism was only a clock concealing national chauvinism.

In reality Mao's theoretical discussion of the problem of the universal and the particular preceded the emergence of any successful strategy in practice. The essay 'On Contradiction', first given as a series of lectures to the Anti-Japanese Military and Political College in Yenan, is dated 1937. The theory of people's democratic revolution which explained the 'particular features' of colonial and semi-colonial situations and related them to the strategic principles of people's war was given a full treatment in Mao's essay 'On New Democracy' in

January 1940. Similarly, the Ten Great Relations which set forth the basic principles of China's development strategy taking into account the specific features of Chinese problems were drafted in April 1956, i.e., at least, two year before the Great Leap Forward strategy was propounded. This shows that in course of practice Mao has constantly grappled with the philosophical problems at certain crucial points and arrived at certain formulations which have further guided his policies.

Three Elements

The Law of Particularity further clarifies certain aspects of the Law of Unity of Knowing and Doing and the Law of Analysis. If perception of an individual phenomenon is the first step in knowledge then it necessarily involves comprehending each specific problem or contradiction thoroughly. The less thorough the comprehension of the specific problem the shallower would be the conceptual formulation that is based on it. The shallower the theory the poorer the practice based on that theory. Therefore, a dialectical materialist must understand the essence of each contradiction. It is this essence which differentiates one contradiction from another, one thing from another. The essence of a thing lies in the specificity of its contradictory aspects. Thus the *particular essence* of each aspect of a thing defines the essence of the thing. This is the first point in the Law of Particularity.

Dialectics unites particularity with universality. Only thus can the meaning of the parts as well as the whole be discerned. Once the particularity of the aspects is comprehended the particularity of the contradiction as a whole can be defined. This is done by comparing the position of various contradictions and finding out which of them is the most influential in a certain stage of development of a thing. This is called the principal contradiction. This is the second element in the Law of Particularity.

The third and equally important element is determining the quality of confrontation within different contradictions or the nature of the contradictory relationship. Which contradictions are antagonistic and which are non-antagonistic during a stage of development? Since everything divides into two and struggle is the primary characteristic of a contradiction, antagonism is obviously inherent in all contradictions. But in specific stages of development, certain contradictions are developed and the antagonism between them is more acute than in others. When another stage emerges a non-antagonistic contradiction may become antagonistic. The important implication of this is that the resolution of an antagonistic contradiction generally requires resort to revolutionary armed struggle whereas a non-antagonistic contradiction can be handled with peaceful and presuasive methods.

Thus grasping the particular essence of aspects of a contradiction, identifying the principal contradiction, and distinguishing the antagonistic contradictions from the non-antagonistic ones are the three elements of the Law of Particularity.

Particular Essence of a Contradiction

Criticising the dogmatists in the CPC, Mao wrote in 1937 that the dogmatists do not understand that it is precisely in the particularity of contradiction that the universality of contradiction resides. Nor do they understand how important is the study of the particularity of contradiction in the concrete things confronting us for *guiding the course of revolutionary practice.*[65]

The concept of the thing-in-itself with which Hegel used to define the identity of a thing influenced both Marx and Engel. Lenin elaborated Engels' view on the concept and said that there was no limit to exploring the essence of a thing.[66] Mao pursued this further and pointed out the need for understanding the 'particular essence' of each things as well as the areas of its commonness with other things.[67] To Mao, it is the 'particular essence' of each form of motion which qualitatively distinguishes it from other forms of motion.[68] Thus the distinct character of a thing is as true as its interdependence with things. According to Mao this applies not only to nature, but also to social phenomena. As he put it, 'Every form of society, every form of ideology, has its own particular contradiction and particular essence.'[69] At the same time according to him 'unless we understand the universality of contradiction, we have no way of discovering the universal cause or universal basis for the movement or development of things.'[70] Thus, the dialectics of the particular and the universal can ensure an all-sided analysis and synthesis of things. First of all, we start with observation of particular things and then go on to formulate the knowledge of things in general. From the particular to the general and then to the particular—this is how the process of cognition goes on, each cycle improving our state of knowledge.[71]

Mao suggests that the particular essence of a contradiction can be grasped by discovering the particularity of the two aspects of each contradiction. This means 'understanding what specific *position* each aspect occupies, what concrete *form* it assumes in its interdependence and in its contradiction with its opposite, and what concrete *methods* are employed in the struggle with its opposite...'[72] If we take, for example, the contradiction between the Chinese landlords and the peasantry during the war of resistance against Japan, in order to understand the particularity of the landlords, we have to analyse their position vis-a-vis other classes (powerful in the countryside but without the monopoly of power nationally), their forms (small and patriotic landlords, big landlords, semi-feudal landlords), and what methods were employed to resolve this contradiction (unity with and neutralisation of the patriotic landlords, confiscation of the land of the fleeing landlords, rent reduction campaigns, etc.). The peasantry could be analysed also in the same way. All this requires what Lenin called a 'concrete analysis of concrete conditions'. And what is more important is that 'qualitatively different contradictions can only be resolved by qualitatively different methods.'[73] There is nothing like an 'unalterable formula' to resolve contradictions. Engles perhaps had the same thing in mind when he said that 'every kind of thing ...has a peculiar way of being negated in such a manner that it gives rise to a development...'[74]

This is also Mao Zedong's understanding of creative development of ideology and this provides the background to the CPC's innovations in both revolutionary strategy as well as the strategy of development. The strategy and tactics of people's war were propounded by Mao according to this theory. In post-Liberation China, local initiative in development activities has been constantly encouraged. Among the dialectical principles frequently propagated in China. 'unity' at the central level and 'specifics of the local requirements' were always emphasised.[75] That the particularity of Chinese problems requires Chinese solutions and not mechanical application of methods applied elsewhere has been always underlined in China. Hence the need for the 'creative application' of ideology assumes great importance in specific situations.

The Principal Contradiction

The particularity of a contradiction does not only lie in its particular essence internally but also in its relative position externally. In the long process of development of things there are specific stages and in each stages some contradictions are more powerful than the others. According to Mao, 'One of them is necessarily the principal contradiction (*zhu-yao-de mao-dun*) whose existence and development determines or influences the existence and development of the other contradictions.'[76]

Mao also insists that there is only one principal contradiction at every stage of the development of the process and when another stage emerges a new principal contradiction also emerges. He gives three major instances to explain this. In a capitalist society, the proletariat and the bourgeoisie form the principal contradiction society, the proletariat and the bourgeoisie form the principal contradiction and the other contradictions like the one between the remnant feudal class and the bourgeoisie are non-principal (*fe-zhu-yao*). During a war of imperialist aggression the principal contradiction is between imperialism and the country which is attacked. In this situation all the classes except the traitors temporarily unite against the national enemy for the contradictions among them are non-principal. But there are instances where imperialism operates through the ruling class of a country and the principal contradiction comes to be the one between the masses on the one hand and the alliance of imperialists and the domestic ruling class on the other.

Mao admits that situations like those in the semi-colonies present a *complicated picture*. So it is necessary to find the principal contradiction after careful dialectical materialist investigation. Mao has said that 'once this principal contradiction is grasped, all problems can be readily solved,' otherwise one can be 'lost in a fog' and cannot get to the heart of the problem.

The distinction between fundamental contradiction (*gen-ben-de mao-dun*) and the principal contradiction (*zhu-yao-de mao-dun*) is conceptually clear in that the former applies to an entire process (*gue-cheng*) and the latter to only a stage (*jie-duan*) But Mao's example of the contradiction between the bourgeoisie and the proletariat is somewhat confusing. In the context of the debate on the theory of continuous revolution the Maoists have described the contradiction between the forces of production and the relations of production as 'basic contradiction' (*ji-ben mao-dun*), and the contradiction between the proletariat and the bourgeoisie as the 'major contradiction' (also *zhu-yao-de mao-dun*) during the socialist period. Here 'major' and 'principal' seem to be equated. If socialist stage is the transitional period overlapping with the final stage of the capitalist process and the initial stage of the communist process then the concept of the principal contradiction is appropriate. But if the socialist stage is a long period and a major class contradiction continues throughout this period then it appears to be a fundamental contradiction (*gen-ben-de mao-dun*). In the same way if we study the list of fundamental contradictions in the modern world situation they are *as broad* as this major contradiction. On the other hand, the whole concept of a principal contradiction was motivated by the desire to comprehend the particularity of a stage of development so that an appropriate strategy could be formulated. Thus, the examples that Mao gives do leave grounds for confusion even though the basic distinction between the fundamental contradiction and the principal contradiction is clear.

Antagonistic and Non-Antagonistic Contradictions

The particularity of a contradiction also lies in the nature and form of the struggle between its opposites. At different stages of development of a thing, its contending forces have different degrees of intensity in their confrontation. In the 1937 essay 'On Contradiction', Mao Zedong discussed this question and pointed out that antagonism was a 'particular manifestation of the struggle of opposites'. It is true that contradictions between the oppressor and the oppressed classes are bound to contain an element of antagonism. But some of these contradictions remain latent and only at definite stages do they manifest antagonism.[77] As Mao put it, 'Some contradictions are characterised by open antagonism, others are not. In accordance with the concrete development of things, some contradictions which were originally non-antagonistic (*fel-dui-kang-xing*) develop into antagonistic (*dui-kang-xing*) ones, while others which were originally antagonistic develop into non-antagonistic ones.'[78]

The 1937 treatment of this point stressed, as did Mao's other writings, the need for understanding the particularity of a stage of development and handling contradictions according to the concrete demands of that stage. On the basis of this perspective, Mao formulated his theory of new democracy and under it the strategy of a four-class united front with the national bourgeoisie in it. The contradiction between the proletariat and the national bourgeoisie which had an element of antagonism in it was basically understood as non-antagonistic at that time so that there could be a united front against three enemies, namely imperialism, feudalism, and bureaucrat-capitalism. The contradictions between these three groups on the one hand and the constituents of the united front on the other were antagonistic. This approach was further clarified in Mao's essay, 'On the People's Democratic Dictatorship' published in June 1949. Methods of dictatorship were to be applied to the handling of antagonistic contradictions whereas democratic methods of persuasion and education were to be used in case of non-antagonistic contradictions.

In his 1957 speech, 'On the Correct Handling of Contradictions Among the People' Mao delved deeper into these concepts and explained their application to the contemporary problems facing China. By antagonistic contradictions he meant 'the contradictions between ourselves and the enemy (*di wo zhi-jien de mao-dun*)' while 'the contradictions among the people (*ren-min nei-bu de mao-dun*)' were non-antagonistic contradictions. He stressed that the concept of 'the people' varies in 'content in different countries and in different periods of history.'[79] Mao said that those who supported the building of socialism in China at that point were among the 'people' and those who opposed it were the 'enemies of the people.'

Mao's 1957 speech criticised two erroneous lines of thinking. First was the rightist viewpoint within and outside the CPC which thought that class contradictions had disappeared with the socialist transformation which had taken place in the PRC. As against this, Mao emphasised the existence of numerous non-antagonistic contradictions and also some continuing basis of antagonistic contradictions in the socialist society. The second viewpoint which Mao criticised exaggerated the threat of counter-revolution in China and showed excessive alarm at the Hungarian uprising in 1956. He pointed out that they underrated the achievements of long years of popular revolutionary struggle and the success in the suppression of counter revolutionaries in China. Between these two extremes Mao asked for clearly distinguishing between the antagonistic and non-antagonistic contradictions and correctly handling them.

Among the examples of non-antagonistic contradictions that Mao gives are: The contradictions between the working class and the peasantry, between the workers and peasants on the one hand and the intellectuals on the other, and so on, 'Correct handling of contradictions among the people' demands the practice of democracy under centralised guidance and not dictatorship. The 1942 formula of 'unity, criticism, unity' (*tuan-jie, pi-ping, tuan-jie*) was applicable in resolving these contradictions.'[80] Exercise of dictatorship which is to be applied when dealing with contradictions with the enemies implies denial of political rights and resorting to coercion whenever necessary.

An important aspect of this motion is the transformation of a non-antagonistic contradiction into an antagonistic one and vice-versa. The Chinese national bourgeoisie moved from its original antagonistic position vis-a-vis China's working classes and came to be included in the united front: it was generally cooperative with the 'people's democratic' and then the 'socialist' transformation of China's economy. It continued to have a dual character, containing both antagonism and non-antagonism. But its overall position partly depended on its own behaviour and partly on the policy of the CPC to wean it away from the bureaucratic-capitalists.

In other words, the role of party policy is extremely significant in guiding the development of contradictions from one stage to another. If contradictions among the people are not handled properly, antagonism may arise. This may appear, to give only a few instances, in the form of sharp differences between workers and peasants in terms of wages, living standards and cultural level; between the government and the people in the forms of bureaucratism and elitism;

and between the party and the masses also in the same form. This is why the comprehension of particularity of the various contradictions in terms of their antagonistic or non-antagonistic character and adoption of appropriate methods for handling them are of great importance.

The Law of Particularity can be stated as follows: *A contradiction is defined in terms of the particular essence of its two aspects, its relative position vis-a-vis other contradictions to determine the principal contradiction of the stage, and whether its opposites are antagonistic or not at a given point of time.*

Law of Particularity in Practice

We have already seen that the innovations of the CPC have been based on the philosophical premise of the dialectic of particularity and universality. Mao's writings make it clear again and again that dialectics cannot be reduced to any 'unalterable formula'. In what conditions does one stage develop into another and a new principal contradiction emerge? In what conditions do the opposite aspects of a contradiction change their places? In what conditions does an antagonistic contradiction develop into a non-antagonistic one? Identification of these *conditions,* in the absence of precise objective proven criteria, still belongs to the subjective realm of human leadership. To what extent the subjective comprehension corresponds to the objective situation can only be tested through practice. In his 1957 speech Mao said, in the context of handling political contradictions: 'The views set out above are based on China's specific historical conditions. Conditions vary in different socialist countries and with different Communist Parties. Therefore, we do not maintain that other countries and Parties should or must follow the Chinese way.'[81]

Since the early 1960s when the Sino-Soviet split became wide, the Chinese gave up explaining their innovations in terms of 'China's specific historical conditions'. Lin Biao's 1965 essay on people's war asserted the universal significance of China's path of the people's democratic revolution for colonial situations. And since the Cultural Revolution the Maoists have combated revisionism not with reference to the Chinese conditions, but in universal theoretical terms of continuing revolutionary class struggle in a socialist society.

But in spite of the universalist perspective which the Chinese communists claim to uphold they seem to have built into it the Law of Particularity, which asks activists to 'creatively apply universal laws to the concrete conditions' of their situation in course of continuous practice, investigation, and study, Thus, the formulation of the dialectical materialist law of particularity clarifies their perspective but leaves the main burden of its practice to the practitioner.

VI. DIALECTICS OF THE DIALECTICAL METHOD

The four laws of materialist dialectics have been presented here by way of summing up the Marxist theory of cognition and practice as it has emerged through the Chinese communist experience. As was pointed out at the beginning, these are steps for comprehending a problem as well as solving it. The two cannot be separated. The first law does not allow their separation. Modern social science seems to have surrendered itself to the pleasures of abstract theorisation and many groups of European Marxists have also joined the bandwagon. Only lately has there come about an increasing awareness in the third world countries of the fact that social science and social practice are inseparable. Thus the Law of Unity of Knowing and Doing has come to be the eminent of the four laws.

The Law of Analysis and Synthesis arise out of the first law and represent the essence of the Marxist theory for guiding practice. Analysis and synthesis are themselves inseparable. Comprehending a contradiction is incomplete without the effort to resolve it, while resolution of a contradiction cannot even begin without its analysis. Thus, Mao's use of the notion 'One Divides into Two' becomes an effective tool of analysis. These two concepts, analysis and synthesis, in a way, liberate materialist dialectics from the grip of the Hegelian triad of thesis, anti-thesis, and synthesis. They seek to firmly root the grasping and handling of contradictions in materialist struggle of the opposites.

The Law of particularity appears conspicuously in Mao's treatment of dialectics. In a commentary on Mao's discussion on contradiction in the early 1950s Cornforth pointed out Mao's emphasis on 'concrete analysis of concrete conditions' and how dialectics was not a set of formulate. Cornforth wrote in 1953 (i.e., when Mao was a 'respectable' Marxist in the entire international communist movement):

> The keynote of Mao's article, 'On Contradiction,' is the insistence that Marxist dialectics does not consist of a set of formulae from which can be deduced the answer to all problems. But on the contrary, the essence of the Marxist dialectical method is that it is a method of studying things as they really are, in their interconnection and movement, and that it does not apply a preconceived scheme and try to make everything fit into it.[82]

While Mao's preoccupation with the particularity of specific situations has earned him compliments from Cornforth, that very orientation got him poor marks from Althusser. Althusser considered the essay 'On Contradiction' as 'generally descriptive' and 'in certain respects abstract.'[83]

One can say that Mao's treatment of the Law of Particularity acquires importance only if its links with the universality are understood. It is true, as Cornforth says, that Mao was for concrete analysis of concrete things. But it is also true that concrete things to Mao were contradictions in the sense Marx, Engels, and Lenin used the term. The universality of contradictions and their development through changing aspects provide meaning to the notion of particularity. Neither the principal contradiction nor an antagonistic relationship are conceivable without comprehending the nature of the contradiction itself, i.e., without dividing one into two and analysing the relationship between the opposing aspects. Therefore, those commentators on Mao who treat Mao's innovations in terrns of rules of concrete analysis or rules of pragmatic management of problems miss the very basis of the Law of Particularity.

Althusser's charge that Mao is too descriptive may seem preposterous to the Chinese communists. Moa has, indeed, discussed philosophy only in relation to concrete problems facing his party and his people. This style of philosophical discussion was new to the tradition of philosophy. But he brought dialectics back to earth by referring to situations around him. His extensive use of traditional Chinese concepts and sayings, numerous examples which he gave from Chinese novels, and his stress on relating dialectics to the actual conditions of life—all these helped in communicating the abstract laws of materialist dialectics to the members of the CPC and later to the Chinese population as a whole.

Does Mao's discussion of dialectics still remain *abstract in certain respects* as Althusser complains? Does Mao talk about dialectics outside the framework of the Marxist conception of society and history? Althusser seems to have formed this impression on the basis of an isolated reading of Mao's essays of 1937. If one looks at the course of developments in China, the character of the Sino-Soviet ideological debate, the debate on class struggle within the CPC, and the emphasis since the beginning of the Cultural Revolution on the 'theory of continuing the revolution under the dictatorship of the proletariat', it becomes clear that Mao's ideas have been put across only in relation to the Marxist conception of society and history. Mao's enormous stress on class struggle as the main mode of practice of materialist dialectics is of special significance. Moreover, Mao's post-Liberation writings, some of which have become available recently, are full of philosophical expositions dwelling upon original Marxist classics.

Mao's philosophical innovations will continue to be debated in the current ideologically-charged atmosphere in the international communist movement. But, as our discussion of the four laws of materialist dialectics shows, Mao's contributions do not show any basic deviation from Engels' treatment of the subject. However, the gap between subjective formulation of objective laws on the one hand and the objective laws themselves on the other forms a contradiction by itself. At present the four laws can be taken to be the principal aspect of this contradiction in that they seem to correspond to reality and guide practice. But as we have seen in the case of each of the laws they need to be continuously tested in practice, refined, and tested against so that the gap becomes progressively narrow.

NOTES

1. *Miscellany of Mao Tse-tung Thought*, translation of *Mao Ze-dong Si-Xiang Wan-sui* (hereafter referred to as *MMT*), *JPRS*, No. 61269-1, p. 218. These are translations of the Red Guard publications of Chairman Mao's writings published in 1967 and 1969.
2. Vsevolod Holubnychy, 'Mao Tse-tung's Materialist Dialectics', *The China Quarterly*, No. 19, July-September 1964.

3. *MMT* II, p. 384.
4. Mao Tse-tung, 'On Practice', in *Four Essays on Philosophy,* Peking: Foreign Language Press, 1968, p. 4.
5. Maurice Cornforth, 'Some Questions about Laws of Dialectics', *Marxism Today,* Vol. 9, No. 11, November 1965.
6. Emile Burns sees in Cornforth's article 'a certain departure from the materialist outlook.' But he too does not suggest how one can concretely relat-knowledge with practice. *Marxism Today,* Vol. 9, No. 12, December 1965.
7. Louis Althusser, 'Contradiction and Overdetermination,' *New Left Review,* No. 41, January-February 1967. Also in *For Marx*, New York: Vintage, 1970.
8. Althusser has been criticised by John Lewis for the most indefensible of reasons. His accustaion that Althusser is guilty of determinism and metaphysical materialism (Lewis says that 'transcendence' has always served the ruling class) still do not touch Althusser's main argument. Lewis's plea for Marxist humanism is well-taken. But unless the overall class character of the situation at a particular stage of revolution guarantees humanism, this kind of concern for humanism becomes idealist. See John Lewis, 'The Althusser Case', *Marxism Today,* Vol. 15, No. 1 and 2, January and February 1972; and Louis Althusser, 'Reply to John Lewis (Self-criticism)', *Marxism Today,* Vol. 15, No. 10, October 1972.
9. Lucio Colletti, 'Marxism and the Dialectic', *New Left Review,* No. 93, September-October 1975.
10. Mao Tse-tung, 'On Practice', op. cit., p. 11.
11. Ibid., p. 20.
12. Ibid., p. 3.
13. According to an official publication this controversy is dated 1955-64. *Three Major Struggles in China's Philosophical Front,* Peking: Foreign Language Press, 1973, p. 31. 'The Ten Great Relations' speech of Mao in April 1956 did embody this approach of transforming idea into matter. Referring to this in August 1964 Mao said: 'I wrote the first ten articles of the Double ten Articles. I discussed how substance changes into spirit and spirit into substances.' *MMT*, p. 398.
14. Ibid., p. 35. A very interesting discussion of matter and idea of a table appeared in the *People's Daily* of 16 July 1963. Its translation appeared in *China News Analysis,* No. 518, 29 May 1964.
15. Mao Tse-tung, *Four Essays on Philosophy,* op. cit., p. 136.
16. Ibid., p. 134.
17. Ibid., p. 58.

18. *Three Major Struggles in China's Philosophic Front,* op. cit., p. 32.
19. 'The question whether objective truth can be attributed to human thinking is not a question of theory but is a *practical* question. In practice man must prove the truth, that is, the reality and power, the this-sidedness of his thinking...the coincidence of the changing circumstances and of human activity càn be conceived and rationally understood only as *revolutionary practice.*' *Selected Works of Marx and Engels,* Moscow, 1970, pp. 13-14.
20. 'Feuerbach and End of Classical German Philosophy', *Selected Works of Marx and Engels,* op. cit., p. 375. Discussing the dialectical notion of matter Engels says elsewhere: 'In this way, by the *activity of human beings,* the idea of *causality* becomes established, the idea that one motion is the cause of another,' *Dialectics of Nature,* Moscow, 1954, p. 230.
21. 'The standpoint of life, of practice, should be first and fundamental in the theory of knowledge', V. I. Lenin, *Materialism and Empirio-Criticism,* Moscow, 1964, p. 129. Lenin adds something more which is interesting: practice can never 'either confirm nor refute any human idea *completely*'. In other words every idea is subject to endless development. In Mao this is the continuous process of development from knowledge to practice and then to knowledge.
22. Mao Tse-tung, 'On Practice', op. cit., p. 16.
23. V. I. Lenin, op. cit., p. 123.
24. Most probably Mao had not read Lenin's *Materialism and Empirio-Criticism* by the time he wrote 'On Practice'. But he must be aware of its contents through other books on Marxism.
25. Marx attributed the first misrepresentation of dialectics to proudhon, see *Selected Works of Marx and Engels,* op. cit., p. 30. Engels distinguished several polarities like 'positive' and 'negative' in *Dialectics of Nature* (op. cit., p. 211). Lenin commented that 'Gorgias put *either-or* to the fundamental questions. But that is not true dialectics; it would be necessary to prove that the object must be necessarily in one or another determinations, not in and for itself'. See V. I. Lenin, 'Conspectus of Lectures on the History of Philosophy', Philosophical Notebooks—*Collected Works,* Vol. 38. Moscow, 1963, pp. 273-4.
26. Mao Tse-tung, 'On Contradiction', op. cit., p. 29.
27. 'In the past we did not deal very clearly with analysis (*fen-xi*) and synthesis (*zong-he*). We understand analysis a little better, but not much has been said about synthesis. I have asked Ai Ssu-ch'i about it, and he said that now we speak only about conceptual analysis and synthesis, not objective and practical synthesis and analysis.' Mao Tse-tung, 'Talk on Philosophy', (18 August 1964), in *MMT,* p. 390.

28. In his 'Talk on Problems of Philosophy' dated 18 August 1964, responding to a query from K'ang Sheng, Mao said: 'Engels spoke about the three categories, but I don't believe two of them (unity of opposites is the most basic law; transmutation between quality and quantity is the unity of opposites between quality and quantity, but there is no negation of negation)', *MMT*, p. 393. In Chinese edition it is also clear. '*En-ge-si jianq-le san ge fan-zhou, Wo bu xiang-xin liang-ge*' *Mao Ze-dong Tung-zhi shi dong-dai zui wei-da de Ma-ke-si-Lie-ning-zhu-yi-zhe* (August 1969), p. 558. In my opinion this statement should not be taken too literally. In many other places Mao himself uses the concept of 'negation of negation'.
29. Mao Tse-tung, 'On Contradiction', op. cit., p. 26.
30. *Serving the People with Dialectics,* Peking: Foreign Language Press, 1972, pp. 10-18. See also note 32, *supra.*
31. Mao Tse-tung, 'On Contradiction' op. cit., p. 28.
32. There is an interesting report as to how a team of weathermen in Kwangsi used the dalectical laws, made a distinction between internal and external causes and by combining local folk beliefs about weather variation with scientific knowledge, considerably improved their weather-forecasting. *Serving the people with Dialectics,* op. cit., pp. 19-25.
33. Mao Tse-tung, 'On Contradiction', op. cit., p. 43. *Mao Ze-dong de wu pian zhe-xhe-zhu-zho,* Peking, 1970, p. 63.
34. In *Dialectical and Historical materialism* Stalin's analysis was of a different nature. He asked the question: What is the chief force in the complex of conditions of the material life of society which determines the character of the social system and the development of society from one system to another? As a commentator explains, by this Stalin meant 'The mode of production of material values, food, clothing, homes, fuel, instruments of production, etc., indispensable for the life and development of society.' James Klugmann, 'Stalin and Dialectical Materialism', *Communist Review,* April and June 1953.
35. Mao refers to the Chinese bourgeois-democratic revolution as a process which between 1911 and 1937 had six stages of development. Mao Tse-tung, 'On Contradiction', op. cit., p. 44.
36. Ibid., p. 31.
37. Ibid., p. 60.
38. Ibid., p. 67.
39. Ibid., p. 68.
40. 'Uniting Two into One', this concept was first used in *Dong-xi lun* written by Fang I-chih in 1653. Li Shen-i discussed its metaphysical

meaning in *Zhe-xue Yan-jiu.* No. 3, 1965, translation in *Chinese Studies in Philosophy,* Vol. VI, No. 1, Fall 1974.

41. P'an Hsiao-yuan took a middle position in the debate in his articles, 'The Law of Contradiction should be a Dialectical Unity of Dividing One into Two' and 'Uniting Two into One', *Xin jian-she,* No. 7, July 1964, *SCMM,* No. 433. The summary of the debate from the Maoist viewpoint was presented by a reporter in 'A New Polemic on the Philosophical Front', *Hong Qi,* No. 16, 31 August 1964. Also see Chin Jan, 'Revolutionary Dialectics or Reconciliations of Contradictions?' *Xin Jian-she,* No. 7, 20 July 1964, *SCMM,* No. 434; 'Study and Apply Revolutionary Dialectics Through the Present Polemic in Philosophy', *Zhong-guo qing-nian,* No. 17, 1 September 1964.
42. Chih Heng, 'Master the Dialectical Method of One Dividing into Two', *Hong Qi,* No. 11, 1 November 1974, *SPRCM,* No. 799, p. 2.
43. Yen Feng, 'Master the Dialectical Viewpoint on Unity of Opposites', *Hong Qi,* No. 9, 28 August 1975, *SPRCM,* No. 799, p. 2.
44. Engels described contradiction thus: 'Even simple mechanical change of position can only come about through a body being at one and the same moment of time both in one place and in another place, being in one and the same place and also not in it. And the continuous origination and simultaneous solution of this contradiction is precisely what motion is', *Anti-Duhring,* op. cit., p. 167.
45. 'Dialectics is the teaching which shows how opposites can be and how they happen to be (how they become) *identical*— under what contradictions they are identical, becoming transformed into one another—why the human mind should grasp these opposites not as dead rigid, but as living, conditional, mobile, becoming transformed into one another.' 'Conspectus of Hegel's Science of Logic', V. I. Lenin, *Collected Works,* Vol. 38, p. 109.
46. Mao Tse-tung, 'On Contradiction', op. cit., p. 68.
47. *MMT,* p. 393.
48. *MMT,* p. 392.
49. *MMT,* p. 393.
50. *Anti-Duhring,* op. cit., p. 196.
51. Ibid., p. 188.
52. Ibid., p. 192. Echoing this Mao in 1958: 'The dialectics of Greece, the metaphysics of the Middle Ages, the Restoration... It is the negation of negation', *MMT,* p. 98.
53. 'Conspectus of Hegel's Science of Logic', op. cit., Vol. 38, p. 97.
54. *MMT,* pp. 207-8. 'The other kind of established opposite does not

exist in nature, but it possesses material conditions... What nature does not have can be built artificially, but there must be a material basis.'

55. *MMT*, p. 50.
56. Ibid., p. 98. Forecasting that if China turned chauvinist then its opposite would emerge, Mao has said: 'Should we stop struggling for the construction of a socialist power just because we are afraid of big nation chauvinism? Even if it should appear, it will march toward the opposite direction, and something correct will replace it.'
57. *MMT*, p. 393, Chinese edition, p. 558.
58. '...in nature, in a manner exactly fixed for each individual case, qualitative changes can only occur by the quantitative addition or quantitative subtraction of matter or motion (so-called energy).' Engels, *Dialectics of Nature,* op. cit., p. 63.
59. Ibid., p. 65.
60. *MMT*, p. 62.
61. 'The First Speech (8 May 1958) at the Second Session of the Eighth Party Congress', *MMT*, p. 95.
62. 'Talk on Sakata's Article', 24 August 1964, *MMT*, p. 399.
63. Mao Tse-tung, 'On Contradiction', op. cit., p. 54.
64. Ibid., p. 54.
65. Ibid., p. 30.
66. Lenin, *Philosophical Notebooks,* op. cit., p. 88.
67. Mao Tse-tung, 'On Contradiction', op. cit., p. 35.
68. 'Dialectics is the study of contradiction in the very essence of objects.' Lenin, *Philosophical Notebooks,* op. cit., p. 253.
69. Ibid., p. 36. Actually 'the particular contradiction constitutes the particular essence', Ibid., p. 35.
70. Ibid., p. 35.
71. This is not the same as inductive logic. Induction does not take into account the *process* of interaction within and between things. Therefore, dialectics takes the valid points of both induction (particular to the general) and deduction (general to the particular) and goes beyond them in studying interconnections through the process of analysis and synthesis. Engels discusses this in *Dialectics of Nature,* op. cit., p. 228.
72. Mao Tse-tung, 'On Contradiction', op. cit., p. 40 (emphasis added).
73. Ibid., p. 38.
74. *Anti-Duhring,* op. cit., p. 196.
75. 'And not the Kao Kang kind of centralisation which meant excessive centralisation', *MMT*, pp. 224-5.
76. Mao Tse-tung, 'On Contradiction', op. cit., p. 51. '*Qi-zhong bi-you yi-zhong shi zhu-yao-de mao-dun, you yu ta-de cun-zai he fa-zhan, gui-ding*

huo ying-xing zhe qi-ta mao-dun de cun-zai he fa-zhan.' Wu-pian Zhe-Xue Zhu-zuo, ibid., p. 76.

77. Marx and Engels wrote in the Communist manifesto: 'Hitherto every form of society has been based ... on the antagonism of the oppressing and oppressed classes. But in order to oppress a class, certain conditions must be assured to it under which it can, at least, continue its slavish existence.' *Selected Works,* Vol. I, op. cit, p. 119. Thus by implication, when these conditions change the nature of antagonism also changes.
78. Mao Tse-tung, 'On Contradiction', op. cit., p. 70. *Mao-zhu-xi de wu-pian zhe-xue zhu-zuo,* ibid., p. 104.
79. Ibid., p. 80.
80. This meant 'starting from the desire for unity, resolving contradictions through criticism or struggle and arriving at a new unity on a new basis', ibid., p. 87.
81. Mao Tse-tung, 'On the Correct Handling of Contradictions Among the People', in *Four Essays on Philosophy,* op. cit., p. 120.
82. Maurice Cornforth, 'Mao Tse-tung on Contradiction', *Communist Review.* November 1953, p. 336. The Maoists may not accept Cornforth's interpretation of antagonistic contradictions which says: 'These are contradictions which work out *without antagonism,* by a series of changes and mutual adjustments of their terms... in Socialist Society when all exploitation of man by man is abolished, there are still contradictions, but no antagonism.'
83. In his 1962 essay, 'Contradiction and Overdetermination', Althusser disposes of Mao with two footnotes, one of which says in part: '...Mao's essay, inspired by his struggle against dogmatism in the Chinese Party, remains generally *descriptive,* and in consequence it is in certain respects *abstract.* Descriptive: his concepts correspond to concrete experiences. In part abstract: the concepts, though new and rich in promise, are presented as *specifications* of the *dialectic* in general rather than as *necessary implications* of the Marxist conception of society and history.' (*For Marx.* op. cit., p. 94.)

Appendix

MAO ZEDONG: A BIOGRAPHICAL CHRONOLOGY

I. The Young Mao: 1893–1920

1893 26 December: Born in Shaoshan in Xiangtan country, Hunan province. Father: Mao Jonsheng, mother: Wen Qimei.

1900 Started learning classics in a primary school.

1905 Removed from school by his father and put to agricultural work on the family land.

1907 Made to marry a girl six years elder than himself.

1908 Ran away from home and joined the Tungshan Primary School in Hsinghsiang country. Here he was inspired by the reformist writings of Gang Yuwei and Liang Qichao.

1911 Off to Changsha. Joined the Wuchang Revolutionary Army on 15 October.

1912 Disenchanted with Revolutionary Army because of Yuan Shikai's liaison with warlords. Attended Hunan First Middle School, Changsha.

1913 In Hunan First Normal School where he studied till the end of 1918.

1914 Read F. Paulsen's *A System of Ethics.*

1915 Took part in a campaign against the school authorities opposing the raising of the tuition fees. Elected as the Secretary of the Students Society.

1917 Selected as a model student. Chairman of the Students Society. Met Li Lisan in the summer. Mao and Lai Hesen set up *Xin-min Xue-hui* (New People's Study Society). Greatly influenced by Chen Duxiu's Writings in *Xinn qing-nian* (*New Youth*). Full of excitement he gave the news of the Bolshevik Revolution first his *sao* (elder brother's wife).

1918 Told his friend Xiao You that even though Dr. Sun Yat-sen was a revolutionary leader, his movement lacked military power. Paid attention to physical exercise. Went to Peking and joined the Peking University Library as an Assistant Librarian. Came in contact with prominent University intellectuals like Chen Duxiu. Li Dazhao and Yang Changji. Fell in love with Yang's daughter Yang Kaihui. Did extensive readings. Friends noted his anarchist ideas. Also began to move towards Marxism.

1919 *January*: Attended an anti-warlord conference in Peking.
February: Went to Shanghai and then to Changsha.
March: Bereaved at mother's death (either March or later that year).
May: Organised rallies in Changsha in sequence with the 4 May incident. Formed Hunan Students Organisation.
July: Founded and edited the *Xiang-jiang Ping-lun (Hsiang River Review)*, in which he wrote, 'The Great Union of the Popular Masses'. The paper was closed down after a month.
August: Edited another student paper, *Xin Hunan (New Hunan),* soon suppressed by the authorities.
November: Wrote nine essays on the 'Darkness of the Feudal Society.'
December: Activity participated in organising a student strike against the Provincial Governor. Forced to leave the province.

1920 *February-June*: In Peking and Shanghai. Talks with Ch'en Tu-hsiu in Shanghai on Marxism.
July: Back in Changsha. Set up a radical bookstore with a friend Miss Tao Szu-yung. Became the Director of the Primary School section attached to the First Teachers' Training School, Changsha. Founded Russian Affairs Study Group. Mao has acknowledged the decisive impact of three books that he read around this time: *The Communist Manifesto,* Kautsky's *class Struggle* and Kirkup's *History of Socialism.* From then on, considered himself a Marxist.
September: Mao and his colleagues of the New People's Study Society set up a 'Communist Group' in Changsha
December: Organised a 'Socialist Youth League' in Changsha.

II. Leader of the Chinese Communist Movement: 1921-1949

1921 1 *July*: As one of the twelve delegates, Mao attended the First Congress of the CPC in Shanghai.
October: In Changsha. Secretary of CPC Hunan Committee. Head of Hunan branch of Ali-China Federation of Labour. Married Yang Kaihui.

December: Set up a party cell among the miners of Anyuan collieries.

1922 1 *May:* Organised a general strike in Hunan.

July: Unable to attend the CPC Second Congress (could not spot the venue).

September: With Ho Shusheng founded Self-Education College in Changsha. Along with Li Lisan and Liu Shaoqi organised a strike of the Anyuan miners. Son An-ying born.

November: Resigned directorship of the Primary Section of the First Teachers' Training School in Changsha. Became the General Executive of the Hunan Trade Union Federation and relinquished this post the following year.

1923 *April:* Human's Governor Zhao Hengti ordered Mao's arrest. Mao moved to Shanghai.

June: Elected to the Central Committee at the Third Congress in Canton. Replaced Zhang Guotao as the head of the Party's Organisation Department. Supported Chen Duxiu's resolution favouring KMT-CPC joint control ofTrade Unions as against Chang's line of independent organisation under CPC control. Mao and Yang Kaihui's second child Anqing was born.

1924 *January:* Attended the First Congress of the KMT as a member of the nine-man Hunan delegation. Served as one of the three communists on a nineteen-member Committee to examine the new KMT constitution. Elected as an alternate member of the KMT's Central Executive Committee. Elected to CPC's Politbureau in the Third Conference in Canton.

August: Spoke on the agrarian situation at the Peasant Movement Training Institute in Canton.

Autumn: Active in the Peasant Movement in Hunan. Editor of the KMT journal, *Political Weekly* in Canton.

November-December: Worked among peasants of his native country.

1925 *January:* Could not attend the CPC Fourth Congress because of illness. Not included in the Politbureau.

August: Became Director of the Peasant Movement Training Institute at Canton. Also Secretary, KMT's Propaganda Department.

November-December: Left for Shanghai to campaign against the Hunan Governor for his brutal suppression and killing of the Anyuan miners.

1926 *January:* Delivered a report on propaganda work at the KMT Second Congress in Canton and stressed the work on the peasant front. Assumed the newly created post of the Head of the Peasant Department of the CPC in Shanghai.

March: Wrote 'An Analysis of the Classes in the Chinese Society' whose publication was rejected by Chen Duxiu in the CPC organ *Guide Weekly* for its radical land policy.
May: Expelled from the Propaganda Department post of the KMT.
20 *December:* Delivered the key-note speech to the First Hunan Peasants Association Congress.

1927 *4 January-5 February:* Made an investigation of rural conditions in five countries near Changsha.
March: Published 'Report on an investigation in the Peasant Movement in Hunan'. Sent his wife Yang Kaihui and children to his mother-in-law's house because of the danger of being discovered by the enemy. He was never to see her again.
April: Elected as alternate member of the Central Committee in the CPC Fifth Congress in Wuhan. Elected Chairman of the All-China Peasants Association established immediately after the Congress. Elected to the KMT's five-member Land Committee.
August: Organised peasant movement in Hunan. Participated in the Nanchang Uprising. Elected as alternate member of CPC's Provisional Politbureau led by Chu Qiubai.
September: Led the Autumn Harvest Uprising in Hunan as the Secretary of the CPC's Front Committee. Detained in Liuyang (Hunan) by the local militia, but luckily was not recognised and was able to escape.
October: Established a revolutionary base in Chingkangshan.
November: Removed from the CPC Politbureau for the failure of the Autumn Harvest Uprising. Mao and Yang's third child Anlong was born.

1928 *April:* Met Zhu De and merged their troops into the Fourth Red Army. Probably *June:* Married He Zizhen, a Changsha normal school graduate.

1929 Engaged in expansion and consolidation of the Jiangxi Soviet with Juichin as its centre. Set up a Soviet in Fukien.
September: Suffered from a severe attack of malaria, cured by Dr. Nelson Fu.

1930 *January:* Wrote the famous letter 'A Single Spark can Start a Prairie Fire.'
June: Hesitantly accepted Li Lisan line of attacking cities.
6 November: Became Head of the Front Committee with the Special Committee and Army Committee under Zhu De.

1931 *November:* Elected by the First Congress of Soviets as the Chairman of the Central Soviet Government with headquarters at Juichin.

1932-34 Serious differences with the Party's central leadership headed by Wang Ming.

1934 *January:* Re-elected as the Chairman of the Soviet government at the Second All-China Congress of the Soviet.
October: Evacuation of the Juichin area in the face of KMT's armed attacks. Long March began.

1935 *January:* Elected as Chairman of the CPC Central Committee at the Tsunyi Conference.
July: Elected to the Executive Committee of the Communist International at the latter's Seventh Congress in Moscow.
October: Arrival at Paoan in Shaanxi province.
December: Spoke of broad national revolutionary united front at the Wayaopao Conference of the Politbureau.

1936 *July:* Interviewed by Edgar Snow.
December: Xi'an Incident. Mao wrote 'Strategic Problems of China's Revolutionary War'.

1937 *Moved to Yenan.*
25 August: Published his Ten-Point National Salvation Programme.

1938 *March:* Wrote 'On Protracted War'.
October: Carried the Central Committee against Wang Ming's opposition to his UF tactics at the Sixth Plenum.

1939 Married Lan P'ing later known as Jiang Qing.

1940 *January:* Wrote 'On New Democracy'.

1941 *5 May:* Speech, 'Reform Our Study.'

1942 *1 February:* Speech, 'Rectify the Party's Style of Work', in a newly set up Central Party School—an important document of the Zhengfeng (rectification) campaign.
·*May:* Lectures at the Yenan Forum on Art and Literature.

1943 Brother Mao Tse-min killed by the enemy.
July: Liu Shaoqi described Mao as 'a strong and great revolutionary'. Position within the Party strengthened.

1944 *November:* Met US Ambassador, Hurley in Yan'an.

1945 *April:* Seventh Congress of the CPC, presented report 'On Coalition Government'. Re-elected as Party Chairman by the Seventh Central Committee.
August: Participated along with Zhou Enlai in negotiations with the KMT in Chongqing.

1946 *July:* Gave the strategic directive entitled 'Smith Chiang Kai-shek's Offensive by a War of Self-Defence.'

August: Spoke about 'All reactionaries are paper tigers' in a conversation with Anna Louise Strong.

1947 *March:* Evacuated Yenan under KMT attack.
June: KMT ordered arrest of Mao.
October: Announced the new land law.

1948 *March:* Warned against 'left deviation' in the Party which involved attacks on middle peasants.
May: Gave call for a Political Consultative Conference.
November: Announced the numerical superiority of the PLA to the KMT troops.

1949 *January:* Peking liberated by the PLA.
21 April: Ordered the crossing of the Yangtse river and beginning of the Southern campaign.
September: Addressed the Political Consultative Conference.
1 October: Proclaimed the establishment of the People's Republic of China.

III. Leader of the People's Republic of China: 1949-1976

1949 *16 December:* Arrived in Moscow.

1950 *February:* Sino-Soviet Pact of Friendship, Alliance and Mutual Assistance, and also a trade agreement signed in Moscow.
June: Addressed the Third Plenum of the Central Committee on economic tasks. Land Reform Law adopted.
8 October: Ordered the Chinese People's Volunteers to march to Korea to support Kim Il-sung's forces.

1951 *October:* Publication of Vol. I of *Selected Works of Mao Tse-tung.*
November: Gave instructions on the movement against 'Three Evils' (corruption, waste and bureaucracy).

1952 *6 April:* Gave important instructions on the post-liberation work in Tibet.

1953 *January:* Called for combatting 'bureaucracy, commandism and violations of law and discipline.'
February: Resolution on Mutual Aid Teams adopted.
March: Death of Stalin. Mao paid tribute calling him 'the greatest genius of the present age and great teacher of the world communist movement.'
June: Inner-Party differences with Liu Shaoqi who was for consolidation of the 'new-democratic order' while Mao was in favour of moving towards socialism.
December: Resolution on Agricultural Producers Cooperatives.

1954 *February:* Fourth Plenum of the Central Committee. Mao was away on holiday and was not present.
September: First National People's Congress adopted the new Constitution of the PRC. Mao elected as the Chairman of the Republic. Mao and Khrushchev conferred in Peking with show of great cordiality.

1955 *March:* Addressed the National Conference of the CPC on the economy, the issue of 'Gao Gang and Rao Shushi anti-party alliance.'
July: Report on Agricultural Cooperativisation.
October: Sixth Plenum of the Central Committee—argued for swift transition towards socialist agriculture.

1956 *January:* announced the twelve-year programme of agricultural development. *Socialist Upsurge in China's Countryside* published.
25 April: Made the speech 'On the Ten Major Relationships' at a Politbureau meeting which was officially published only in December 1976.
2 May: Spoke on 'Let Hundred Flowers Blossom and Let Hundred Schools of Thought Contend' at the Supreme State Conference.
September: Presided over the Eighth Party Congress which passed resolutions on the Second Five-Year Plan.

1957 *27 February:* Made a speech, 'On the Correct Handling of Contradictions among the People' at the Supreme State Conference.
November: Visited Moscow to participate in the celebrations of the Fortieth Anniversary of the October Revolution. Made the statement, 'East wind prevails over the west wind.'

1958 *May:* Presided over the Second Session of the Eighth Party Congress which adopted a new General Line for Socialist Construction and chalked out the strategy of the Great Leap Forward.
28 November-10 December: Sixth Plenum of the Central Committee started making adjustments in the economic strategy. Mao resigned Chairmanship of the Republic.

1959 *August:* Eighth Plenum at Lushan. Confrontation with Peng Dehuai on the development strategy. P'eng dismissed from the post of Defence Minister.
September: Khrushchev visited Peking after the Camp David meeting with Eisenhower.

1960 *October:* Publication of Vol. IV of the *Selected Works of Mao Tse-tung.*

1961 14-18 *January:* Presided over the Ninth Plenum which announced basic changes in the 1958 economic strategy.

1962 24-27 *September:* Made an important speech at the Tenth Plenum explaining his thesis on continuing class struggle in Socialist society.

1963 *February:* Mao initiated nation-wide campaign, Socialist Education Movement at a work conference. The campaign had already begun in Hebei and Hunan in autumn of 1962.

April: Gave directive on political work in the army.

May: Prepared the 'Draft Resolution on Some Problems in Current Rural Work.'

1965 *September:* At a Central Work Conference of the CPC (reportedly an enlarged meeting of the Standing Committee of the Politbureau), Mao demanded initiation of a rectification campaign, but failed to carry majority with him.

October end: Left Beijing for Shanghai and other regions. Returned only after nine months.

10 *November:* Shanghai's *Wen-hui Pao* published ideological criticisms against Wu Han's play, *The Dismissal of Hai Jui.*

1966 24 *April:* Approved the report of the investigation committee which recommended the dismissal of the PLA chief, Luo Ruiqing.

16 *May:* Politbureau Circular on the Cultural Revolution, decision on the dismissal of Peng Zhen, Mayor of Peking.

16 *July:* Swam in the Yangtze river.

12 *August:* Presided over the Eleventh Plenum of the Central Committee which adopted a sixteen point decision concerning the Cultural Revolution.

18 *August:* Appeared in the first major Red Guard rally in Tiananmen Square in Beijing.

31 *August:* Described as 'Supreme Commander.'

1967 23 *January:* On Mao's initiative PLA was ordered to intervene 'to support the broad masses of the left.'

1968 13-21 *October:* Presided over the Twelfth Plenum of the Eighth Central Committee which formally dismissed Liu Shaoqi from all posts.

1969 1-23 *April:* Presided over the Ninth Party Congress. The revised Party Constitution announced that Mao Tse tung Thought was the Marxism of the present era.

1970 1 *May:* Had a cordial conversation with the Indian Charge'd Affaires at a reception. This marked the beginning of a new phase of slow normalisation of Sino-Indian relations.

20 *May:* Gave the call 'People of the World!'Unite and Defeat the US Aggressors and all their Running Dogs.'

23 *August-6 September:* Second Plenum of the Ninth Central Committee: Mao circulated a note entitled 'My Views' initiating a

process of correcting some of the deviations of the Cultural Revolution.

1971 *July:* Met US Secretary of State Henry Kissinger. This started the process of normalisation of Sino-US relations.

13 *September:* Lin Biao died in an aircrash after an abortive coup attempt against Mao.

1 *December:* Joint Editorial carried new instructions from Mao, Three Do's and Three Don't's.

1972 21 *February:* Met US President Richard Nixon in Beijing.

27 *September:* Met Japanese Prime Minister Kakuei Tanaka in Beijing.

1973 24-28 *August:* Presided over the Tenth Party Congress. The revised Party constitution removed the mention of Mao Tse-tung Thought being the Marxism of the present era.

1974 *April:* Vice-Premier Deng Xiaoping addressed the Special Session of the UN General Assembly on the *Three Worlds Thesis* of Mao Tse-tung.

1975 *January:* Fourth National People's Congress where Premier Zhou Enlai announced the 'Programme of four modernisation' in the name of Mao Tse-tung who did not attend the session.

1976 8 *January:* Death of Premier Zhou Enlai.

5 *April:* Pro-Zhou demonstrations at the Tiananmen Square in Beijing.

7 *April:* Resolution by the Politbureau in the name of Mao and the Central Committee dismissing Teng from various posts and appointing Hua Guofeng as Premier.

9 *September:* Mao died.

7 *October:* Politbureau decision to arrest the Gang of Four.

1977 *April:* Vol. V of *Selected Works of Mao Tse-tung* published.

August: Eleventh Party Congress. The revised Party constitution declared Mao as the greatest Marxist of the present times.

Bibliography

I. Selected Works of Mao Tse-tung

Ch'en, Jerome, *Mao*, Englewood Cliffs, N.J.: Prentice-Hall, 1969.

——, *Mao Papers*, New Delhi: Oxford University Press, 1970.

Lee, James and Dilley, *Gray Index to Selected Works of Mao Tse-tung and Selected Military Writings of Mao Tse-tung*, Hong Kong: Union Research Institute, 1968.

Mao Tse-tung, *'Bian-zheng-fa Wei-wu-lum'* On Dialectical Materialism in *Minzhu, Democracy*, Shanghai: March 1940. Dennis J. Doolin and Peter J. Golas (translated), *China Quarterly*, No. 19 (July-September 1964).

——, *Four Essays on Philosophy*, Peking, Foreign Languages Press, 1968.

——, 'The Great Union of the Popular Masses', Stuart R. Schram (translated), *China Quarterly*, No. 49 (January-March 1972).

——, *Mao Ze-dong xuan-ji, Selected Works of Mao Tse-tung*, 4 vols., in a one-volume pocket edition, Peking: 1968.

——, *Mao Ze-dong xuan-ji, Selected Works of Mao Tse-tung*, Vol. V, Peking: 1977.

——, *Mao zhu-xi de wu pian zhe-xue-zuo (Five Philosophical Writings of Chairman Mao)*, Peking: 1970. This carries an additional speech by Mao in March 1957 at the CPC's National Propaganda Conference which does not appear in the English edition.

——, *Mao zhu-xi dui Peng, Huang, Chang, Chou fan-dang ji-duan de pi-pan, Chairman Mao's Criticism of the P'eng-Huang-Chang-Chou Anti-Party Clique*, c. 1967. Translations in *Chinese Law and Government*, Vol. I, No. 4, Winter 1968-69.

——, *Miscellany of Mao Tse-tung Thought*, translations from the Red Guard collections in 1967 and 1969 of Chairman Mao's writings *Mao Ze-dong si-xiang wan-sui*, US Department of Commerce, Joint Publication

Research Service, *JPRS,* Nos. 61269-1 and 61269-2, 2 February 1974.

——, *Mo Takuto shu (Mao's Collected Works),* 10 vols., Takeuchi Minoru (ed.) Tokyo: 1971-72.

——, Speeches at the Supreme State Conferences and Talks with Foreign Visitors, *Chinese Law and Government,* Vol. IX, No. 3, Fall 1976.

——, *Selected Works of Mao Tse-tung,* 4 vols. Peking: Foreign Languages Press, 1965 reprint.

——, *Selected Works of Mao Tse-tung,* Vol. V, Peking: 1977.

——, *Quotations from Chairman Mao Tse-tung,* Peking: foreign Languages Press, 1966.

Schram, Stuart R. (translated and with introduction), *Mao Tse-tung: Basic Tactics,* N.Y., London: Praeger and Pall Mall Press, 1966, 1967.

——, *The Political Thought of Mao Tse-tung,* New York: Praeger, revised edition, 1969. Many of the pieces here are Schram's own translations of Mao's original publications. Schram frequently points out the discrepancies between the official Selected Works and the original versions.

——*Mao Tse-tung Unrehearsed: Talks and Letters 1956-71,* London: Penguin, 1974.

Starr, John Bryan and Dyer, Nancy Ann, *Post-Liberation Works of Mao zedong,* Berkeley: Center for Chinese Studies, 1976. (Index)

II. Mao and China's New-Democratic Revolution

Adie, W.A.C., *Chinese Strategic Thinking under Mao Tse-tung,* Canberra: Australian National University Press, 1973.

Brandt, Conrad *et.al.* (eds.), *A Documentary History of Chinese Communism,* London: Allen and Unwin, 1952.

Ch'en, Jerome, *Mao and the Chinese Revolution,* London: Oxford University Press, 1965.

Chen, Theodore H.E. (ed.), *The Chinese Communist Regime: Documents and Commentary,* New York: Praeger, 1967.

Chiang Kai-shek, *China's Destiny,* New York: Roy Publishers, 1947.

Compton, Boyd (ed.), *Mao's China: Party Reform Documents,* Seattle: University of Washington Press: 1966.

d'Encausse, Helen C. and Schram, Stuart R. (eds.) *Marxism and Asia,* London: Allen Lane, The Penguin Press, 1969.

Degras, Jane (ed.), *The Communist International 1919-1943 Documents,* London: Oxford University Press, 1956.

Deshingkar, Giri, 'Maoist Strategic Doctrine', *India International Centre Quarterly,* Vol. 3, No. 4, 1976.

Dorrill, William F., 'The Fukien Rebellion and the CCP: A Case of Maoist Revisionism', *China Quarterly,* No. 37, February-March 1969.

Griffith, Samuel, *Mao Tse-tung on Guerrilla Warfare,* New York: Praeger, 1961.

Han Su-yin, *The Morning Deluge: Mao Tse-tung and the Chinese Revolution, 1893-1953,* London: Jonathan Cape, 1972.

Heinzig, Dieter, 'The Otto Braun Memoirs and Mao's Rise to Power', *China Quarterly,* No. 46, April-June 1971.

Ho Kan-chin, *A History of the Modern Chinese Revolution,* Peking: Foreign Languages Press, 1960.

Hsu Kwan-San, 'Liu Shao-chi and Mao Tse-tung 1922-1947', *Chinese Law and Government,* Vol. III, Nos. 2 and 3, Summer-Fall, 1970.

Hsueh Chun-tu, *Revolutionary Leaders of Modern China,* London: Oxford University Press, 1970.

Hu Hua *et. al.* (eds.), *Zhong-guo Xin-min-zhu-yi Geming de Can-Kao Zi-liao (Reference Materials on the History of the New Democratic Revolution),* Shanghai: 1951.

Johson, Chalmers, *Peasant Nationalism and Communist Power,* Stanford: Stanford University Press, 1962.

Kuo, Warren, *Analytical History of the CCP,* 4 vols., Taipei: Institute of International Relations, 1966.

Lin Piao, *Long Live Victory of the People's War,* Peking: Foreign Languages Press, 1965.

Lowe, Donald M., *The Functions of 'China' in Marx, Lenin and Mao,* Berkeley and Los Angeles: The University California Press, 1966.

Lu Wen, 'A Refutation of Comrade Yang Hsien-chen's Absurd Views which Distort New Democracy to Mean Capitalism', *Jing-ji Yan-jiu, Economic Research,* No. 2 (20 February 1965); *Selections from China Mainland Megazines, SCMM,* No. 464, 12 April 1965.

Mine, Hilary, 'People's Democracy and the Dictatorship of the Proletariat', *World News and Views,* Vol. 30, No. 17, 29 April 1950.

Mohanty, Manoranjan, 'Maoist Revolutionary Strategy: A Reinterpretation', *The Institute for Defence Studies and Analysis Journal,* Vol. II, No. 3, January 1970.

——, *Revolutionary Violence: A study of the Maoist Movement in India,* New Delhi: Sterling, 1977.

Ng, Yong-sang, 'The Poetry of Mao Tse-tung', *China Quarterly,* No. 13, January-March 1963.

North, Robert, *Moscow and the Chinese Communists,* Stanford: Stanford University Press, 1963.

Pak, Hyobam (ed.), *Documents of the Chinese Communist Party 1927-1930.* Hong Kong: Union Research Institute, 1971.

Rue, John E. *Mao Tse-tung in Opposition 1927-35*, Stanford: Published for the Hoover Institution on War, Revolution and Peace, Stanford University Press, 1966.

Schram, Stuart R., 'From the "Great Union of the Popular Masses" to the "Great Alliance"', *China Quarterly*, No. 49, January-March 1972.

——, *Mao Tse-tung*, London: Penguin, 1967.

——, 'On the Nature of Mao Tse-tung's "Deviation" in 1927', *China Quarterly*, No. 18, April-June 1964.

Schwarts, Benjamin, *Chinese Communism and the Rise of Mao*, New York: Harper, second edition, 1958.

——, 'The Legend of "the Legend of Maoism"', *China Quarterly*, No. 2, April-June 1960.

Selden, Mark, *The Yenan Way in Revolutionary China*, Cambridge, Massachusetts: Harvard University Press, 1971.

Sen, Mohit, *The Chinese Revolution and Maoism*, New Delhi: C.P.I., 1975.

Snow, Edgar, *Red Star over China*, New York: Penguin, revised edition, 1972.

Sobolov, A., 'People's Democracy as a Form of Political Organization of Society', *Communist Review*, London: January 1952.

Swarup, Shanti, *A Study of the Chinese Communist Movement 1927-35*, London: Oxford University Press, 1966.

Van Slyke, Lyman P. (ed.), *The Chinese Communist Movement: A Report of the United States War Department, July 1945*, Stanford: Stanford University Press, 1968.

——, *Enemies and Friends: United Front in Chinese Communist History*, Stanford: Stanford University Press, 1967.

Vladimirov, P.P., *China's Special Area*, Bombay: Allied Publishers, 1974.

Wilson, Dick, *The Long March 1935*, New York: Avon Books, 1971.

Wittfogel, Karl A., 'The Legend of Maoism', *China Quarterly*, No. 2, April-June 1960.

Wittfogel, Karl A., Schwartz, Benjamin, and Sjaardema, Henryk, 'Maoism'

——, 'Legend', or 'Legend of a "Legend"', *China, Quarterly*, No. 4, October-December 1960.

Yakhontoff, Victor, *The Chinese Soviets*, New York: Coward-McCann, 1934.

Yin Ching-yao, 'Mao Tse-tung's Theory of Two Stages and Two Alliances', *Issues and Studies*, Vol. IX, No. 3, December 1972.

III. Mao and the Socialist Revolution

Archer, Jules, *Mao Tse-tung: A Biography*, New York: Pocket Books, 1972.

Barnett, A.D.(ed.), *Chinese Communist Politics in Action*, Seattle: University of Washington Press, 1969.

Baum, Richard, *Prelude to Revolution: Mao, the party and the Peasant Question 1962-1966,* New York: Columbia University Press, 1975.

Bandyopadhyaya, Jayantanuja, *Mao Tse-tung and Gandhi,* Bombay: Allied, 1973,

Bennett, Gordon, 'China's Continuing Revolution: Will it be Permanent?', *Asian Survey,* Vol. X, No. 1, January 1970.

Bowie, R.R. and Fairbank, J.K. (eds.), *Communist China 1955-1959:Policy Documents with Analysis,* Cambridge, Massachusetts: Harvard University, Press, 1962.

Bridgham, Philip, 'Mao's Cultural Revolution in 1967: The Struggle to Seize Power', *China Quarterly,* No. 34, April-June 1968.

——, 'Mao's "Cultural Revolution": Origin and Development', *China Quarterly,* No. 29, January-March 1967

Ch'en Shao-Yu (Wang Ming), *China: Cultural Revolution or Counterrevolution?*, Moscow: 1969.

Chao Yang, 'Conscientiously Study Chairman Mao's Theory of Continuing the Revolution', *Peking Review,* 20 January 1970.

Chen Yung-ping, *Chinese Political Thought: Mao Tse-tung and Liu Shao-ch'i,* The Hague: Najhoff, 1966.

Cohen, Arthur, *The Communism of Mao Tse-tung,* Chicago: The University of Chicago Press, 1964.

Delyusin, Lev, *Socio-Political Essence of Maoism,* New Delhi: Sterling, 1977.

Deshpande, G.P., *China's Cultural Revolution,* Bombay: Economic and Political Weekly, 1971.

Documents of Chinese Communist Party Central Committee: September 1956-April 1969, Hong Kong: Union Research Institute, 1971.

Documents of the Eighth Congress of the Communist Party of China, Peking: Foreign Languages Press, 1956.

Documents of the Second Session of the Eighth Congress of the Communist Party of China, Peking, FLP, 1958.

Documents of the Ninth Congress of the Communist Party of China, Peking: FLP, 1969.

Documents of the Tenth Congress of the Communist Party of China, Peking: FLP, 1973.

Documents of the Eleventh Congress of the Communist Party of China, Peking: FLP, 1977.

Domes, Jurgen, *The Internal Politics of China 1949-72,* London: C. Hurst and Co., 1973.

Dorrill, William F., 'Transfer of Legitimacy in the Chinese Communist Party: Origins of the Maoist Path', *China Quarterly,* No. 36., October-December 1968.

Dutt, Gargi, and Dutt, V.P., *China's Cultural Revolution,* Bombay: Asia Publishing House, 1970.

Fitzgerald, C.P., *Mao Tse-tung and China,* London: Hodder and Stoughton, 1976.

Gray, Jack and Cavendish, Patrick, *Chinese Communism in Crisis,* London: Pall Mall Press, 1968.

Gupta, Krishna Prakash, 'Marxism-Leninism Mao Tse-tung Thought: Visions and Revisions', *China Report,* Vol. X, Nos. 5 and 6, September-December 1974.

Han Su-yin, *The Wind in the Tower: Mao Tse-tung 1953-1975,* London: Jonathan Cape, 1975.

Hsiung, James Chieh, *Ideology and Practice: The Evolution of Chinese Communism,* New York: Praeger, 1970.

Ito Kikuzo and Minoru Shibota, 'The Dilemma of Mao Tse-tung', *China Quarterly,* No. 35, July-September 1968.

Jain, J.P. *After Mao What?,* New Delhi: Radiant Publishers, 1976.

Johnson, Chalmers (ed.), *Ideology and Politics in Contemporary China,* Seattle: University of Washington Press, 1973.

Lee, Chen-Chung, 'Trotsky's Theory of "Permanent Revolution", and Mao Tse-tung's Theory of the "Continuous Revolution"', Part I and Part II, *Issues and Studies,* Vol. VIII, Nos. 7 and 8, April and May 1972, Part III, *Issues and Studies* Vol. VIII No.11, August 1972, Part IV in Vol. IX, No. 2, November 1972.

Leo, Goodstadt, *Mao Tse-tung: The Search for Plenty,* London: Longman, 1972.

Levy, Richard, 'New Light on Mao: His Views on the Soviet Union's Political Economy', *China Quarterly,* No. 61, January-March 1975.

Lewis, John W., *Leadership in Communist China,* Ithaca: Cornell University Press, 1963.

——(ed.), *Party Leadership and Revolutionary Power in China,* London: Cambridge University Press, 1970.

Lifton, Robert J., *Revolutionary Immortality: Mao Tse-tung and the Chinese Cultural Revolution,* New York: Random House, 1968.

Maitan, Livio, *Party, Army and Masses in China,* London: NLB, 1976.

Meisner, Maurice, 'Leninism and Maoism : Some Populist Perspectives on Marxism-Leninism in China', *China Quarterly,* No. 45, January-March 1971.

——, 'Utopian Goals and Ascetic Values in Chinese Communist Ideology', *Journal of Asian Studies,* Vol. XXVIII, No. 1, November 1968.

Present-day China: Socio-economic Problems (Collected Articles), Moscow: Progress Publishers, 1975.

Rice, Edward, *Mao's Way,* Berkeley: University of California Press, 1972.

Robinson, Thomas (ed.), *China's Cultural Revolution,* Berkeley: University of California Press, 1971.

Scalapino, Robert A. (ed.) *Elites in the People's Republic of China,* Seattle: University of Washington Press, 1972.

Schram, Stuart (ed.), *Authority, Participation and Cultural Change in China,* London: Cambridge University Press, 1973.

Schram, Stuart R., 'Mao Tse-tung and Liu Shao-chi 1939-1968', *Asian Survey,* Vol. XII, No. 4, April 1972.

——, 'Mao Tse-tung and the Theory of Permanent Revolution', *China Quarterly,* No. 46, April-June 1971.

Schurmann, Franz, *Ideology and Organization in Communist China,* Berkeley: University of California Press, 1968, revised edition.

Schwartz, Benjamin, *Communism and China: Ideology in Flux,* Cambridge: Massachusetts: Harvard University Press, 1968.

Sladkovsky, M.I. (ed.), *Leninism and Modern China's Problems,* Moscow: Progress Publishers, 1972.

Snow, Edgar, *The Long Revolution,* New York: Random House, 1971.

Solomon, Richard H., *Mao's Revolution and the Chinese Political Culture,* Berkeley: University of California Press, 1971.

Starr, John B., 'Conceptual Foundations of Mao Tse-tung's Theory of Continuous Revolution', *Asian Survey,* Vol. XI, No. 6, June 1971.

——, *Ideology and Culture: An Introduction to the Dialectic of Contemporary Chinese Politics,* New York: Harper and Row, 1973.

——, 'Revolution in Retrospect: The Paris Commune Through Chinese Eyes', *China Quarterly,* No. 49, January-March 1971.

Tan Chung, 'Maoism to Remember', *Institute for Defence Studies and Analyses (IDSA) Journal,* Vol. IX, No. 3, January-March 1977.

Townsend, James, *Politics in China,* Boston: Little, Brown, 1974.

Uhalley, Jr., Stephen, *Mao Tse-tung: A Critical Biography,* New York: New Viewpoints, 1975.

Von der Kroef, Justus M., 'Lenin, Mao and Aidit', *China Quarterly,* No. 10, April-June 1962.

Wakeman, Jr., Frederic, 'The Use and Abuse of Ideology in the Study of Contemporary China', *China Quarterly,* No. 61, January-March 1975.

Wheelwright, E.L. and McFarlane, Bruce, *The Chinese Road to Socialism,* New York: Monthly Review Press 1970.

Yeh Ch'ing (Fen Tso-hsuan) *Inside Mao Tsu-tung Thought* by Stephen Pan, T.H. Tshan (translated and edited), Hocksmille, New York: Exposition Press, 1975.

IV. Maoist World-View

Boorman, Howard L., 'Mao Tse-tung as Historian', *China Quarterly*, No. 28, October-December 1966.

Boardman, Robert, *Britain and the People's Republic of China 1949-74*, London: Macmillan, 1976.

Bressi, Giovanni, 'China and Western Europe', *Asian Survey*, Vol. XII, No. 10, October 1972.

Chiao Kuan-hua, *Speech by Chiao Kuan-hua*, Chairman of the Delegation of the People's Republic of China at the Plenary Meetings of the Sessions of the UN General Assembly, 1971, 1972, 1973, 1974, 1975 and 1976, Peking: FLP.

Clubb, O. Edmund, *China and Russia*, New York: Columbia University Press, 1971.

Cranmer-Byng, John, 'The Chinese View of Their Place in the World: An Historical Perspective', *China Quarterly*, No. 53, January-March 1973.

Dai Shen-yu, *China, the Superpowers and the Third World: A Handbook on Comparative World Politics*, Hong Kong: Chinese University, 1971.

Dutt, V.P., *China and the World*, New York: Praeger, 1966.

Eto, Shinkichi, 'Motivation and Tactics of Peking's New Foreign Policy', *China in the Seventies*, Hamburg: Institute of Asian Affairs, 1975.

Fitzgerald, C.P., *The Chinese View of Their Place in the World*, London: Oxford University Press, 1955.

Ginsberg, Norton, 'On the Chinese Perception of a World Order', Tang Tsou and Ho Ping-ti (eds.) *China in Crisis*, Chicago: University of Chicago Press, 1968, Vol. 2.

Girling, John, *Peking and People's Wars*, London: George Allen and Unwin, 1969.

Gittings, John, 'New Light on Mao: His View of the World', *China Quarterly*, No. 60, October-December 1974.

——, *Survey of the Sino-Soviet Dispute 1963-1967*, London: Oxford University Press, 1968.

——, *The World and China 1922-1972*, London: Eyre Methuen 1974.

The great Debate, Bombay: People's Publishing House, 1964.

Hsiao, Gene T. (ed.), *Sino-American Detente and Its Policy Implications*, New York: Praeger, 1974.

Jain, J.P., *China in World Politics*, New Delhi: Radiant, 1976.

Larkin, Bruce, *China and Africa 1949-1970*, Berkeley: University of California Press, 1971.

Lawrence, Alan, *China's Foreign Relations Since 1949*, London: Routledge and Kegan Paul, 1975.

Lovelace, Daniel, *China and 'People's War' in Thailand 1964-1969*, Berkeley: Centre of Chinese Studies, China Research Monographs, 1971.

More on the Great Debate, Bombay: People's Publishing House, 1964.

Mozingo, David, *Chinese Policy toward Indonesia 1949-1967*, Ithaca: Cornell University Press, 1976.

Ojha, Ishwar C., *Chinese Foreign Policy in an Age of Transition,* Boston: Beacon Press, 1971.

Scalapino, Robert A., *Asia and the Road Ahead: Issues for the Major Powers,* Berkeley: University of California Press, 1975.

Schurmann, Franz, *The Logic of World Power: An Inquiry into the Origins, Currents and Contradictions of World Politics,* New York: Pantheon, 1974.

Service, John S., *The Amerasia Papers: Some Problems of US-China Relations,* Berkeley: University of California, Centre for Chinese Studies, 1971.

Sinha, Mira, 'The Maoist World System and India's Place in It', *The Institute for Defence Studies and Analyses Journal,* Vol. III, No. 3, January 1971.

Speeches welcoming the Delegation of the PRC by the UN General Assembly President and Representative of Various Countries at the Plenary Meeting of the Twenty-sixth Session of the UN General Assembly, 15 November 1971, Peking: FLP, 1971.

Tang Tsou, *America's Failure in China,* Chicago: University of Chicago Press, 1963.

Teng Hsiao-ping, 'Speech at the Special Session of the UN General Assembly', *Peking Review,* No. 15, 12 April 1974.

Taylor, Jay, *China and Southeast Asia: Peking's Relations with Revolutionary Movements,* New York: Praeger, 1974.

Treadgold, Donald (ed.), *Soviet and Chinese Communism: Similarities and Differences,* Seattle: University of Washington Press, 1967.

US Department of State, *The China White Paper,* 2 vols., Stanford: Stanford University Press, 1967.

Van Ness, Peter, *Revolution and China's Foreign Policy: Peking's Support for Wars of National Liberation,* Berkeley: University of California Press, 1970.

Whiting, Allen, *The Chinese Calculus of Deterrence: India and Indo-China,* Ann Arbor: University of Michigan Press, 1975.

——, 'New Light on Mao: Quemoy, 1968: Mao's Miscalculations', *China Quarterly,* No. 62, April-June 1975.

Wilcox, Francis (ed.), *China and the Great Powers: Relations with the United States, the Soviet Union and Japan,* New York: Praeger, 1974.

Yin Ching-yao, 'Peiping's Foreign Policy and Tactics', *Issues and Studies,* Vol. VII. No. 7, April 1971.

Zagoria, Donald S., *The Sino-Soviet Conflict 1956-61,* New York: Atheneum, 1969, revised edition.

V. On Dialectical Materialism

'A New Polemic on the Philosophical Front', *Hong Qi,* No. 16, 31 August 1964, translation in *SCMM,* No. 434.

Althusser, Louis, 'Contradiction and Overdetermination', *New Left Review,* No. 41, January-February 1967.

——, *For Marx,* New York: Vintage, 1970.

——, 'Reply to John Lewis (Self-criticism)', *Marxism Today,* No. 10, October 1972.

Bhattacharya, Janaki Ballabva, *Negation,* Calcutta: Indian Studies: Past and Present, Sanskrit Pustak Bhandar, 1965.

Chang Tsu-Ch'eng 'Combining Two into One Means No Revolution', *Hong Qi,* Nos. 23-24, 22 December 1964, translation in *SCMM,* No. 453.

Chih Heng, 'Master the Dialectical Method of One Dividing into Two', *Hong Qi,* No. 11, 1 November 1974, *Selection from People's Republic of China Magazines, SPRCM,* No. 799.

Chih Jan, 'Revolutionary Dialectics or Reconciliations of Contradictions?', *Xin Jian-she,* No. 7, 20 July 1964, translation in *SCMM,* No. 434.

Chomsky, Noam, *Problems of Knowledge and Freedom,* London: Fontana, 1972.

Cohen, Arthur, *The Communism of Mao Tse-tung,* Chicago and London: University of Chicago Press, 1964.

Colletti, Lucio, 'Marxism and the Dialectic', *New Left Review,* No. 93, September-October 1975.

Cornforth, Maurice, *Dialectical Materialism,* Calcutta: National Book Agency, 1957.

——, 'Mao Tse-tung on Contradiction', *Communist Review,* November 1953.

——, 'Some Questions about Laws of Dialectics', *Marxism Today,* Vol. 9, No. 11, November 1965.

Doolin, Dennis and Golas, Peter, 'On Contradiction' in the Light of Mao Tse-tung's Essay 'On Dialectical Materialism', *China Quarterly,* No. 19, July-September 1964.

Engels, F., *Anti-Duhring,* Moscow: FLPH, 1954.

——, *Dialectics of Nature,* Moscow: FLPH, 1954.

Freiberg, J.W., 'The Dialectic in China: Maoist and Daoist', *Bulletin of Concerned Asian Scholars,* Vol. 9, No. 1, January-March 1977.

Glaberman, Martin, 'Mao as a Dialectician', *International Philosophical Quarterly,* Vol. 8, March 1968.

Hoffman, John, *Marxism and the Theory of Praxis,* London: Lawrence and Wishart, 1975.

Holubnychy, Vsevolod, 'Mao Tse-tung's Materialistic Dialectics', *The China, Quarterly,* No. 19, July-September 1964.

Hyppolite, Jean, *Studies on Marx and Hegel,* New York: Harper Torchbooks, 1969.

Jay, Martin, *The Dialectical Imagination: The Frankfurt School and the Institute of Social Research 1923-1950,* Boston: 1973.

Jordan, Z.A., *The Evolution of Dialectical Materialism,* New York: St. Martin's Press, 1967.

Klugmann, James, 'Stalin and Dialectical Materialism', *Communist Review,* April and June 1953.

Korsch, Karl, *Marxism and Philosophy,* New York: Monthly Review Press, 1970.

Lefevre, Henri, *Dialectical Materialism,* London: Jonathan Cape, 1968.

Lenin, V.I. 'Conspectus of Lectures on the History of Philosophy', *Philosophical Notebooks—Collected Works,* Moscow: FLPH, 1963, Vol. 38.

——, *Materialism and Empirio-criticism,* Moscow: FLPH, 1964.

Lewis, John, 'The Althusser Case', *Marxism Today,* Vol. 15, Nos. 1 and 2, January and February 1972.

——, 'Discussion on the Laws of Dialectics', *Marxism Today,* Vol. 10. No. 1, January 1966.

Marcuse, Herbert, *Negations: Essays in Critical Theory,* London: Penguin, 1972.

Marx and Engels, *The German Ideology,* Moscow: FLPS, 1959.

P'an Hsiao-yuan, 'The Law of Contradiction Should be a Dialectical Unity of "Dividing One into Two", and "Uniting Two into One"' *Xin Jian-she, New Constructions,* No. 7, 20 July 1964, translation in *SCMM,* No. 433.

P'an Yu-kuo, 'Dividing One into Two versus Grasping the Living Thought', *Hong Qi,* No. 1, 6 January 1965, translation in *SCMM,* No. 454.

Rue, John E., 'Is Mao Tse-tung's "Dialectical Materialism" a Forgery?', *The Journal of Asian Studies,* Vol. XXVI, No. 3, May 1967.

Rumiantsev, 'Maoism and the Anti-Marxist Nature of Maoist Philosophy', *Kommunist,* No. 2, 1968, translation in *Chinese Studies in History and Philosophy,* Vol. II, No. 4, Summer, 1969.

Sartre, Jean-Paul, *Search for a Method,* New York: Vintage, 1968.

Schram, Stuart, 'Mao Tse-tung as a Marxist Dialectician', *China Quarterly,* Vol. 29, January-March 1967.

Serving the People with Dialectics, Peking: FLP, 1972.

Sharma, Dhirendra, *The Negative Dialectics: A Study of the Negative Dialecticism in Indian Philosophy,* New Delhi: Sterling, 1974.

Singh, Randhir, *Reason, Revolution and Political Theory,* Bombay: PPH, second edition, 1977.

Stalin, J.V., *Dialectical and Historical Materialism,* Calcutta: National Book Agency, 1975.

'Study and Apply Revolutionary Dialectics through the present Polemic in Philosophy', *Zhong-guo Qing-nian,* No. 17, 1 September 1964.

'Study Well the Theory of Knowledge of Dialectical Materialism', *Hong Qi,* No. 1, January 1971, *SCMM,* No. 698, 29 January 1971.

Three Major Struggles on China's Philosophical Front, Peking: FLP, 1973.

Welter, Gustav Andreas, *Dialectical Materialism: A Historical and Systematic Survey of Philosophy in the Soviet Union,* New York: Praeger, 1958.

Yen Feng, 'Master the Dialectical Viewpoint on Unity of Opposites', *Hong Qi,* No. 9, 28 August 1975, *Selections from People's Republic of China Press, SPRCP,* No. 841.

Index

Africa 25, 65, 142-3, 146, 154-5
Afro-Asian nations 140
agrarian armed struggle 31-2
agrarian reforms in the Soviet areas 32
agrarian revolution 44, 127
agricultural cooperatives 85
Albania 61
Algeria 25
Althusser, the French Marxist 168-9, 201-2
American imperialism 156
American invasion 64
American presence in Western Europe 160
Angola 25
antagonism 59, 193
antagonistic 196
anti-colonial struggle 37
    and anti-feudal struggle 18
anti-imperialist 156
    and anti-feudal 33
    character 29
    contradiction 143, 153
    mobilisation 42
    revolution 142
    struggle 139, 147, 152, 156
    united front 157
anti-Japanese military movement 32
anti-Japanese united front 32-3
anti-KMT united front 34
anti-rightist campaigns 89
armed struggle 20, 50, 149
    against imperialism and colonialism 140
ASAFLA 142-3, 147, 156
Asia 25, 65, 143, 146, 154
    national liberation movements in 142
atom bomb 144

Bangladesh 160
Basic Line 79-80, 92, 114, 120, 129
    of the CPC 148
Bolshevik revolution 25, 29, 138
Borodin 31
bourgeois ideology 116
bourgeois ownership 127
bourgeois-democratic revolution 37, 126
bourgeoisie 118, 120-21
    and the proletariat, struggle between 121
bureaucratic-capitalists 198

capitalism 107, 154, 187, 189
in agriculture 45
in China 39
to socialism 81, 145
capitalist restoration 123, 150
capitalist road 113
capitalist trends 129
Chang Hsueh-liang 33
Che Guevara 54-5
Chen Boda 79, 84, 105, 120-21
Chiang Kai-shek 30-31, 35
strategy 32
Chile 160
China 25, 36, 110, 126, 128, 143, 157, 161
against the Japanese 139
and the Soviet Union, relations between 94
comprador and landlord classes 54
counter-revolution in 198
current world-view 160
Democratic League 58
development strategy 192
economic and military backwardness 157
foreign policy 150, 162
performance 158
handicrafts and capitalist industry 85
international struggle against revisionism 148
new democratic revolution 63, 155
people's democratic revolution 142, 146
policy in Western Europe 161
political integration of 29
provisional constitution 57
revisionism in 79
revolutionary 50
experience 25
people's war 179
slower economic growth 63
socialism in 197
socialist construction in 18
socialist revolution and construction in 80
view of the world 153
working classes 198
work-motivation, service mentality, solidarity 48
China-India war 94
Chinese communist experiences 166
Chinese Communist Movement 1921-1949 210
Chinese communist outlook 179
Chinese communist practice 48, 168
Chinese communist theoreticians 81
Chinese communist writings terms 76
Chinese communists 21, 59, 114, 128-9, 165, 201
Chinese economy 130
Chinese experience 25
Chinese foreign policy 20
behaviour 160
Chinese history 18
Chinese landlords 194
Chinese masses 40
Chinese new-democratic revolution 62
Chinese peasantry 44
Chinese people and Marxism-Leninism 43
Chinese people's democratic revolution 64
Chinese press 104
Chinese revolution 18, 20-21, 26, 28, 30, 37, 41, 43-4, 46, 62-3, 127, 138, 147

Chinese revolutionary 52, 140, 144
 environment 39
 experiences 20
 movement 18, 48, 173
 strategy 176
 war 64
Chinese society 18
 'middle elements' in the 41
Chinese Soviet government 54
Chinese Soviet Republic 32
Chinese working class 56
Chinese world-view 149, 153, 159-60
civil war 33
 and the National War 50
 between the KMT and the CPC 51
class conciliation embodied 156
class contradiction and class struggle 113
class contradictions 97
class struggle 18, 87-9, 95-7, 99-100, 106, 109-10, 115-8, 120, 122-3, 126, 128, 144, 149, 156, 167, 171, 173-4
Colletti, Lucio 169-70, 183
colonial and feudal oppression 25
colonialism 155, 157
Common Programme 57
 of the CPPCC 158
Communist Parties in the agrarian, anti-feudal, anti-imperialist countries 62
Communist Party 125
 of China (CPC) 18
 of India (CPI) 63
 of India (Marxist) (CPI-M) 64
 of the Soviet Union 63
comprador bourgeoisie 40, 138
Confucianism 21
Confucius 105
consciousness 125
 and thinking 124
continuous revolution 128
contradictions 149, 152-3, 156, 169, 177-8, 189, 192-3
 between the US and the USSR 152
 correctly 158
 focus of 142
 principal 155-6, 195
Cornforth, Maurice 168-9
counter-revolution 88
counter-revolutionary war 139
CPC 30, 34, 40, 46, 80, 85, 89, 93, 116, 127-8, 138, 141-2, 145, 151, 154, 173, 187, 193, 202
 and the CPSU 141
 Basic Line 113
 ideological documents of the 143
 leadership 19, 41
 new Constitution of the 118
 world-view of the 139-40, 158
 original world-view 159
CPSU 142, 145
 leaders 144
Cuban missiles crisis 94
Cultural Revolution 48, 60, 82, 87, 97-8, 101-2, 105-6, 109-10, 117-8, 120, 171, 199, 202
 as idealistic deviation 128
 beginning of the 119
cultural struggle 106
Czechoslovakia 113, 148

Debray, Regis 55
Democratic League 57
Democratic Party of Workers and Peasants 57

democratic revolution 126
Deng Xiaoping 109-10, 151, 156-7, 173
dialectical materialism 171, 174
dialectical materialist formulation 145
dialectics 202
dictatorship 108
Dimitrov, Georgi 34
Dimitrov on people's democracy 61

East European revolutions 62
East Wind 142, 155
Eastern Europe 155
eight-grade wage system 107
Eighth Party Congress 80-1, 84, 90, 92, 120-21
    Communique 90
    of the CPC 82
Engels 21, 103, 114, 166, 168, 175, 182, 184, 186, 188, 190, 193-4, 201-2
equilibrium and socialist revolution 127
Europe 151, 154
    eastern 61
European Economic Community 155, 160
European Marxists 167-8, 200
exploiting and exploited classes 119, 144

fascist Germany 138
feudalism 39-40, 138, 195, 197
    to communism 127
foreign imperialism 95
four-class united front 65
four laws of dialectics 167
France 161
fundamental contradiction 141-3, 180, 196

Gao Gang 117, 191
General Line 79, 83-4, 90, 121
General Line of Socialist Construction (GLSC) 77, 79
GPCR 102, 105, 118, 148
Great Chinese Revolution of 1925-27 33
Great Leap Forward 174, 179
    strategy 182
Great Production Movement of 1940 55
Great Proletarian Cultural Revolution (GPCR) 84, 98
guerilla warfare 52, 55-6
Gulf states 160

harmonious 116
Hegel 184, 186, 193
Hegelian idealism 168
Hegelian laws of dialectics 178
Hegel's three famous laws 176
Hinduism 22
Holubnychy 166
Hua Guofeng 26
Hungarian events 86
Hungary 113

idealism 124
ideological criticism 119
ideological struggle 89, 99, 117
imperialism 40, 54, 138, 143, 145, 149, 152, 180, 197
    and colonialism 139
    and feudalism 18
    and feudalism, fighting against 41
    and reaction 144
    and social imperialism 153

and social imperialism 153
and the oppressed nations 155
imperialist aggression 195
imperialist and social imperialist countries 149, 152, 159
imperialist power 189
imperialist system 144
India 25
Indian Ocean 151
Indo-China 25, 63
liberation of 155
victory of liberation forces of 64
inner-party struggle 117-8, 129
international anti-imperialist united front 142, 147, 155
international communist movement 19
international revolutionary movements 140
International United Front 138

Japan 33, 40
Japanese aggression 27, 36
in Manchuria 32
Japanese armed forces 36
Japanese forces and the KMT forces 55
Japanese imperialism 36
Japanese troops 45
Jiang Qing 156
Jiangxi Soviet 54-5

Kant 183
Kardelj 86
KMT 32, 36, 40
against the Japanese 34
forces 54
knowledge-practice-knowledge cycle 176
Korean war 139-40
Kuomintang Revolutionary Committee 58

land reforms 35
landlords 32, 39, 194
and big bourgeoisie 61, 117
Latin America 25, 142-3, 146, 154
Law in Marxist Tradition 175
Law of Analysis 167, 176, 180, 190, 192
and Synthesis 200
Law of Particularity 167, 192-3, 199, 201
Law of Synthesis 184, 190
Law of Unity 170
of Knowing and Doing 167, 172, 175, 192, 200
Laws of Dialectics 168
Lenin 21, 29-30, 41, 45, 48, 103, 113-4, 141, 148, 166, 174, 176, 182, 187, 190, 194, 201
stress 183
Leninist precept 144
Li Li-san 31, 44
Li Zepeng 53
liberation, and revolution 157
liberation struggle 25
Lin Biao 45, 49, 54-5, 77, 79, 94, 100-06, 117-8, 129, 146-7, 149-50, 155, 199
Liu Shaoqi 59, 77, 79, 80, 82, 84, 87, 91, 94, 99, 120, 173, 191
living standards and cultural level 198

Malaya 63
Mao Zedong 18-9, 26, 28, 33, 36-7, 41, 46, 49-50, 60-61, 75, 79, 83-5, 87, 89-91, 93, 97-8, 101-3, 110, 113, 117, 119-20, 127,

129-30, 139, 142, 144, 148, 165-6, 168-9, 171-2, 174-6, 178-9, 182, 185-6, 188, 190, 194-5
continuous revolution 129
famous speech of February 1957 86
innovations 191
philosophical innovations 202
revolutionary strategy 51
statement of 20 May 1970 156
Tenth Plenum speech 114
theory of new democracy 27
thought 78, 104
Maoism 21
Maoists 106, 124-5, 173
class 64
dialectical materialist method 146
dialectics 166
'guerilla warfare' 19
in China 82
leadership 47
lines 84
method of dialectical materialist analysis 143
notion of new-democracy 61
revolutionary outlook 27
World-View 136
Marx, Karl 37, 39, 48, 91, 103, 114, 125, 169-70, 175, 184, 193, 201
Marxism 22, 103, 116, 168
in Europe 165
true 124
Marxism-Leninism 21, 28, 77, 104
framework of 145
Mao Zedong Thought 114
Marxists 79, 116
circles 170
classics 202
conception of society and history 202
Leninist 142, 145
principle 105
revolutionary theory 26, 48
theory 92
notion of dialectics 125
proposition 123
theory 122, 124, 126, 190
theory of bourgeois-democratic revolution 37
theory of knowledge 175
view on the peasantry 45
mass campaigns 129
mass enthusiasm 19
mass mobilisation 19
mass nationalism 29
materialist dialectics 200, 202
materialist struggle 200
May Fourth Movement 29
of 1919 27

national democratic revolution 147
new-democratic form 59
new-democratic revolution 37, 59, 64
Ninth Congress 150, 152
Formulation 149
Nixon to China 150
Non-Antagonistic Contradictions 141, 196, 198
North America 147
North Korea 64
and Vietnam 161
nuclear armaments 115
nuclear weapons 144

October Revolution 150, 187
oppressed nations 149, 160

and imperialism 149

Party-Building 50
peasant movement 32
peasant society 18
peasantry 127
Peng Dehuai 79, 93, 117, 173, 191
Peng Zhen 99, 100
People's Democracies 61-2, 65
people's democratic dictatorship 56, 59, 81
people's democratic revolution 64, 127
People's Republic of China (PRC) 20, 27, 42, 80, 214
people's struggle against the super-powers 153, 156
People's War 52, 55
against US imperialism 146
of liberation 54
principles of 49
with guerilla war 64
permanent revolution 127-8
philosophical premise 124
political degeneration 19
political power 59
in eastern Europe 62
political struggles, conscious 123
politics and ideology 116
power struggle 99
PRC 59
production and superstructure 124
productive forces 122
proletarian movements 29
proletariat 120-1
and the bourgeoi, contradiction between 180
and the bourgeoisie 195
dictatorship of 62
of the 126
psychological security 59

Qiao Guanhua 150-52, 161

Red Army 32-3, 36, 40, 51, 54-5
revisionism 93, 104
struggle against 148
revolution and counter-revolution 91
revolutionary activism 162
Revolutionary Armed Struggle 139, 193
revolutionary era 17
revolutionary people's war 171
revolutionary struggle 145, 156
class 118, 124, 182
revolutionary theory 125
Roy, M.N. 29, 31, 41
ruling classes 95
Rumania 61
rural labourers 44
Russian revisionists 162
Russian revolution 45

Second Plenum of the Ninth Central Committee 79
self-mobilisation by the masses 115
semi-colonial 40
and semi-feudal situation 56
semi-feudal 40
landlords 194
Seventh Party Congress 138, 140, 142
Shaanxi-Gansu-Ningxia 33, 35, 41
Shao Huaze 181
Sino-Japanese war 28, 40, 41, 45-6, 51-2, 55
Sino-Soviet debate 140
ideological 202
Sino-Soviet split 199

six political criteria 118
social democrats in Europe 34
social development 171
social justice 65
social-imperialism 148, 150, 152, 154, 156
social-imperialist 157
socialism 62, 92-3, 96, 106, 108, 113, 116, 142
  and imperialism 144
  in China 18, 65
socialist and democratic forces 56
socialist camp 150, 154, 157
  and the imperialist camp 142
socialist construction 84, 129, 156
socialist development 19
Socialist Education Movement (SEM) 80, 89, 96
socialist foreign policy 160
socialist revolution 29, 81, 120, 123, 162
socialist road 113
socialist society 106, 121-2, 198
socialist system 104, 115, 121
socialist transformation 80, 84-5
South-East Asia 160-1
Soviet Army 61-2
Soviet economic 108
Soviet formulation 86
Soviet influence 160
Soviet revisionists 151
  social imperialism 150
Soviet type of dictatorship of the proletariat 61
Soviet Union 62, 93, 115, 138, 148, 155, 157, 159, 162
  and China 162
Sri Lanka 160
Stalin 30, 85, 87, 103, 166, 182, 187
Stalin cult 86
State power 62, 81
stress class struggle 172
struggle against imperialism 146
Struggle-Criticism-Transformation 119
Sun Yat-sen 30, 35, 42, 57
superpowers 139, 145, 150, 152-5, 157

Telengana people's armed struggle in India 63
Ten Great Relations 192
Ten Principles of Operation 53
Tenth Party Congress 84, 90, 105, 116, 120-21, 129, 140, 151,
Tenth Plenum 95
third world 160
Tito 86
Togliatti 143
Trotsky 41, 126-8
  theory and Mao's theory, no similarity 129
  theory of incessant revolution 129
Trotskyites 128
Twentieth Party Congress 144
two-road struggle 182

U.S. imperialism 138
United Front 40, 50
  against imperialism 146
  manifesto 56
United Nations 155, 157
United States 143
Unity-Criticisim-Unity 119
USA 153, 155
  imperialism 139, 146, 150-1, 162
USSR 62, 113, 148, 150, 152, 154, 155, 158, 160, 162

Vietnam 150, 156, 161
  liberation forces in 151
  liberation struggles of the 162

wages 198
warlords 54
Warsaw Treaty forces 148
West Wind 142, 155
Western Europe 147, 160
Western industrial society 21
workers and peasants, differences between the 198
Workers and Peasants Red Army 32, 44
working class 61
  and peasantry 62
world anti-imperialist revolution 147, 162
World War, First 29, 44
World War, Second 25, 27, 60, 63, 138, 153-4
world-view 163
  of the CPC 154
  redefinition of the 148

Yang Hu-cheng 33
Yang Xianzhen 59, 60, 172, 174, 181, 183, 185
  theory of 126
Yao Wenyuan 106
Yugoslavia 162

Zhang Chunqiao 107-8
Zhang Guotao 191
Zheng Feng 47
  campaign 48, 117
Zhou Enlai 83-4, 105, 117-20, 139